teach yourself

shorthand
pitman 2000

teach yourself®

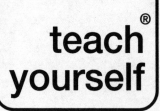

shorthand
pitman 2000
pitman

For over 60 years, more than 40 million people have learnt over 750 subjects the **teach yourself** way, with impressive results.

be where you want to be
with **teach yourself**

For UK orders: please contact Bookpoint Ltd, 130 Milton Park, Abingdon, Oxon OX14 4SB. Telephone: +44 (0) 1235 827720. Fax: +44 (0) 1235 400454. Lines are open 09.00–18.00, Monday to Saturday, with a 24-hour message answering service. Details about our titles and how to order are available at www.teachyourself.co.uk

Long renowned as the authoritative source for self-guided learning – with more than 40 million copies sold worldwide – the **teach yourself** series includes over 300 titles in the fields of languages, crafts, hobbies, business, computing and education.

British Library Cataloguing in Publication Data
A catalogue record for this title is available from the British Library.

First published in UK 1986 by Hodder Headline, 338 Euston Road, London, NW1 3BH.

This edition published 2003

The **teach yourself** name is a registered trade mark of Hodder Headline.

Typeset by Transet Limited, Coventry, England.
Printed in Great Britain for Hodder Education, a division of Hodder Headline Ltd, 338 Euston Road, London NW1 3BH by Cox & Wyman Ltd, Reading, Berkshire.

Hodder Headline's policy is to use papers that are natural, renewable and recyclable products and made from wood grown in sustainable forests. The logging and manufacturing processes are expected to conform to the environmental regulations of the country of origin.

Impression number 10 9 8 7 6 5 4
Year 2009 2008 2007 2006 2005

contents

Preface

It is not surprising that shorthand should have a long history. As soon as writing began about five thousand years ago, men noticed that while they could speak rapidly and listen to and understand what people said equally rapidly, it was another story when they had to write the words down.

For example, in English today, the gap between speech and writing is great. We can speak and listen at 140 to 180 words a minute, but we can write at only 25 words a minute.

So ever since writing started, men have been trying to find quicker ways of doing it. There was certainly shorthand in Roman times, and we know that Cicero, the great orator, had a shorthand writer. In Shakespeare's time some attempts were made (not very successfully) to use shorthand in order to pirate Shakespeare's plays. In Charles II's reign, Samuel Pepys wrote his famous diary in Shelton shorthand – a very good system, though never capable of verbatim note-taking.

Only in the nineteenth century, with the more sophisticated and scientifically based system of Isaac Pitman, did shorthand become a method of writing capable of recording every word of human speech at speeds of up to 250 words a minute and, equally important, of being perfectly transcribed.

One consequence of great social and economic significance was that, as the need for language communications increased with the industrial and commercial revolution, shorthand found (and still retains) a place in the office. Shorthand is also, however, a most valuable skill for any person who has, in the course of earning a living, to use words and writing every day.

The essence of Pitman Shorthand, whether New Era (the older version) or 2000 (first introduced in the early 1970s), lies in the following points:

1 It is a system of writing based on sound and not on spelling.
2 Each of the twenty-four consonants of the English language has a separate stroke to indicate it. There is no such correspondence in ordinary longhand.
3 The consonantal skeleton of a word makes up its 'outline'. For example, the word *package* has an outline that consists of P, K, and J.
4 The twenty vowels and diphthongs of the English language are represented when that is necessary, and more often it is not, by a system of dots and dashes or other small and rapidly executed marks.
5 A number of abbreviating devices are used to show the common collocations of English sounds as, for example, ST and -ING and CON.
6 The most frequently occurring words in the language – words like *and*, *the*, *have* and *for*, and so on – have their own specific one-stroke signs. These are sometimes arbitrary, but more often based on their vowel and consonant structure.
7 Phrasing forms an integral part of the system. That is to say, two, three, four or more words may often be written continuously without a lift of the pen. There are well-tried principles of phrasing that enable this to be done. Phrasing adds greatly to the speed potential and writing ease of the system and in average English material, about twenty to twenty-five per cent of the words are phrased.

Pitman 2000 Shorthand does not differ at all in its essentials – stated above – from Pitman New Era. It does differ in being easier to learn and more consistent in its application of the rules. It still has a speed potential of at least 150 words a minute, and is at least equally easy to transcribe into a handwritten or typed form with complete accuracy.

This book sets out to present the whole of the Pitman 2000 Shorthand version with all its rules explained, including all its phrasing principles. All the points made are illustrated with shorthand examples and with sentence exercises for reading, copying and writing.

The book is intended primarily for those wishing to acquire a full knowledge of the system. It is not written with the aim of enabling a student to become a fast writer. That is another matter. Advice is given from time to time in the course of the book to those who wish to write shorthand fast – that is, at speeds of 100 words a minute or above.

Pitman 2000 Shorthand is not hard to learn. Almost anyone can do it. All it requires is regular daily application and effort. Half an hour's study six days a week is better than six hours' study in two three-hour sessions. As with all skills, regular repetitive practice is needed, and the more frequent and the closer together in time these practices are, the more efficient and effective the learning will be.

It may be that you will find, as so many previous learners of shorthand have done, that the subject will soon begin to exert its own particular fascination. So much the better.

Shorthand still remains, along with typing, a livelihood-earning qualification. Those who are well trained and competent in these skills and who have a thorough mastery of visual English still get jobs – and, indeed, much better jobs than those who enter office life without them. Electronic technology is changing the job of the shorthand-trained secretary, but it is certainly not eliminating it.

In any case, anyone who masters the system will have acquired knowledge and skill that will remain firmly implanted, like the ability to ride a bicycle or to swim, and that knowledge and skill is sure to be of lifelong value.

Introduction

Please read this first before beginning your study of the system.

1 For the most efficient learning of Pitman 2000 Shorthand, it is best to study for half an hour or an hour each day. By setting aside such a period each day, you will economise on time in the long run.

2 It may seem odd, but it is certainly true that learning to read shorthand well is a great aid to learning to write it well. Repetitive reading is necessary in order to become a fast and fluent reader. All the shorthand should be read over again, until it can be read with no hesitation.

3 Do not move on to new material until you are sure you have mastered the section or part-section that you are working on.

4 There are many places in the text where you are given advice about how to write shorthand. In general, though, the following points always apply:

(*a*) Shorthand should be written lightly. This is the most important single point to observe.
(*b*) While all strokes are written lightly, you will learn from the start that some are written a little more firmly, and the distinction has to be made between those that are very light and those that are a little heavier.
(*c*) All the strokes are of uniform size.
(*d*) For practice writing, use a shorthand notebook of good quality, smooth-surfaced paper of traditional size (8″ × 5″) and with 21 lines to a page.

(*e*) Shorthand is best written with a pen that is very smooth and fluent, and flexible enough to make the distinctions between light and heavy easily, or a special shorthand pencil.
(*f*) Space out the shorthand words and phrases evenly and adopt a size about the same as that given in the text. This means that you should get an average of 10 to 15 words on a 4″ line. It is convenient to have a left-hand margin of 1″.

5 The short forms that appear throughout the text are very important. They are short ways of writing the very common words of the language, and they have to be learned by heart. This is no very arduous task as there are only 144 of them. The mere fact that the short forms occur so frequently helps in committing them to memory. But they do need to be learned.

6 The writing of Pitman Shorthand is not concerned with the spelling of words, only sounds. We write shorthand by the sounds of words only. For example, in a word like *lamb*, we write the *b* in longhand, but the word consists of only the three sounds L-A-M and this is what we write in shorthand. Similarly, the spelling of a word like *bough* bears little relationship to the sounds we hear, which are just two: B and the diphthong OW – and these are the two sounds that we write in shorthand. Shorthand is written phonetically. We write the *sounds* and not the spelling.

7(*a*) You will find that there are exercises throughout this book. They are an indispensable and vital part of 'teach yourself'. If you work on them in the way that will be outlined below, you will rapidly build up a vocabulary of the most commonly occurring words, increase your understanding of the rules, acquire accuracy, facility and speed in writing shorthand.
(*b*) Most of the exercises are presented in shorthand; a few are in longhand. Those in longhand are intended as a self-testing device. You convert the longhand into shorthand, and then check your own shorthand against that given in the key. Any mistakes that you make will reveal your weaknesses, and so you can concentrate on these and thus consolidate your knowledge of the system.
(*c*) The shorthand exercises introduce nothing new, but are based wholly on the rules, the words, and the phrasing that the preceding text has presented.

The first thing to do is to read each of the sentences or paragraphs. If you 'get stuck' at any point, try to puzzle out the outlines, but do not spend too much time doing this. Refer to the key. The important thing is first to ensure that you can, without further reference to the key, read every word of the exercise. Equally important is the repetitive work. Go on re-reading, if necessary three or four times, until you can read unhesitatingly at 100 words a minute or more.

When that point is reached, but not before, copy the shorthand from the book into your shorthand notebook. There are 21 lines on a page of a shorthand notebook. Copy only on lines 1, 4, 7, 10 . . ., etc. In this way you will finish up with 7 lines of copied shorthand and you will find that, if you have written the shorthand in the way suggested, you will have about 100 words on a page.

It is very important that when you are fair copying the shorthand, you should not do it mindlessly, but say the words quietly to yourself as you write them in. In this way you create the bond between what is seen, heard and written simultaneously.

Now, by using the first of the blank lines, you can re-copy – once again being sure to *say* the words as you write them – and when you reach the end of the page you will be able to calculate your copying speed.

If when you start on the second blank line you can get somebody to dictate the page to you from the key, that will be helpful. However, when you have filled up your blank lines you can still test your own writing ability, if you have a watch or clock with a seconds hand, by writing the page (or the exercise) into shorthand from the longhand of the key. In this way you can calculate your 'free' writing speed. For example, suppose you wrote 110 words in 67 seconds, then you wrote $110 \div 67$ words in one second, and therefore $110 \div 67 \times 60$ words in a minute = 98 words a minute.

8 When you finally reach the end of the book, you may wish to practise your speed regularly, and this you can do by getting a suitable dictation cassette at the speed you think you can just cope with. These are available from Pitman Publishing Ltd, 128 Long Acre, London WC2E 9AN.

Now you are ready to begin Section 1.

Section 1

Consonants

There are twenty-four consonant sounds in the English language.
Here are thirteen of them:

P B T D CH J

K G M N NG

L W

Note that:

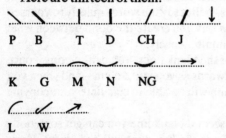

1 The first eight go in pairs. Each pair has the same sound except that the more firmly written of the pair is voiced, and the very light one of the pair unvoiced. That is to say, the vocal cords are used for voiced consonants, but not for the unvoiced ones.
2 The first six are all written downwards.
3 The next five are all horizontals written from left to right. Three of these – M, N, NG (as in *bank* or *song*) – are shallow curves.
4 L is a full-bodied quarter circle written upwards.
5 W begins with a small round hook and is written upwards.
6 All the consonants are the same length.

Consonants joined

Two or more of these consonants can be written one after another without taking the pen from the paper, thus forming an *outline* for a word.

Writing notes When two or more consonants are written together there should be no appreciable pause between ending one stroke and beginning the next. Write very lightly even when making the distinction between such strokes as T and D. Write the outline first, and insert the vowels after completing the outline:

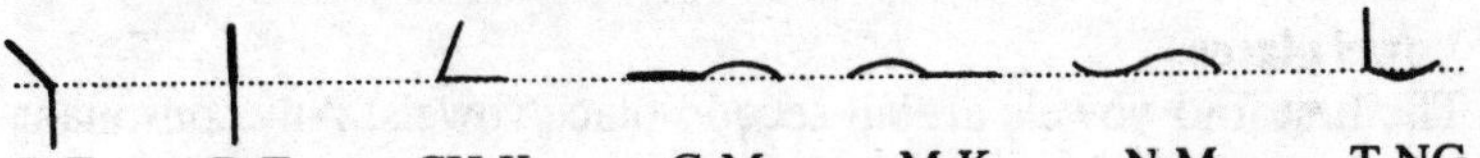

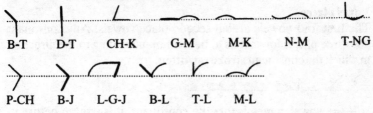

B-T D-T CH-K G-M M-K N-M T-NG

P-CH B-J L-G-J B-L T-L M-L

EXERCISE 1 Practise writing the thirteen consonants several times. Then practise the consonants joined to form outlines.

Vowels

Now we come to the vowels. English has twenty vowels and diphthongs. In this section, we are dealing with eight vowels. Vowels are written with either dots or short dashes.

Vowel	*How written*	*Examples*
AY as in *gate*	heavy dot	 aim may gate
OH as in *code*	heavy dash	 ode dough code
E as in *bet*	light dot	 etch gem bet
U as in *cub*	light dash	 up lung cub
AH as in *palm*	heavy dot	 calm pa palm
AW as in *bought*	heavy dash	 law awl bought

A as in *pack* light dot

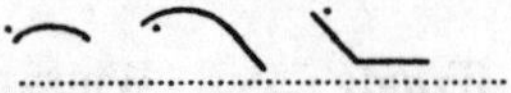

am map pack

O as in *lock* light dash

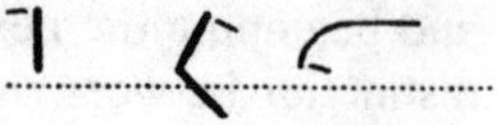

odd job lock

Vowel places

The first four vowels are all second-place vowels. Any consonant has three places for vowels to be written, according to the direction in which the consonant stroke is written:

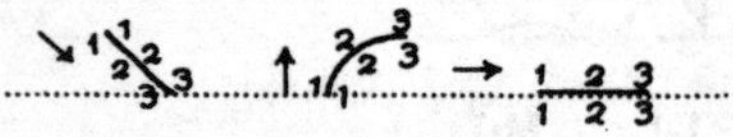
1 2 3
1 2 3
1 2 3
1 2 3

If the vowel comes *before* the consonant, it is written before it, and if it comes *after* the consonant, it is written after it. The examples make this clear:

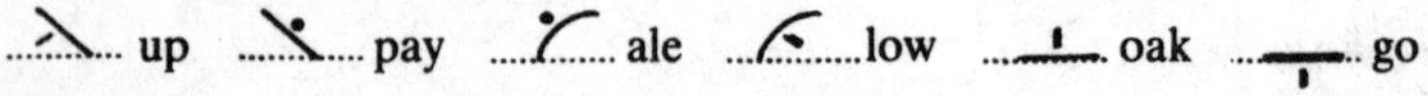
up
pay
ale
low
oak
go

Writing note Notice that dash vowels are written at right angles to the stroke at the point where they are written.

Position of outlines

Now come two rules that run all the way through shorthand.

1 The *first* vowel in a word decides where the outline for that word will be written – *above*, *on*, or *through* the line. All the first four vowels that were shown are second-place vowels. There the examples given are all *on* the line.

2 It is the first upward or downward stroke that *takes* the position – above, on or through the line. All the second group of four vowels are first-place vowels. Therefore they were written with the first upward or downward stroke *above* the line. If an outline consists of horizontal strokes only, then they are written on the line if the first vowel in the word is a second-place vowel, and above the line if the first vowel in the word is a first-place vowel.

Here are the outlines for six more words illustrating these two rules:

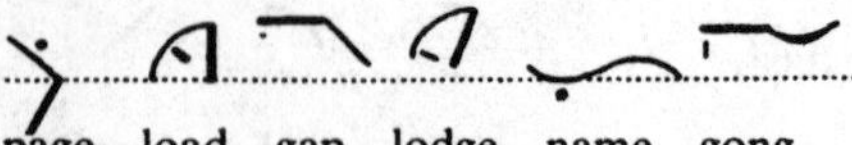

page load gap lodge name gong

EXERCISE 2 Read then copy the following words:

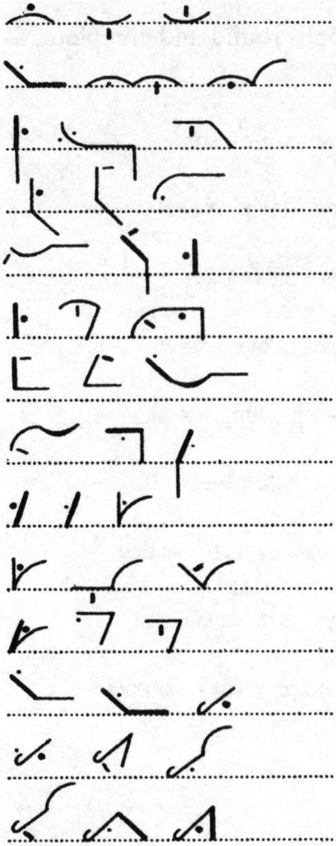

aim know own

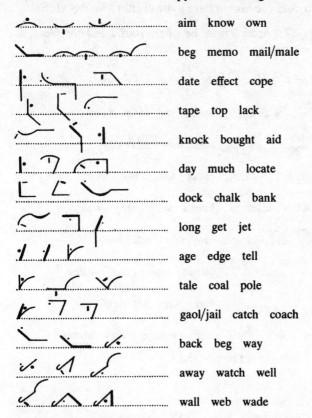

beg memo mail/male

date effect cope

tape top lack

knock bought aid

day much locate

dock chalk bank

long get jet

age edge tell

tale coal pole

gaol/jail catch coach

back beg way

away watch well

wall web wade

EXERCISE 3 Write the following words in shorthand, then check against the key:

(*a*) long get jet age edge tell tale
(*b*) gale pail gaol/jail catch coach back beg
(*c*) way away watch well wall web pack

Circle S

A small circle may be written at the beginning or at the end of any consonant. Initially it represents the sound of S. Finally it represents the sound of S or Z. An initial circle S is read first. A final circle

S is read last. That means that you cannot have a vowel before an initial circle S, and you cannot have a vowel after a final circle S.

Writing note The circle S must be small, round and complete, as shown in the examples:

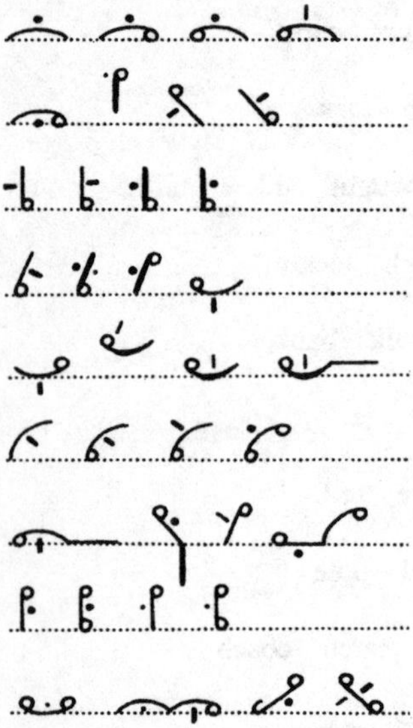

aim aims same some

maize sad soap pose

oats toes aids days

chose ages sage snow

knows song sung sunk

low slow sole sales

smoke spade such scales

stay stays set sets

sense memos ways suppose

All these words should be practised.

SES circle

Nouns ending in the S or Z sound have plurals ending in SES or ZEZ (pace, paces; phase, phases). Verbs ending in S or Z have a third person singular of the present tense which ends in SES or ZEZ (guess, guesses; laze, lazes). The sound also occurs in other words. It is shown by writing the final circle large as shown in the examples, and it is called the SES circle:

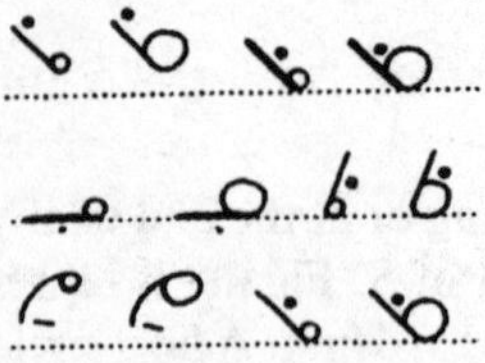

pass passes base bases

guess guesses chase chases

loss losses pace paces

case cases space spaces

sense senses dose/doze doses/dozes

excess access/axes box boxes

The suffix -ING

A very common verbal suffix is -ING. This is shown by a dot placed at the end of the consonant that precedes it. The dot -ING is used only for verbal suffixes: it is not used for words like *king*, *sting*, *awning*, etc.:

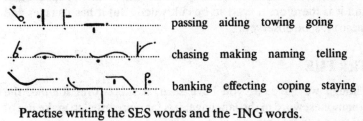

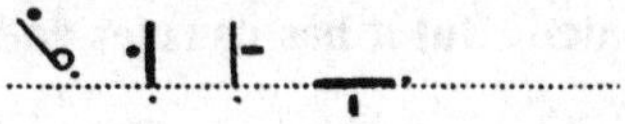
passing aiding towing going

chasing making naming telling

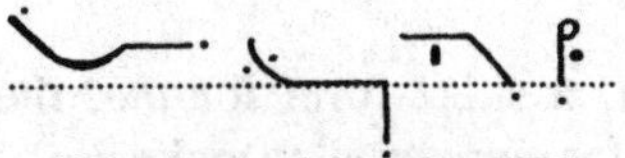
banking effecting coping staying

Practise writing the SES words and the -ING words.

Short forms

Very common and frequently occurring words are represented by shortened outlines and these all have to be learned by heart. Copy and memorise them:

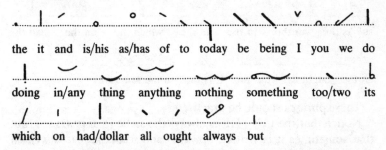

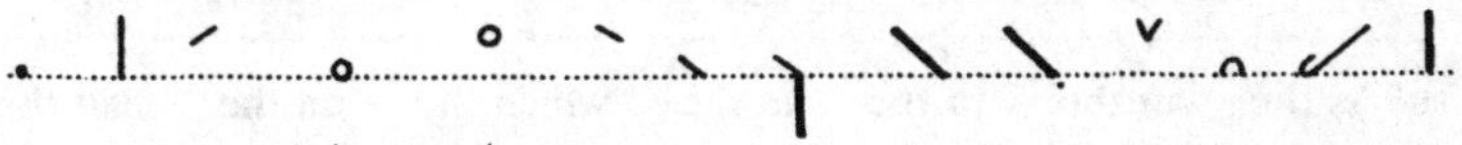
the it and is/his as/has of to today be being I you we do

doing in/any thing anything nothing something too/two its

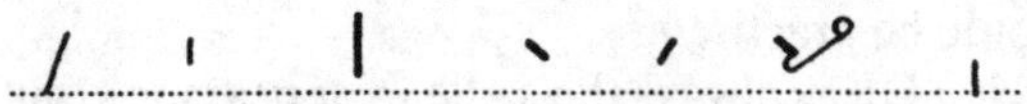
which on had/dollar all ought always but

Notes on short forms Some short forms are very short strokes for very common words, and these strokes are arbitrary, for example *and*, *of*, *on*, *but*. Most short forms, however, have consonant strokes and a position in relation to the line that are connected with the way they are spoken.

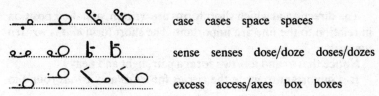

The direction in which short forms are written, and their position in relation to the line are important. The short form *and* is written upwards.

Notice that *to* and *too/two* form a pair, light and heavy.

It is important to write the circles for *is/his* and *as/has* round to the left, that is anticlockwise, 

Phrasing

It is often possible to write two or three or more words in shorthand as one continuous outline without a lift of the pen. There are principles of phrasing which will be explained as we proceed.

Phrasing increases the ease, speed and readability of shorthand, and it is therefore a craft to be cultivated. But it has its rules and these must be observed.

Tick THE

Though we have, as you have seen, a short form for *the*, the commonest word in the language, it is far more usual to make use of a tick as in these phrases:

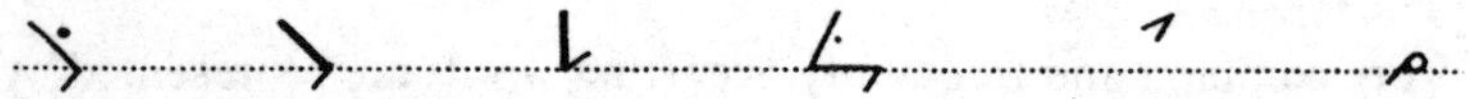

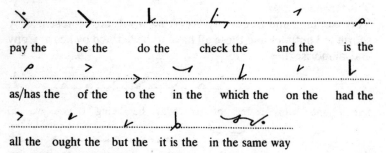

pay the   be the   do the   check the   and the   is the

as/has the   of the   to the   in the   which the   on the   had the

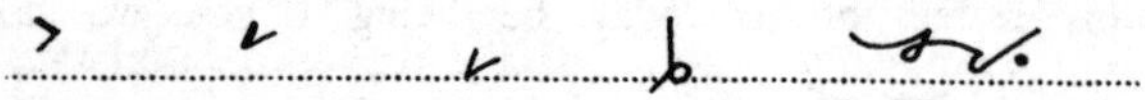

all the   ought the   but the   it is the   in the same way

These phrases should be practised.

Notice that the tick THE is always the same in appearance, but that sometimes it is written upwards and sometimes it is written downwards. The rule is simple. Tick THE can only be written *after* a stroke. Then it is written in the direction that gives the sharper angle.

The phrases *on-the* and *but-the* are given a slight slant to make them easier to write and read.

Circle S for *us*

The circle S may be used in phrases for *us*:

to us   of us   on us

These phrases should be practised.

Punctuation

Punctuation is the same in shorthand as it is in longhand, except for:

full stop 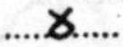 question mark  exclamation mark 

dash  hyphen  parentheses (brackets) 

To show a capital letter, two short light dashes  are written upwards below the outline, as in:

 Tom 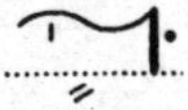 Monday

EXERCISE 4 First read the sentences, without the key if possible. Then copy them, writing as quickly as you can while still concentrating on accurate, well-formed outlines like those in the text. Say the words to yourself as you write.

Follow the instructions given above for all other shorthand exercises in this and subsequent sections:

(*a*) 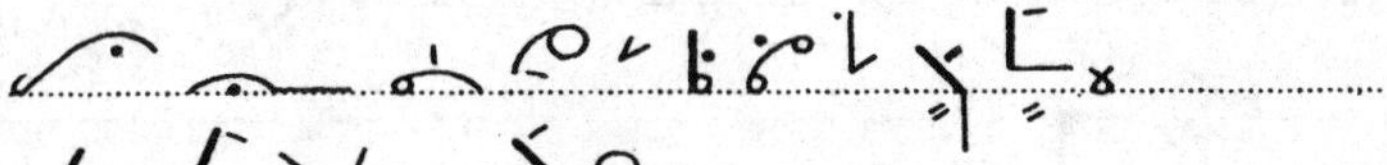

(*b*) 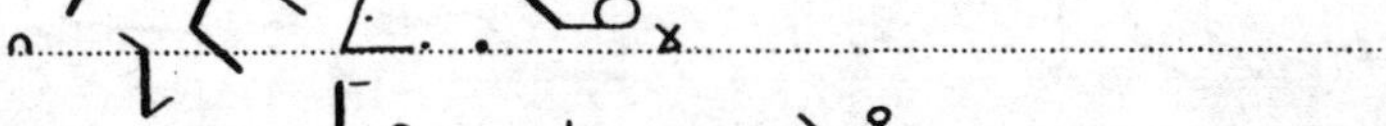

(c) 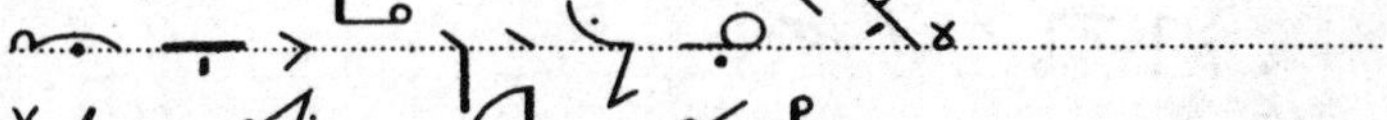

(*d*) 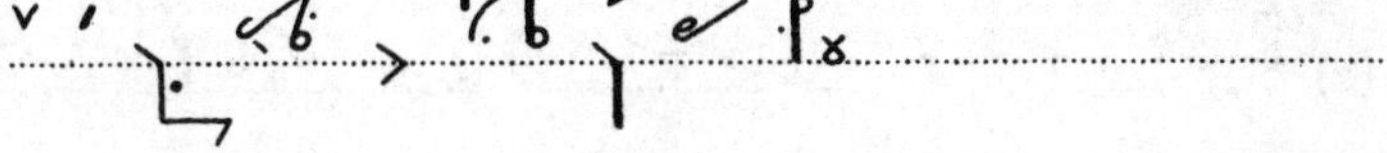

(*e*) 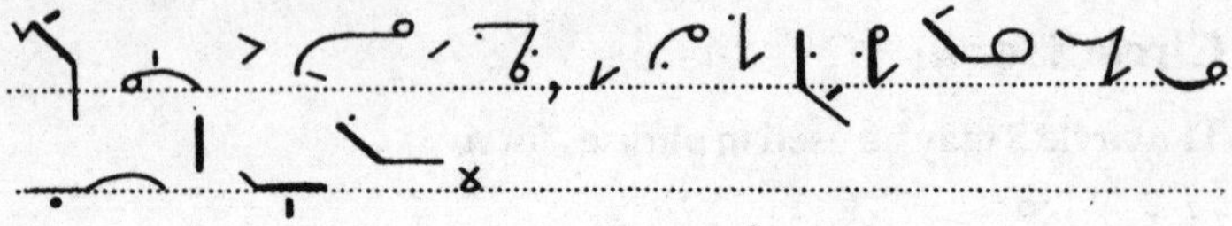

(*f*) 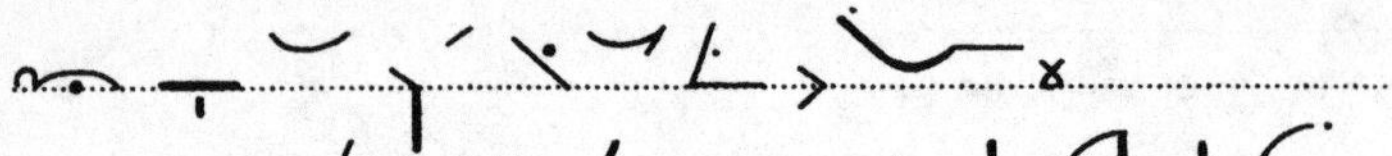

(*g*) 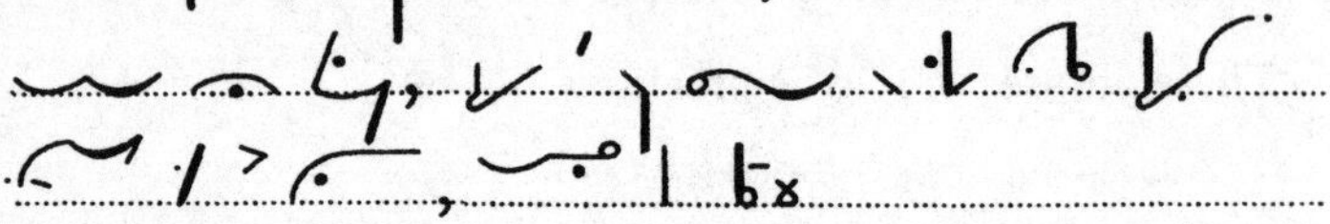

(*h*) 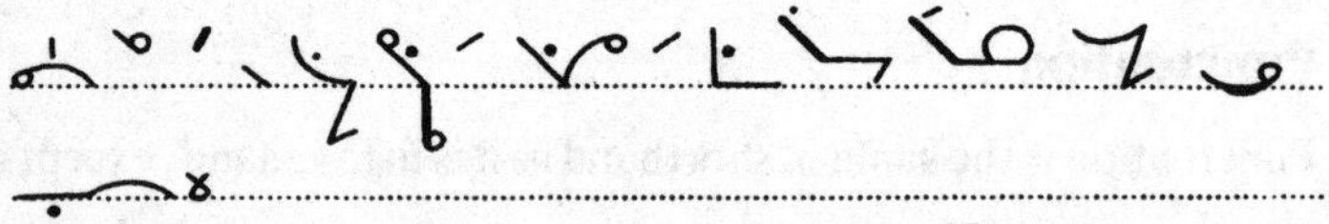

(*i*) 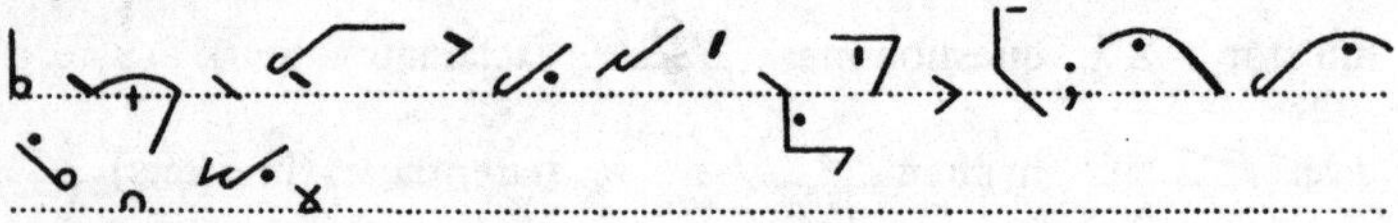

(*j*) 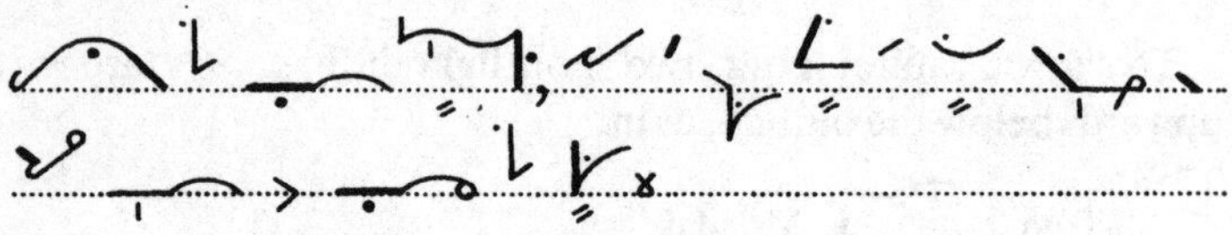

EXERCISE 5

(*a*) 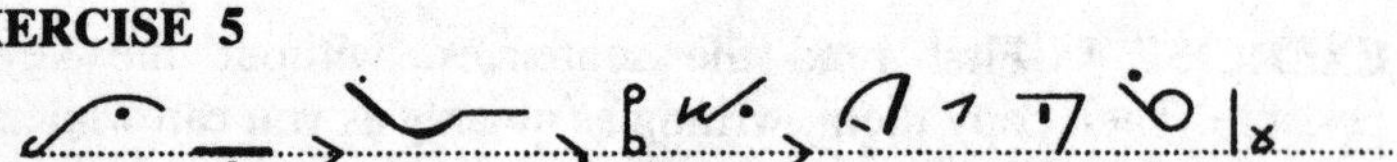

(*b*) 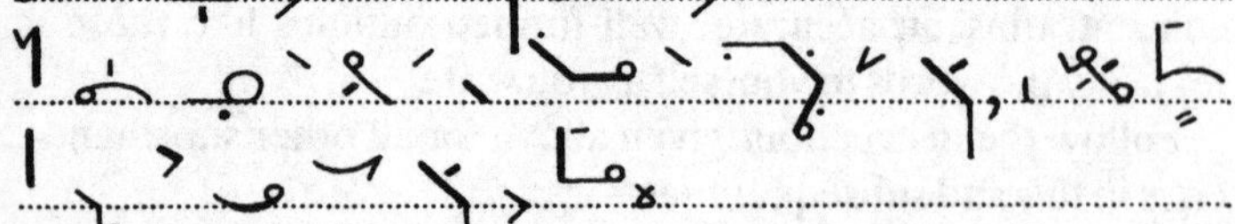

(*c*) 

(*d*) 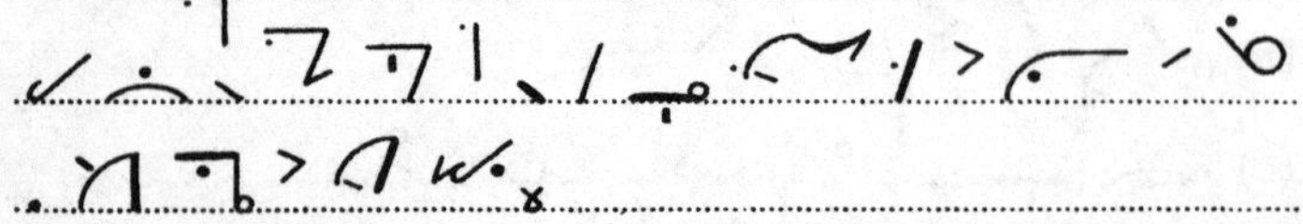

(*e*) 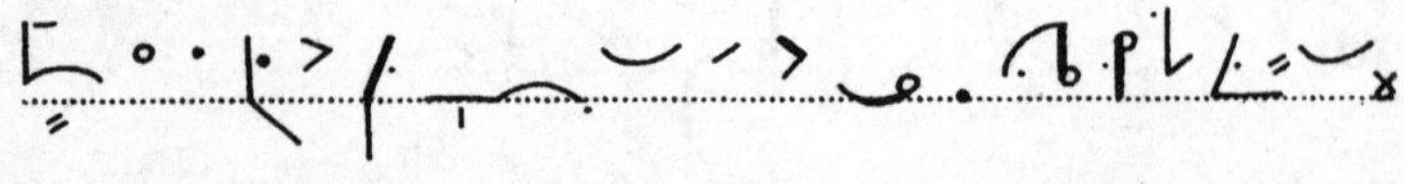

EXERCISE 6 Write the following in shorthand (phrasing is shown by the hyphens):

(*a*) We ought to-take two of-the boats up to-the lake today.
(*b*) I-know something you ought to-do; you ought to bank-the cheques today.
(*c*) It-was snowing along-the edge of-the bay and-I-had no mac.
(*d*) Take all-the baggage to-the docks and stow it in-the space which-the dock allocates to-us.
(*e*) We ought to know-the name of-the tape, because it-is-the same as-the tapes we bought at-the sale on-Monday.

Section 2

Seven more consonants

Here are a further seven consonants:

F V Th TH S SH Y

Note that:

1 the first four of these are pairs, the light stroke being the unvoiced sound and the heavy stroke the voiced sound.
2 the difference between the two *th* forms is that heard in the words *thick* (unvoiced) and *those* (voiced).
3 F, V and SH are full-bodied quarter circles. Th, TH and the stroke for S are shallow curves.
4 all are written downwards except for Y, which begins with the small round hook and goes upwards. Compare 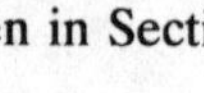 and 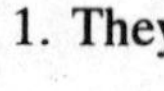 .

Words

The words that follow show all the new consonants in use, along with the consonants and vowels already given in Section 1. They should be read and copied:

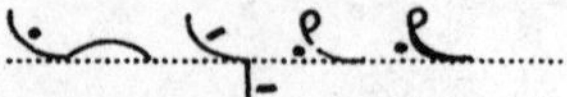 fame photo safe save

 faith facts cafe follow

 vote love vague vale/veil

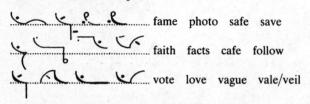

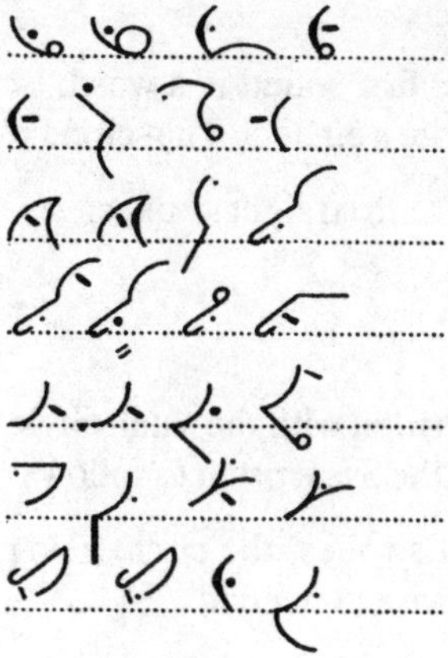

face/phase faces/phases them those

though path maths oath

loth loathe thatch yell

yellow Yale yes yolk

show showing shape shops

cash shed shallow shell

wash washing they chef

Stroke S

Stroke S is used:

1 When S is the only consonant in the word:

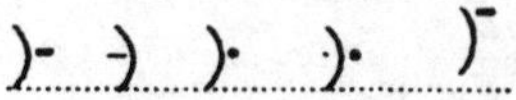

so us say essay saw

2 When a vowel precedes an initial S or when a vowel follows a final S:

ask escape essences peso Nassau

This is one of the many devices in shorthand which enable us to dispense with vowels. For example,  must begin with S, whereas 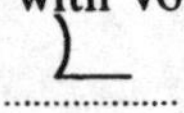 must begin with a vowel before the S (*sack/sock*, *ask*).

3 When a word begins with S + vowel + S/Z:

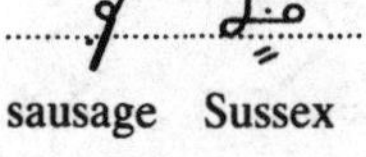

sausage Sussex

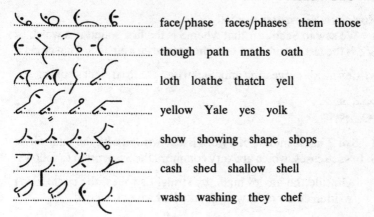

How circle S is written medially

1 We saw in Section 1 that when S is the first sound in a word, or S/Z is the last sound in a word, then we write a circle S. That circle is written inside curves and anticlockwise  to straight strokes:

sex sense

2 S or Z in the middle of a word is also written with the small circle S. In such cases, which are very common, the S is written as follows:

Outside the angles made by straight strokes, the circle being written either clockwise or anticlockwise as needed:

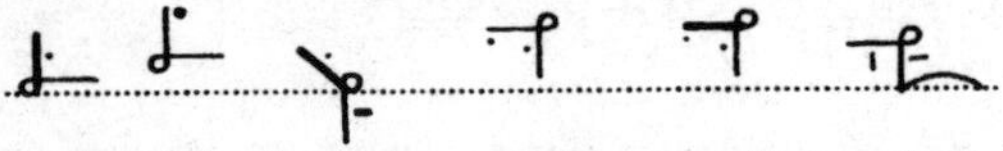

desk task bestow cassette gazette custom

Inside curves, whether the curves are alone or before or after a straight stroke:

mass message mask chosen dozen tassel

Inside the first curve when two curves are separated by S/Z:

fasten unsafe mason lesson

Notice in the last two examples how the circle is completed before the next consonant is written.

After downward curves F, V, Th, TH followed by S/Z and L, or an N followed by S/Z and L, the circle is only taken far enough for the following L to be written out of it:

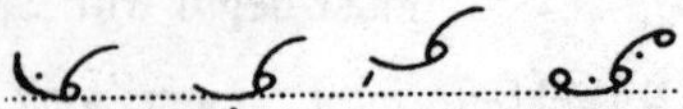

vessel nestle nozzle senseless

EXERCISE 7

(*a*) 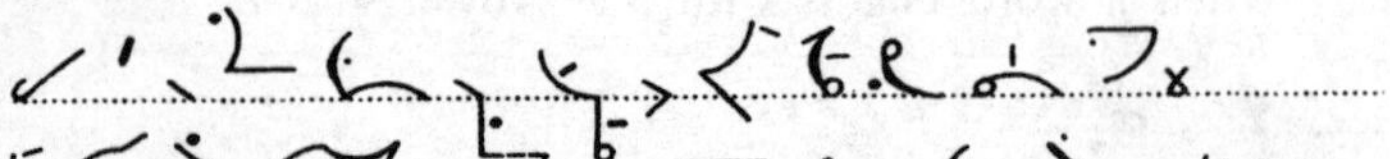

(*b*) 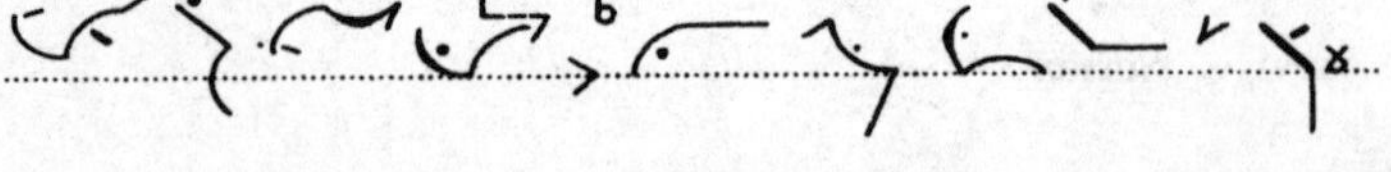

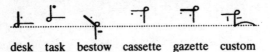

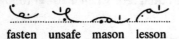

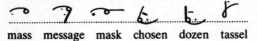

(c)
(d)
(e)

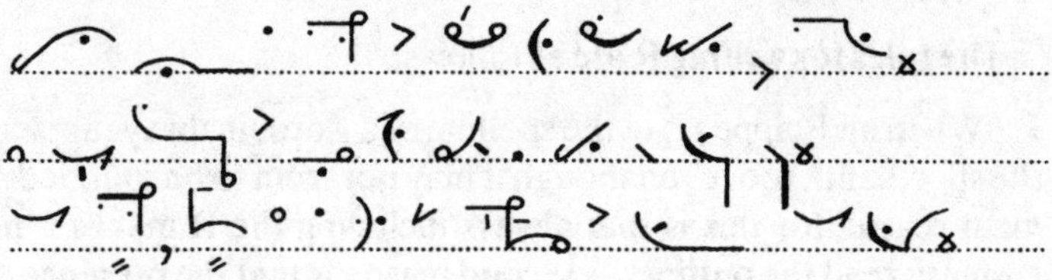

Past tense of regular verbs

1 Regular verbs are those that have only four forms like *touch*. The forms are *touch*, *touches*, *touching*, *touched*. Such verbs are very numerous.

2 The past tense of all regular verbs in English ends in the sound of either T or D. To write such past tenses, disjoin the T or D, whichever is sounded, and write it close up (see page 150 for further rules on disjoining):

ask asked face faced weigh weighed pass passed

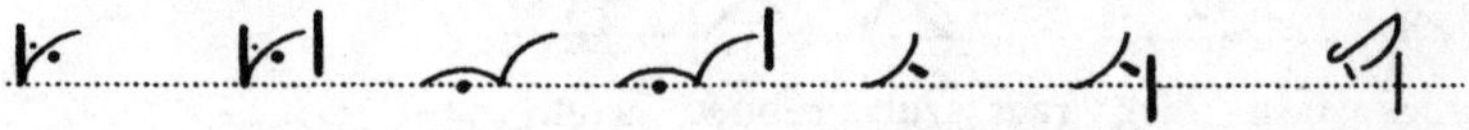

delay delayed mail mailed show showed washed

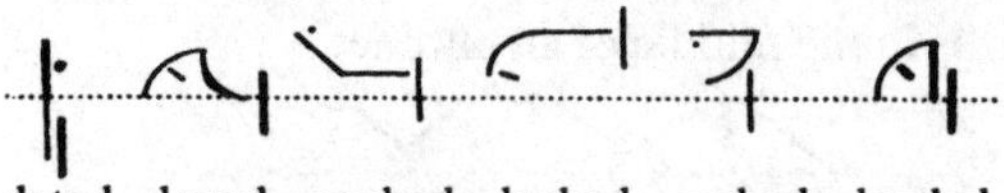

dated loved packed locked cashed loaded

The consonant R

Because R is a very common consonant, there are two ways of writing it. There is a straight stroke written upward 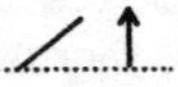 and a full-bodied curve written downwards .

Writing notes Upward R is written at an angle and this plus the fact that it is upward ensures that it can never be mistaken for CH.

Compare  CH-K and  R-K. Both these strokes are light strokes.

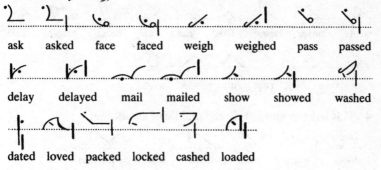

The rules for writing R are as follows:

1 When an R appears in the spelling of a word, it always appears in the shorthand, too, even though it may not seem to be sounded. The main reason for this is that always including the R makes it much easier to read the outline. A second reason is that the presence of an R often modifies the vowel that precedes it.

2 R is always written downward before M:

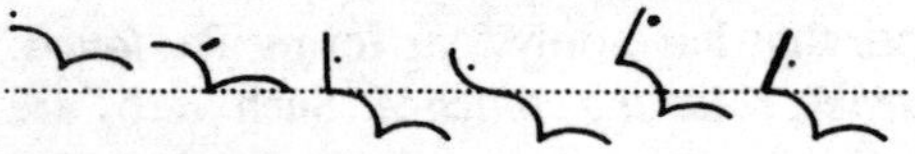

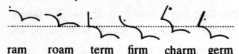

ram roam term firm charm germ

(Note how the ER vowel is written in *term* and *firm*.)

3 R is written upwards when it is the first sound in a word:

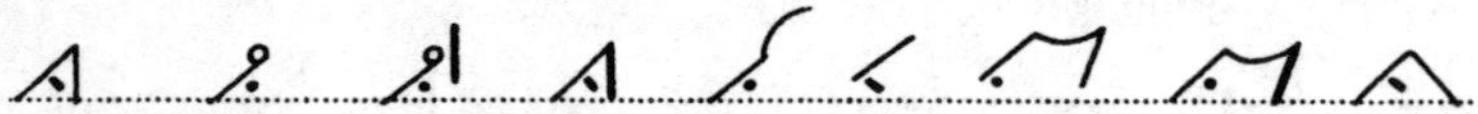

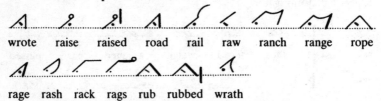

wrote raise raised road rail raw ranch range rope

rage rash rack rags rub rubbed wrath

4 R is written upwards in the middle of an outline:

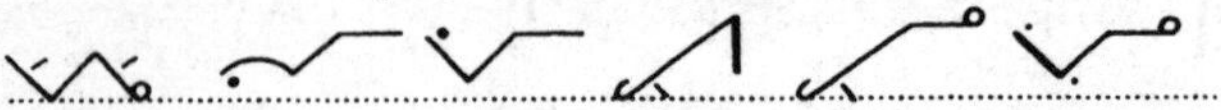

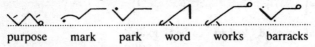

purpose mark park word works barracks

5 R is written upwards when it is the last consonant in a word and is followed by a vowel sound:

burrow borrowed morrow narrow thorough marrow

6 R is written downwards when R is the first consonant in a word and is preceded by a vowel:

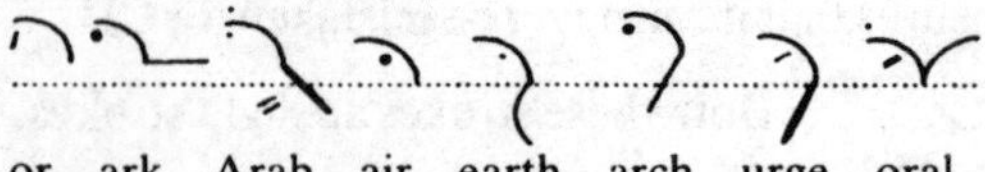

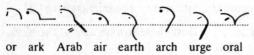

or ark Arab air earth arch urge oral

7 R is written downwards at the end of an outline when R ends the word:

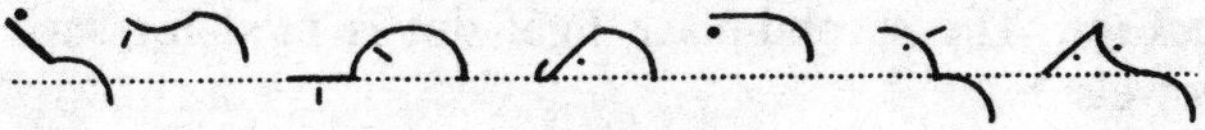

bar nor colour were car error refer

8 Note that the common words ending in sounds -ARE and -ORE (variously spelled) are written with the AY vowel, second-place heavy dot, and with the OH vowel, second-place heavy dash, respectively, as in:

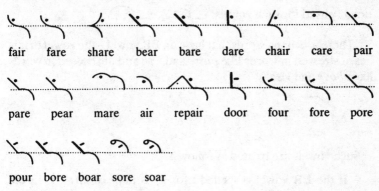

fair fare share bear bare dare chair care pair

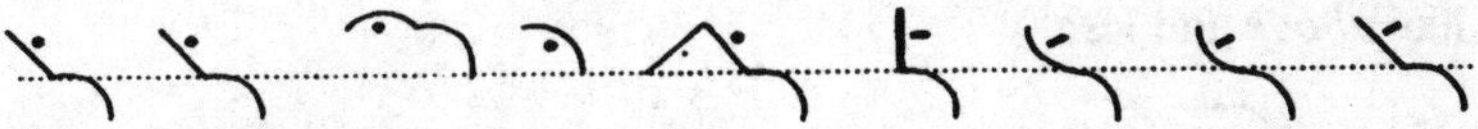

pare pear mare air repair door four fore pore

pour bore boar sore soar

9 When downward R is used in a root outline, it is retained in derivatives from that root, as in:

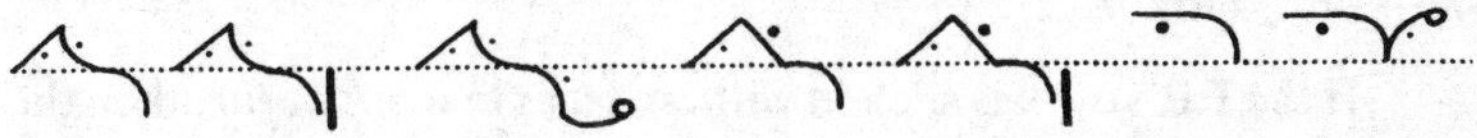

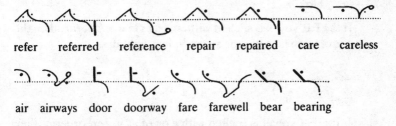

refer referred reference repair repaired care careless

air airways door doorway fare farewell bear bearing

10 Circle S or SES may be added to final downward R:

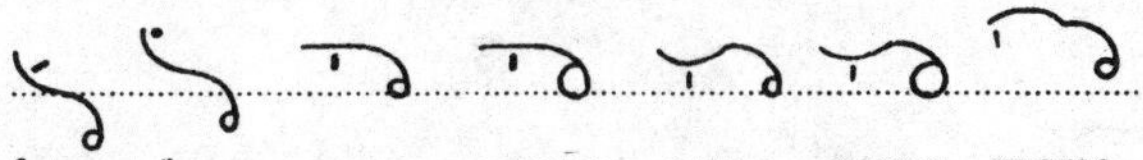

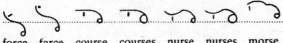

force farce course courses nurse nurses morse

Writing 'neutral' and unstressed vowels

1 Many two-syllable words end in -AGE, unstressed, such as *cabbage*, *package*. The second-place light dot is used for such unstressed vowels:

cabbage package

2 In words like *custom* and *colour*, the second vowel is unstressed and indeterminate in sound. The second-place light dash is conventionally used for such vowels: , .

3 There are many words that have an ER vowel – the vowel that is heard stressed in words like *purse* and *jerk* and unstressed in words like *above* and *visa*:

purse jerk

Such vowels are treated as follows:

If the ER vowel is spelled *i* (or *y*) as in *fir* or *birth*, then the convention is to use the second-place light dot:

fir birth

If the ER vowel is spelled with *o* or *u* as in *work* or *fur*, then the convention is to use the second-place light dash:

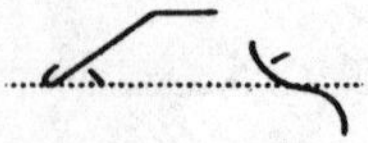

work fur

If the ER vowel is spelled with *e* or *ea* as in *earl* or *term*, then the convention is to use the second-place light dot:

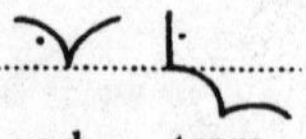

earl term

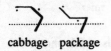

Indicating vowels

Once again, as you will realise, having studied how upward and downward R are used, we have a way of showing vowels without the need to write them in.

If we see a downward R as the first consonant in an outline, then (unless it precedes M) we know there must be a vowel before it. The position of the outline will give us the clue to the vowel. For example, in  there must be a vowel before the R and the vowel must be first-place, so the word is *ark*.

Short forms

Copy and memorise:

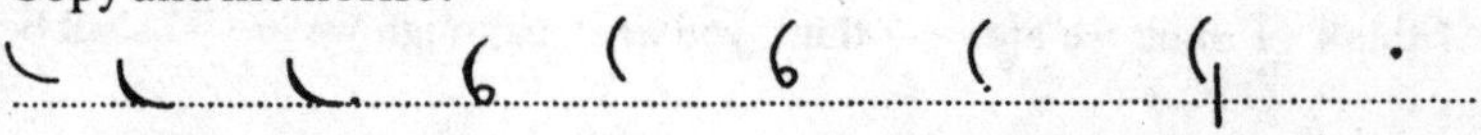

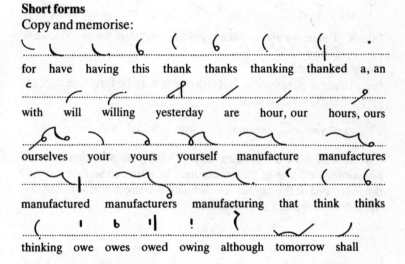

for have having this thank thanks thanking thanked a, an

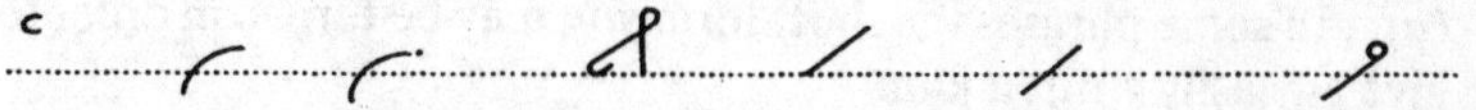

with will willing yesterday are hour, our hours, ours

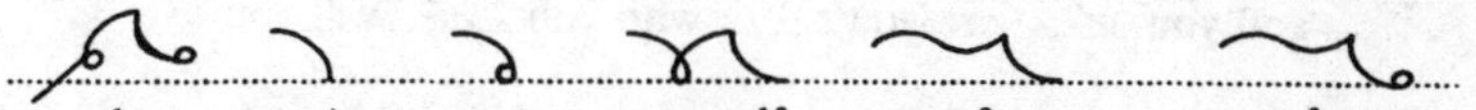

ourselves your yours yourself manufacture manufactures

manufactured manufacturers manufacturing that think thinks

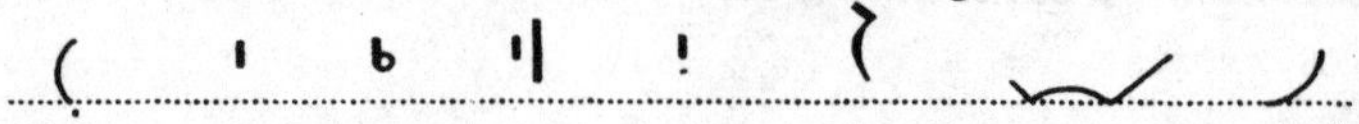

thinking owe owes owed owing although tomorrow shall

Notes on short forms

(*a*) *with* is a small light anticlockwise semicircle written in the first position (above the line).

(*b*) The short forms for *will*, *willing*, *hour/our*, *hours/ours*, *ourselves* are all written *through* the line.

(*c*) Notice how many short forms like *thank* may have circle S added, dot -ING added, disjoined T or D added just like other regular verbs.

(*d*) The short form for *that* is a heavy TH above the line but it is only half the length of a normal TH.

Phrasing

Practise:

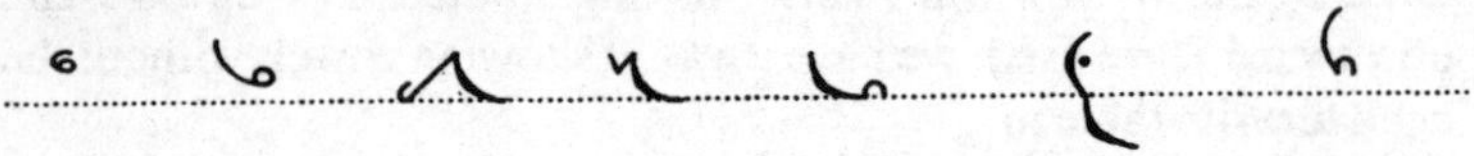

with us for us we have I have have you they have thank you

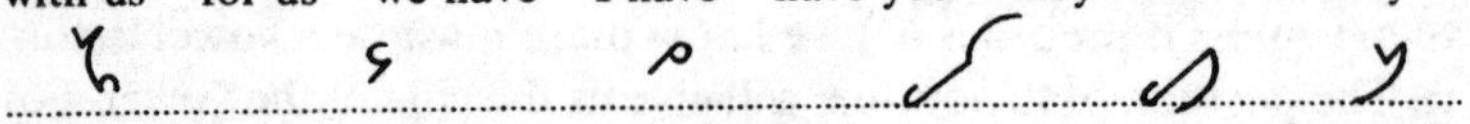

I thank you with the as the, has the we will we shall I shall

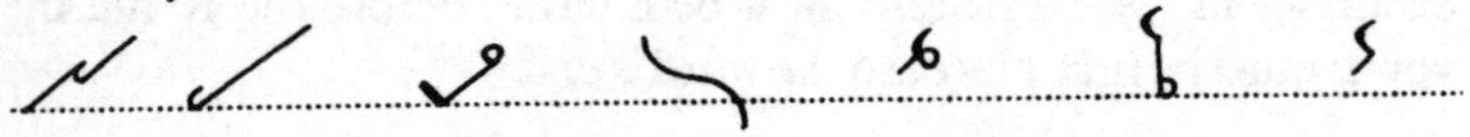

are we we are two hours for your that is the that it is that the

I think I think we are we think you are although we are I shall be

Notes on phrases

(*a*) In some phrases the short form *you* may be turned in order to give an easily written join:

 and you 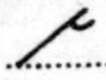 are you  with you  will you

(*b*) Notice how in phrases like *I-thank-you* and *that-it-is* and *I-think* the position of the phrase may be adjusted so that not only the first word of the phrase is written in its correct position, but also the second word of the phrase too.

Intersections

One stroke may be struck through a preceding one to represent a commonly occurring word, as in:

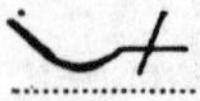 bank charge  customs form

There are thirteen of these intersections in Pitman 2000 Shorthand and *charge* and *form* are the first two of these. A circle S may be added for the plural or to show the possessive, as in:

 your charges  despatch forms

EXERCISE 8

(a) 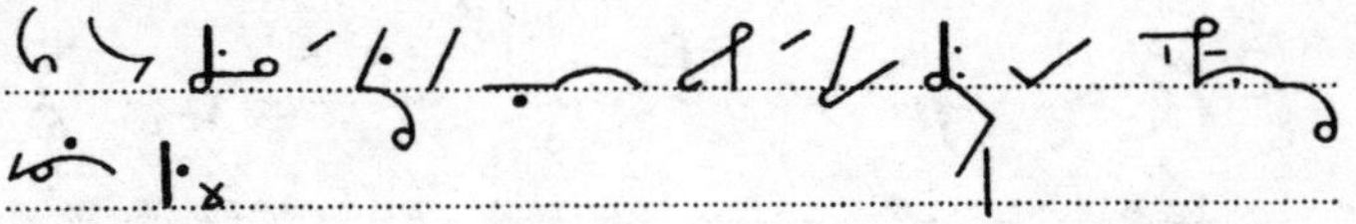

(b) 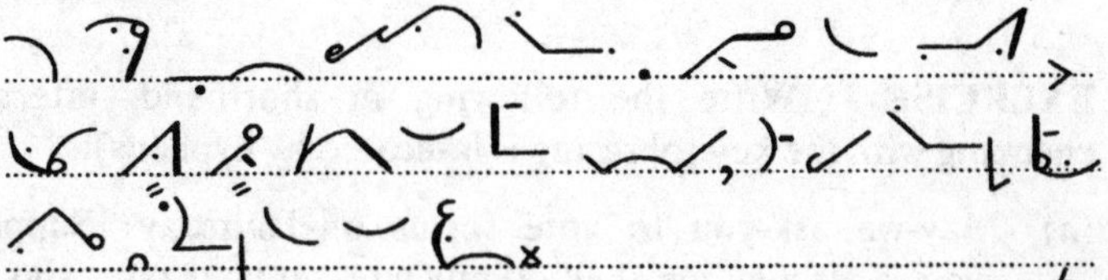

(c) 

(d) 

(e) 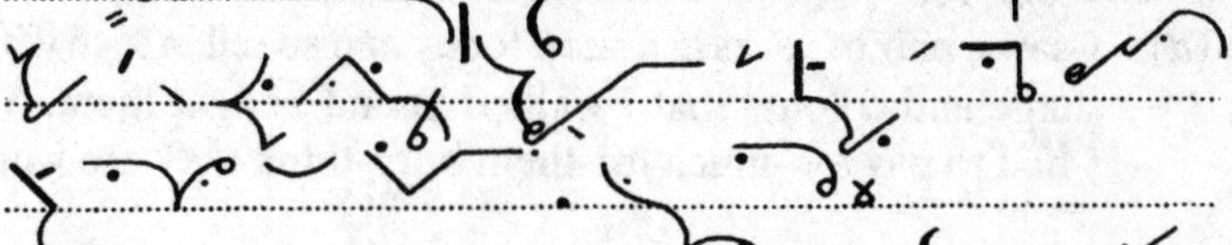

(f) 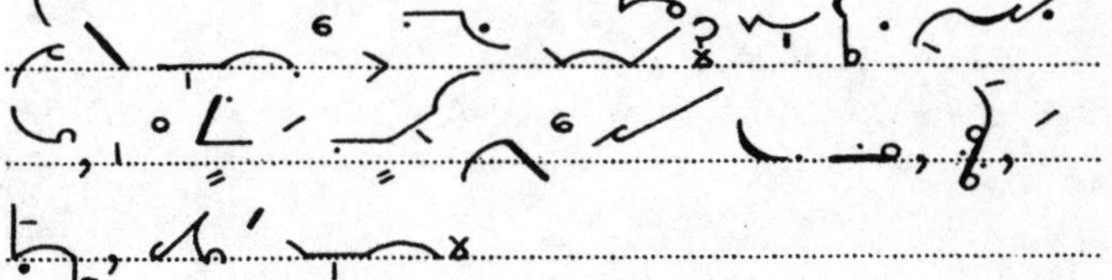

(g) 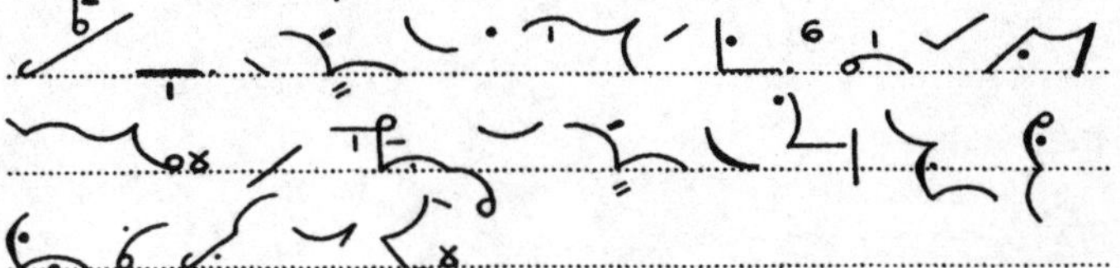

(h) 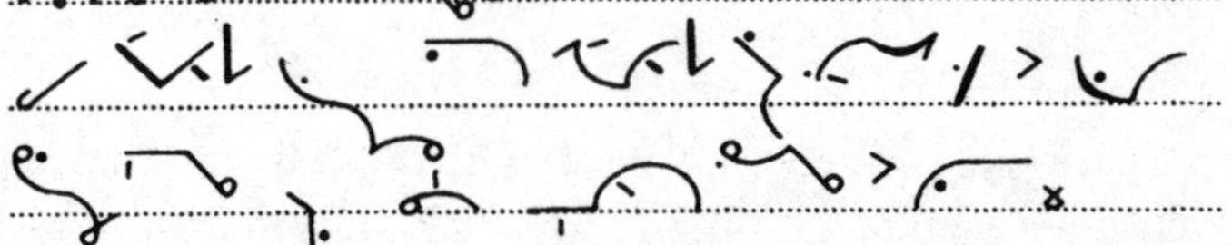

(i) 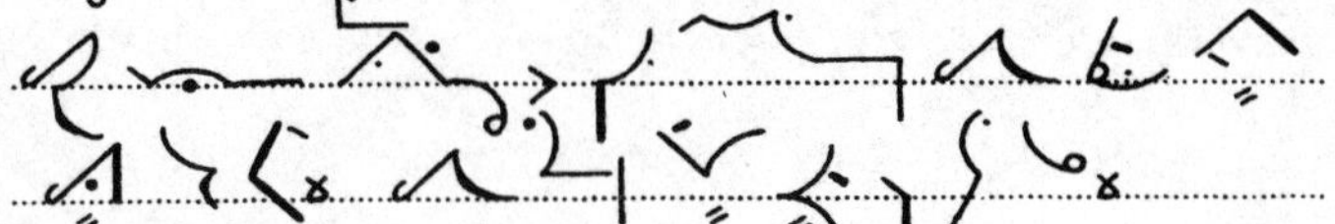

(*j*) 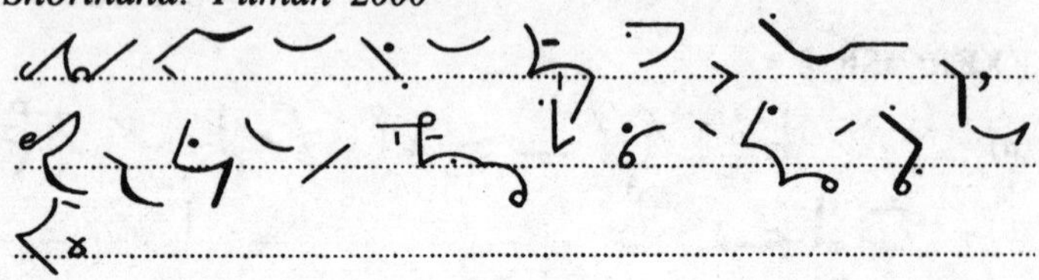

EXERCISE 9 Write the following in shorthand, afterwards checking with the key (phrasing is indicated by hyphens):

(*a*) May-we ask-you to vote for-us on-Thursday? Supposing we-are elected, we-shall-do much to-get your rates and taxes paid.

(*b*) Some of-us will-have to pay-the dock-charges today or they-will take our boxes to-the customs and it-will take-us months to-get them back.

(*c*) They-have worked long hours for-us, and-I-think-we ought to ask them to-come with-us to-the Bungalow Cafe and pay for-them, too.

(*d*) I-saw a pair of vases in a shop today and so fell in love with-the shape and colours that I walked in and bought them. Maybe I-had to pay too-much for-them but I-think they-are worth it.

Section 3

Halving strokes

Halving to add T

In words of only one syllable, any *light* stroke may be halved to add the sound of T.

A circle S may be added to the half-length stroke:

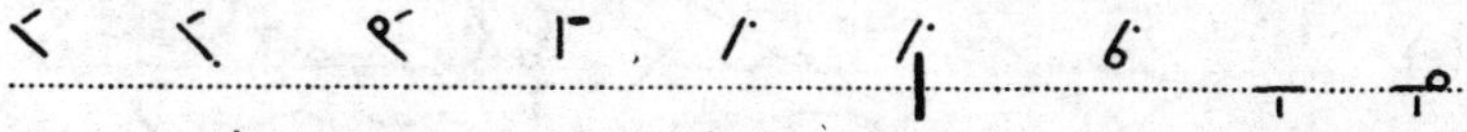

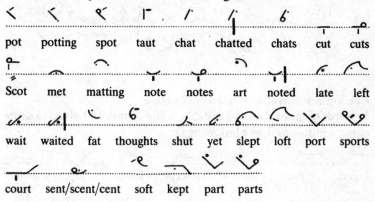

pot potting spot taut chat chatted chats cut cuts

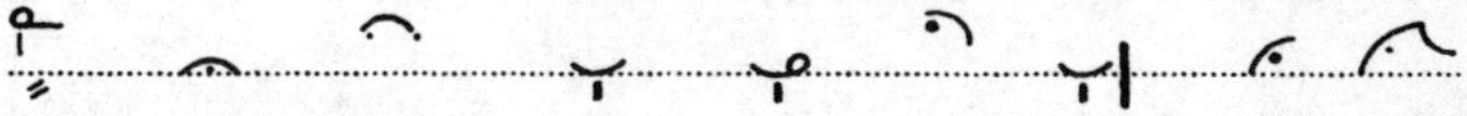

Scot met matting note notes art noted late left

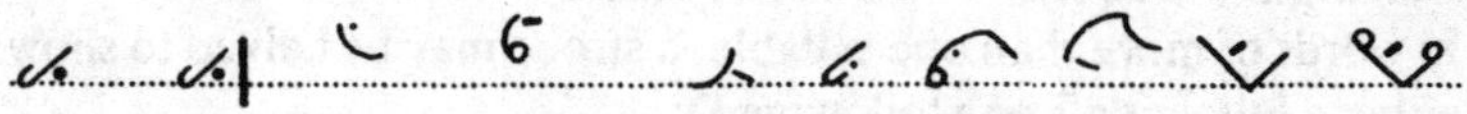

wait waited fat thoughts shut yet slept loft port sports

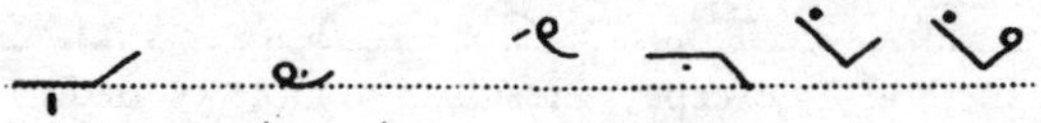

court sent/scent/cent soft kept part parts

Halving to add D

In words of only one syllable, a *heavy* stroke may be halved to add the sound of D.

A circle S may be added to the half-length stroke. The heavy stroke NG is not halved:

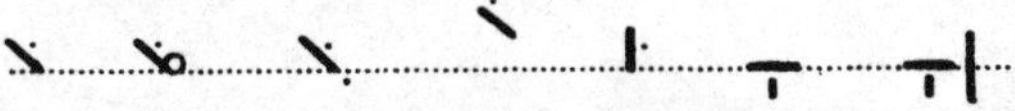

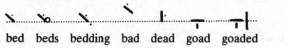

bed beds bedding bad dead goad goaded

EXERCISE 10

(*a*) (*b*) (*c*) (*d*) (*e*)

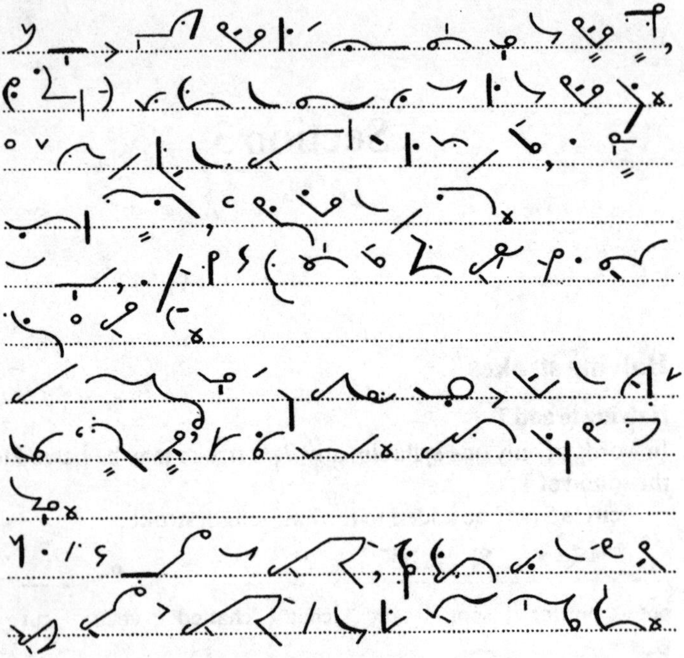

Halving in words of more than one syllable

In words of more than one syllable, a stroke may be halved to show either a following T or a following D:

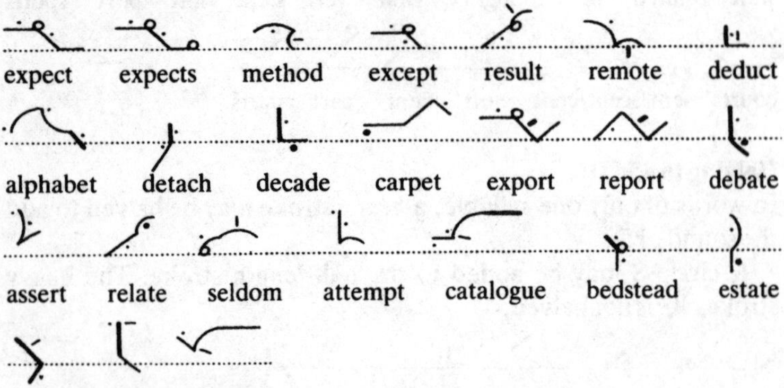

expect expects method except result remote deduct

alphabet detach decade carpet export report debate

assert relate seldom attempt catalogue bedstead estate

budget adopt padlock

When not to halve

Strokes are *not* halved if, as a result, the outline would be difficult to read:

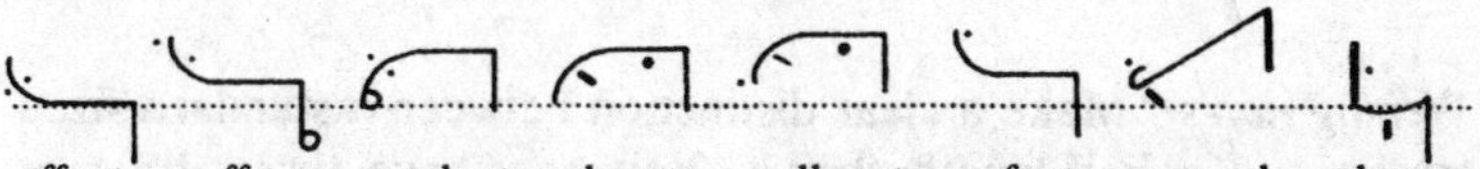

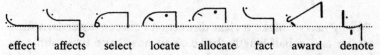

effect affects select locate allocate fact award denote

An upward R, standing alone, is *not* halved for T. It would too closely resemble the short forms *and* or *should*. We write:

rate rates wrote rats

There are a number of words in which an R or an L is followed by a sounded vowel and then by a D. In such words halving is *not* used. If a sounded vowel comes between R or L and D, the full strokes are written:

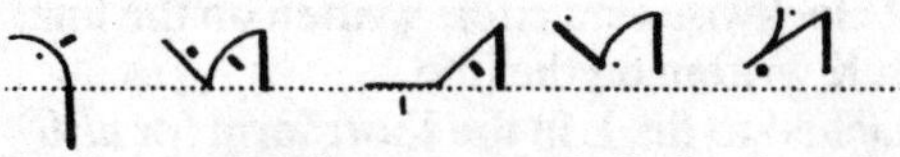

erode payload corrode ballad charade

Remember that upward R, being a light stroke, cannot be halved for D in a word of one syllable.

EXERCISE 11

(*a*) 

(*b*) 

(c) 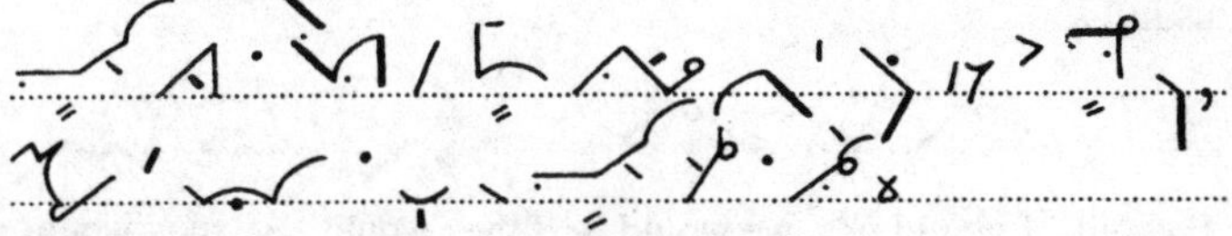

(*d*) 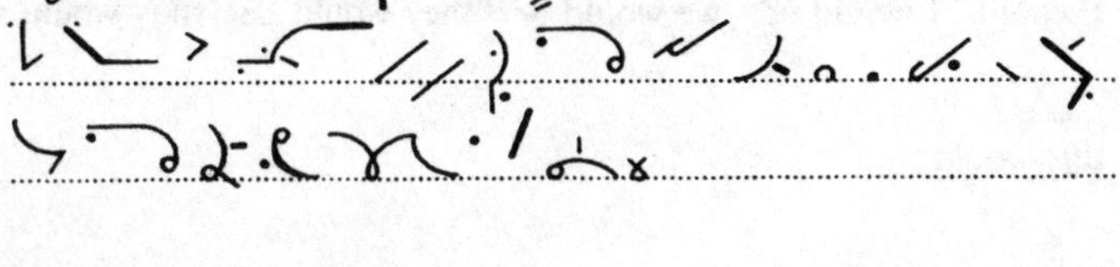

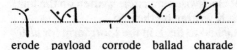

(*e*)

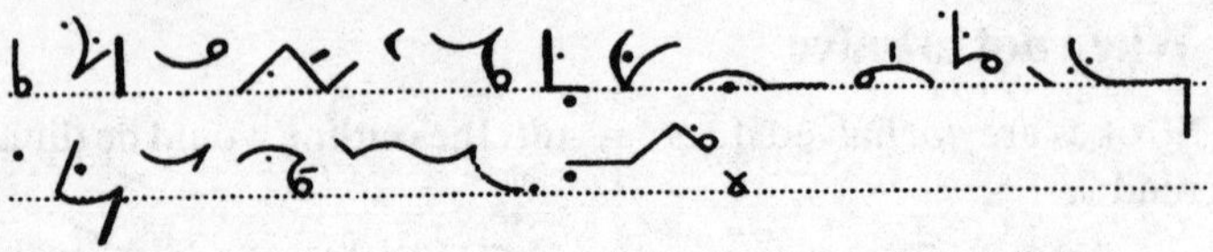

Writing notes Make a clear distinction between a standard-sized stroke and a half-length stroke. You now have three different lengths of stroke: (*a*) standard, (*b*) half-length, and (*c*) some of the short forms like *and*, *on*, *of* and so on which are shorter still.

Short forms

To be copied and memorised:

could would also

Notes on short forms

(*a*) *Would* is a small light clockwise semicircle written on the line.
(*b*) *Could* is a half-length K written on the line.
(*c*) The vowel AW is attached to the L in the short form for *also*.

Phrases

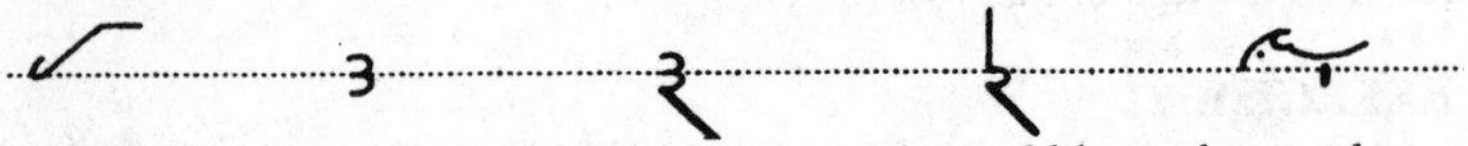

we could would you would you be it would be let you know

let us know let us have in fact

1 In the phrase *in fact* a consonant is omitted.
2 In some phrases *would* can more easily be shown by a W halved, as in:

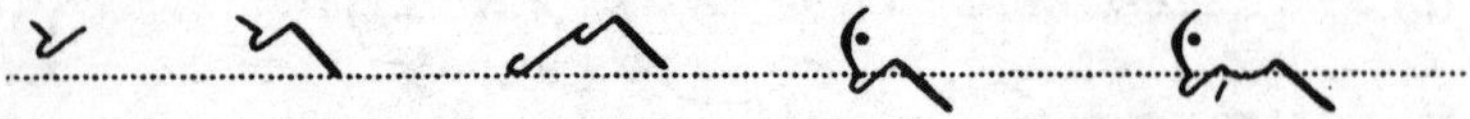

I would I would be we would be they would be they would not be

this would

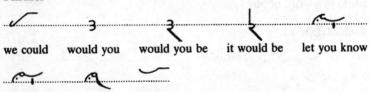

EXERCISE 12

(*a*)
(*b*)
(*c*)
(*d*)
(*e*)

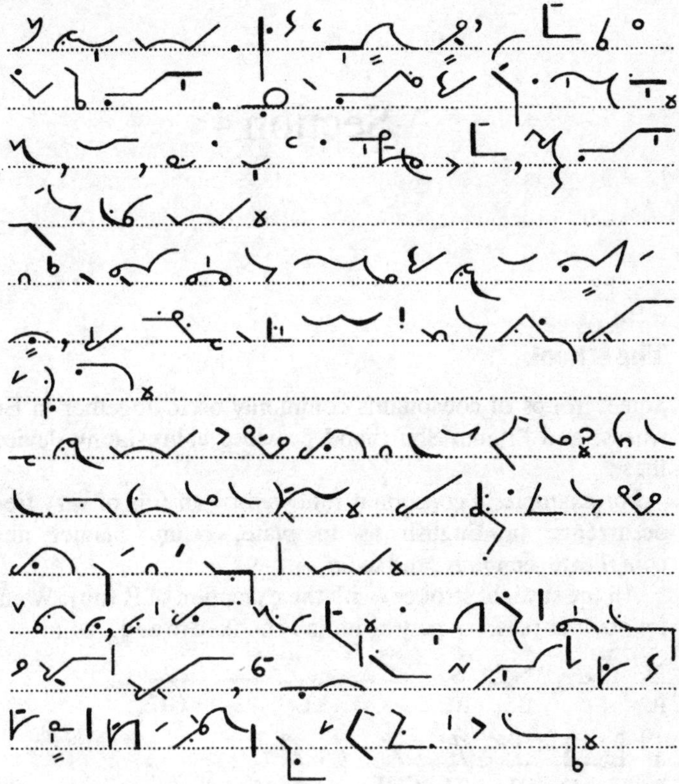

EXERCISE 13 Write the following in shorthand, afterwards checking with the key (phrasing is indicated by hyphens):

(*a*) I-met them at-the-same spot as-we-had met a month ago, but as I-was in-the car I-could fetch-the mats and carpets and load them on Tom's estate car.

(*b*) We-expected to-have a report today with-the results of-the work of-our firm in Canada, but-we-have-not had it yet.

(*c*) Select-the things you would care to purchase in-the pages of-the catalogue, make up-the Purchases-Form and-have it sent to-us today.

(*d*) Although our manufacturers have-not sent-us all-that-we asked for, I-think-we ought to manage at-this month's rates of sales.

Section 4

The L hook

Some groups of consonants commonly occur together in English words, and Pitman Shorthand provides abbreviating devices for these.

For example, a consonant followed by an L is of very frequent occurrence in English as in *pl*ate, *cl*aim, *bl*ame, nu*cl*eus, com*pl*icate, ena*bl*ing, and so on.

All the straight strokes (with the exception of R (up), W and Y – for obvious reasons) may be initially hooked to add L as in:

P PL B BL K KL G GL

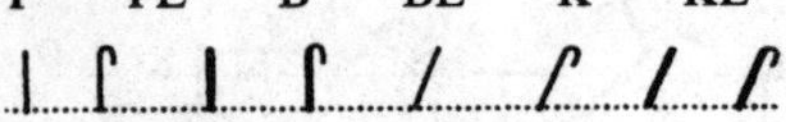

T TL D DL CH CHL J JL

Note that this L hook is always written to the left – anticlockwise. It can be used in one of two ways:

(*a*) consonantally, as in: 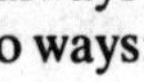 *play* 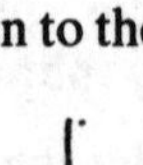 *tablet*

(*b*) syllabically, as in: 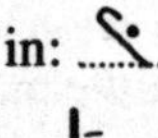 *double*  *tackle*

Here are some examples:

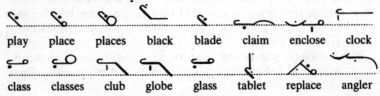

play place places black blade claim enclose clock

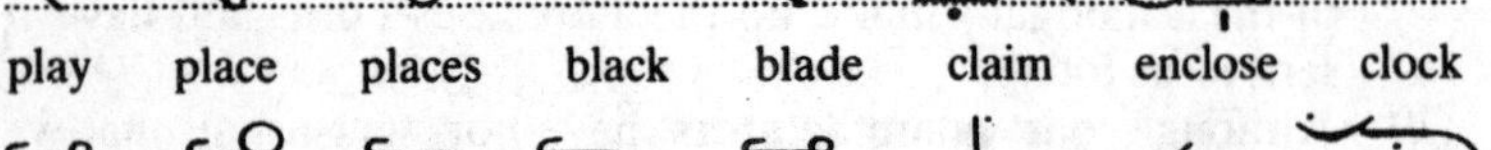

class classes club globe glass tablet replace angler

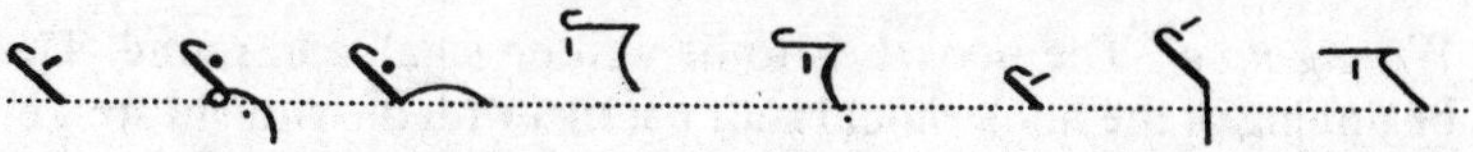

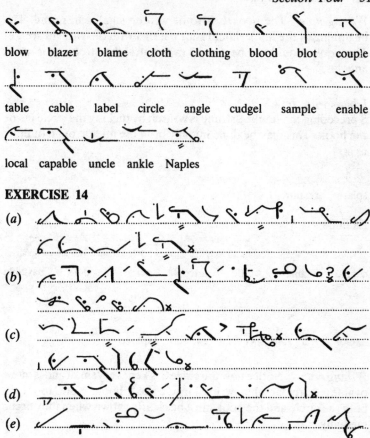

blow blazer blame cloth clothing blood blot couple

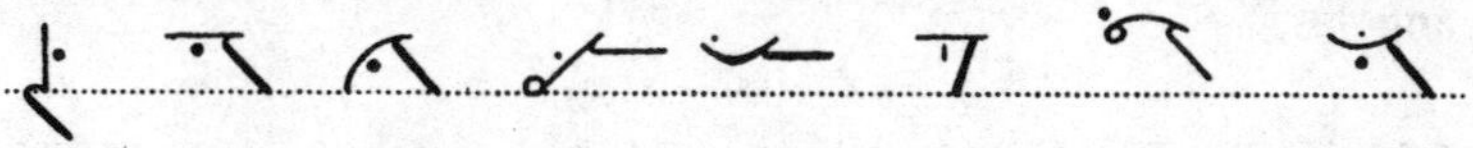

table cable label circle angle cudgel sample enable

local capable uncle ankle Naples

EXERCISE 14

(*a*) 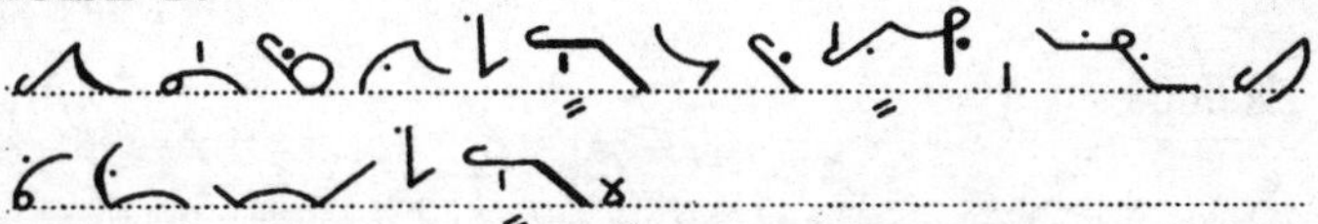

(*b*) 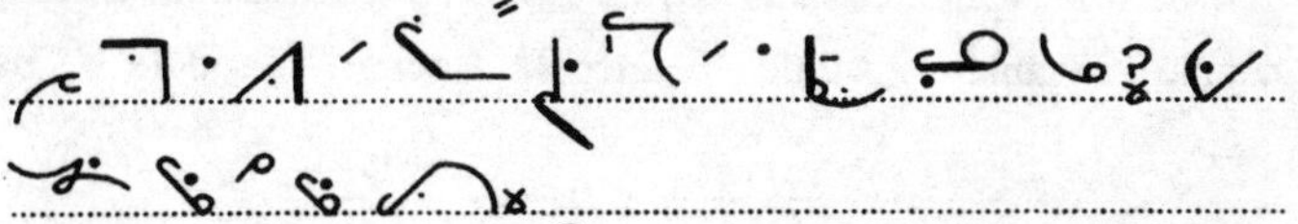

(*c*) 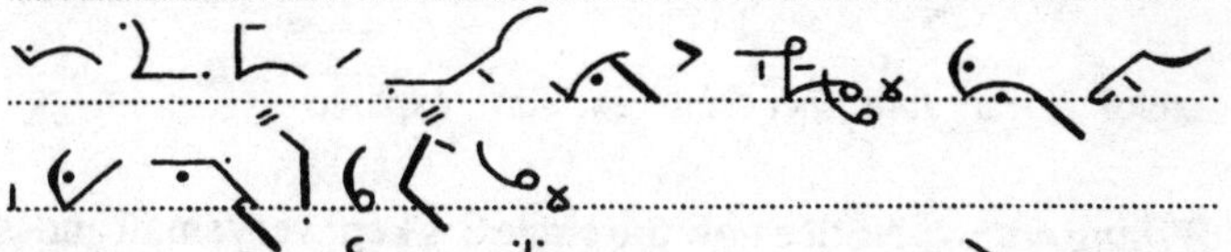

(*d*) 

(*e*) 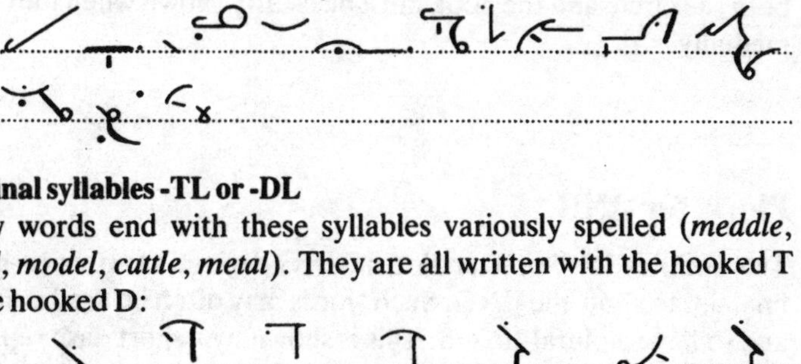

The final syllables -TL or -DL

Many words end with these syllables variously spelled (*meddle*, *pedal*, *model*, *cattle*, *metal*). They are all written with the hooked T or the hooked D:

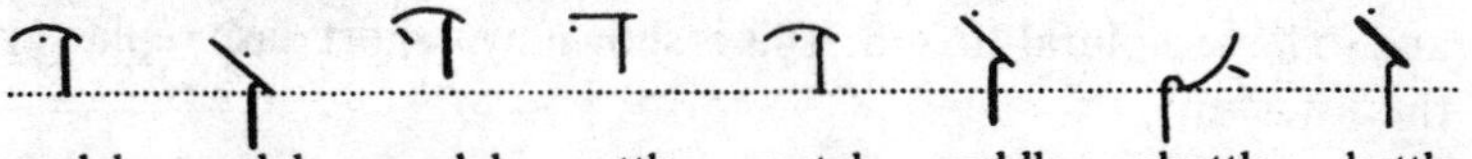

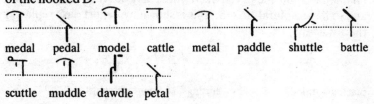

medal pedal model cattle metal paddle shuttle battle

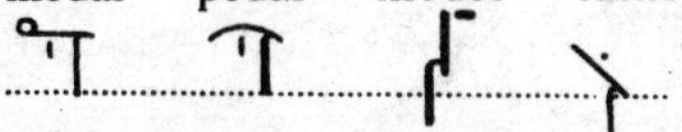

scuttle muddle dawdle petal

Writing note The hook L is to be written small and round. The beginning of the hook should start parallel with the straight stroke. The hook should *not* be turned in towards the stroke, nor made angular.

L hook with circle S

S preceding the hooked stroke is written by tucking the circle inside the hook. This may be done initially or in the middle of an outline, as in:

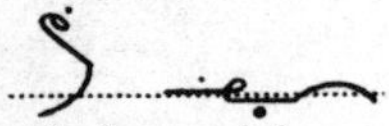

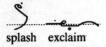

splash exclaim

Examples:

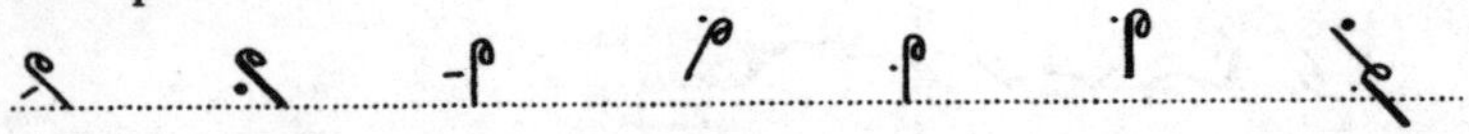

supple sable subtle satchel settle saddle passable

explore traceable pedestal exclaim explode

Writing notes Notice how the circle S is kept very small and is more oval than circular when written inside the L hook. Note, too, how both the circle and the hook must be clearly shown when they occur medially.

Plural for -ING

The outlines for words ending in -ING derived from verbs have a final dot to show the -ING. Such words may often be used as nouns, and so have a plural -INGS. This is shown by a short dash replacing the dot, as in:

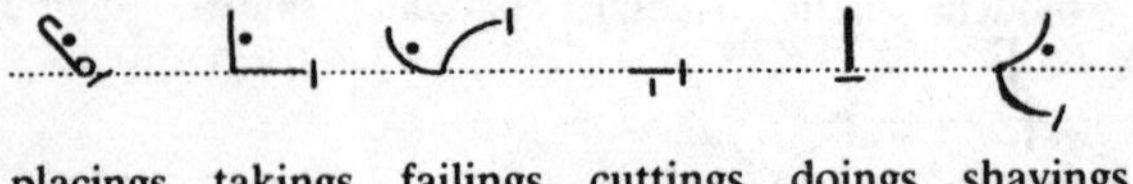

placings takings failings cuttings doings shavings

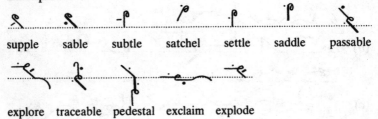

Short forms

To be copied and memorised:

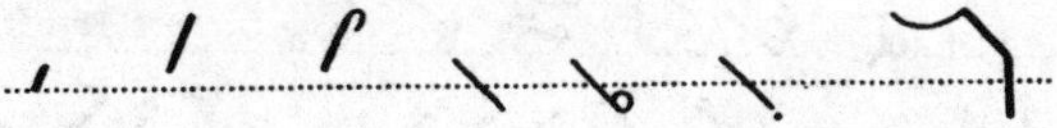

who large largely put puts putting anybody

Note that the short form for *who* is a short heavy downstroke.

Phrases

who is who are able to unable to by all at all let us know

let us have

EXERCISE 15

(*a*)

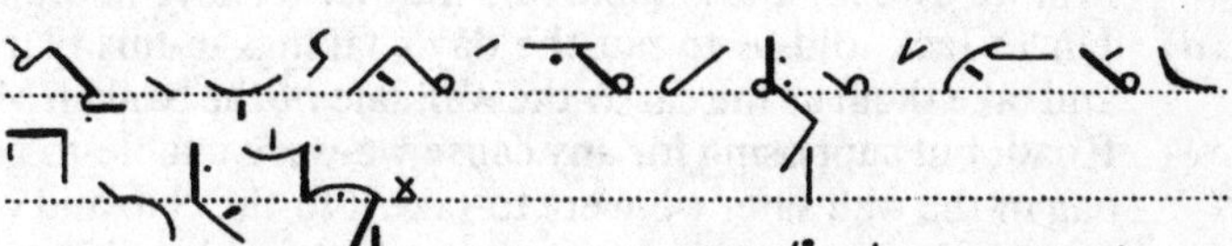

(*b*)

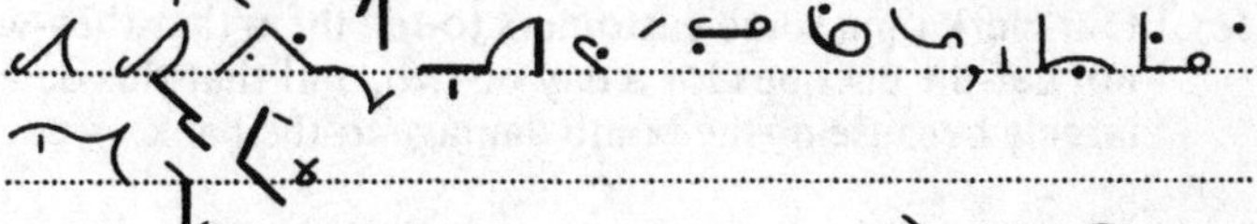

(*c*)

(*d*)

(*e*)

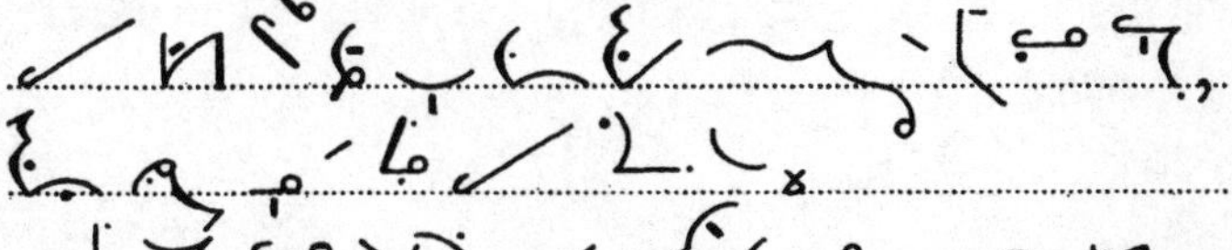

(*f*)

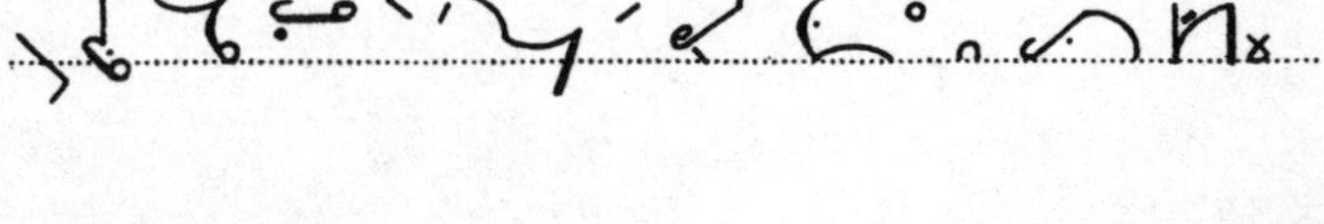

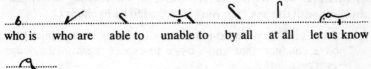

(*g*)

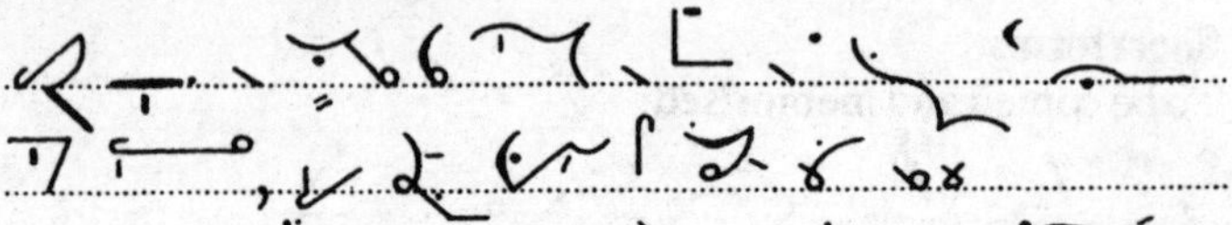

(*h*)

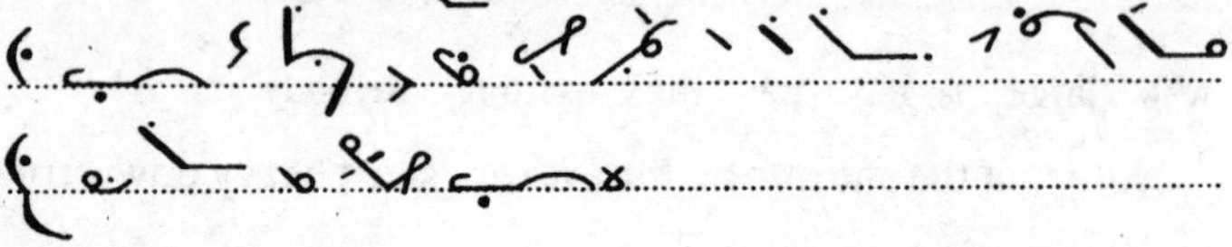

EXERCISE 16 Write the following in shorthand, afterwards checking with the key (phrasing is indicated by hyphens):

(*a*) They said they-would-not-be coming at-all today, but they-have changed that and-we-are to-expect them at-the lodge as-it gets dark.

(*b*) We-have-not enough places at-the table for all of-them and so we-shall ask for a change of date and search for a spot with space for-them all.

(*c*) I-shall catch-the shuttle to Glasgow and be at-the Temple Bar Motel with an hour to spare, in-which I-shall settle up with-the firm we owe for-those sable furs they let-us-have in March.

(*d*) Uncle Jack told-us to put-the day's takings in-this black bag and take them in-the car to-the wall safe of-the bank in Market Road; but supposing for any cause we-were unable-to get-the bag in-the wall safe, we-were to-take it to-the club and wait.

(*e*) Our clerk rang some customers to-tell them that-they-would-not get-the cheques for a day or-two, and-that-this delay was largely because of-the bomb damage to-the bank.

Section 5

Review

Read, copy and then re-read from your own copy each of the four passages that follow:

1

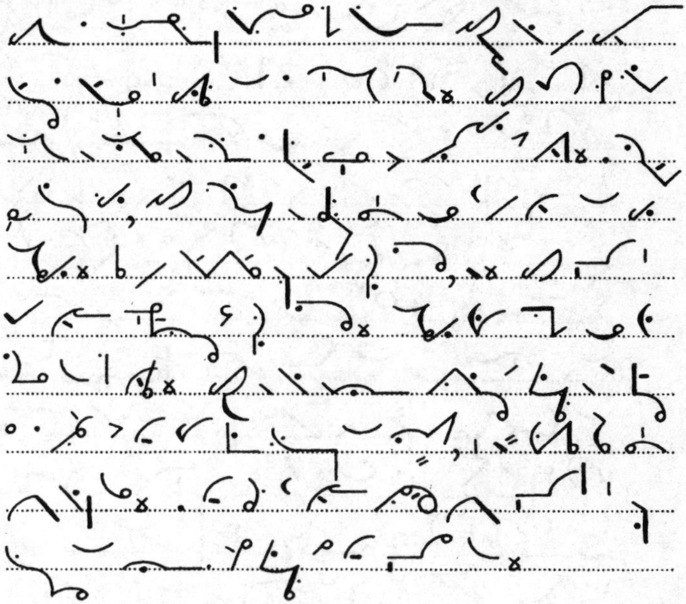

2

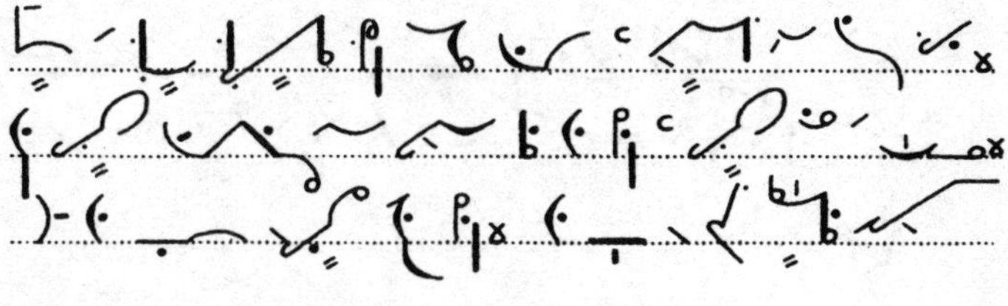

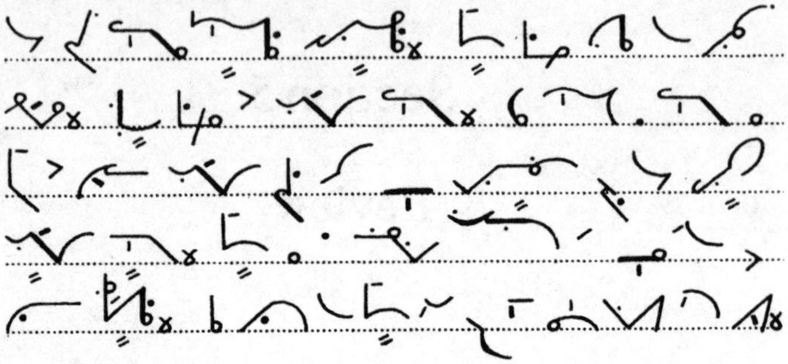

3

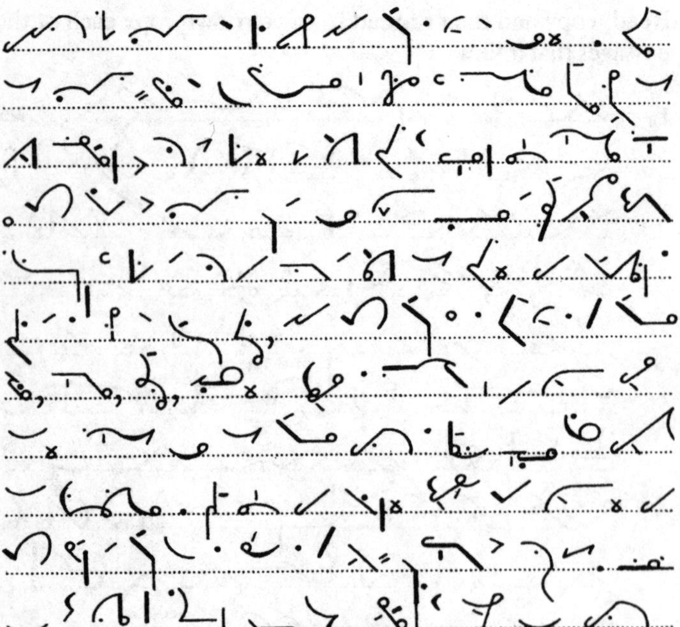

4

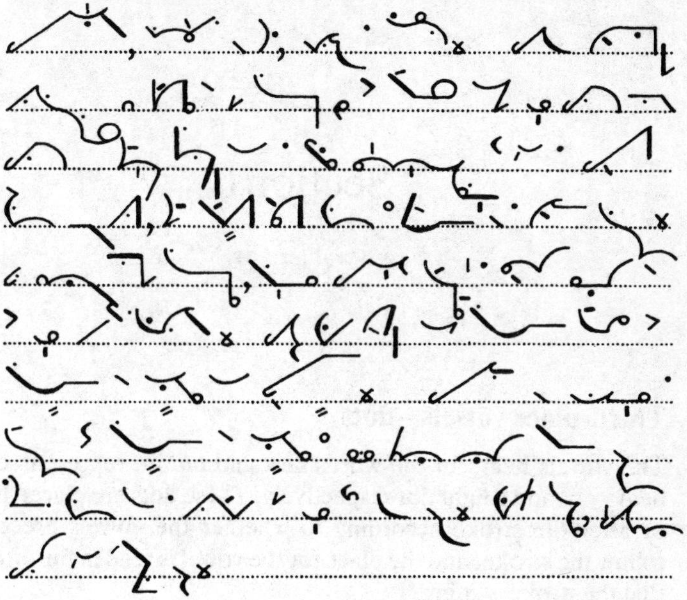

Section 6

Third-place vowels – dots

The vowels heard in the words *beet* and *bit* are represented by a heavy dot and a light dot respectively. These dots are placed before or after the stroke according to whether the vowels precede or follow the stroke, and the place for the vowel is read in the direction that the stroke is going.

L is an upward stroke so vowel-places are read 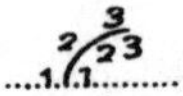 as in the words:

 ill  lee

D is a downward stroke so vowel-places are read  as in the words:

 Dee  did

N is a horizontal stroke from left to right so the vowel-places are read 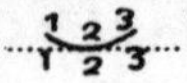 as in the words:

 neat  knit

Now follow two rules:

1 When the first vowel in a word is a third-place vowel, then the first upward or downward stroke is written *through* the line. If the outline consists only of horizontal strokes and the first vowel is a third-place vowel, then the outline is written on the line.

2 When a third-place vowel occurs between two consonants it is written in the third place *before* the *second* consonant. (The reason for this rule is to keep the vowel out of angles where it might be hard to write or read.)

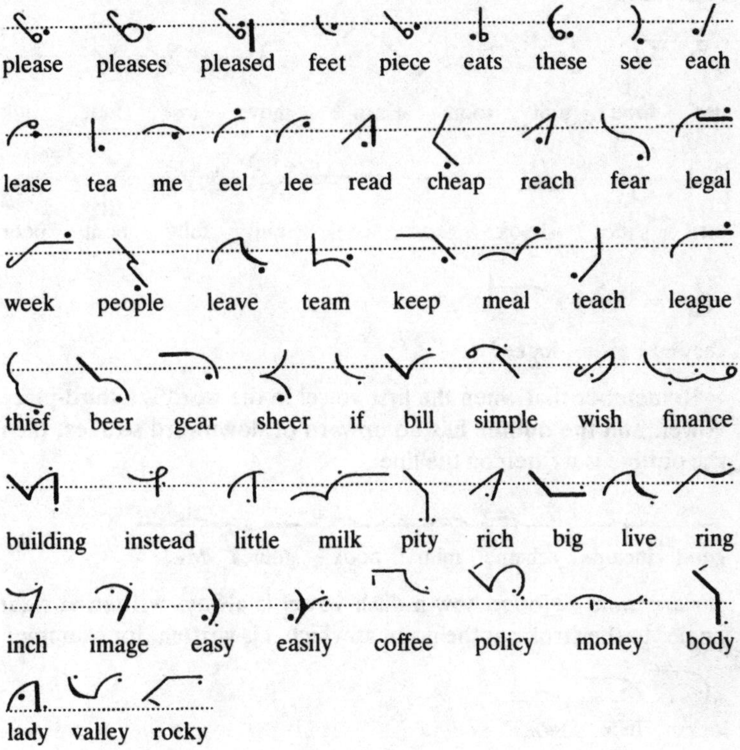
please pleases pleased feet piece eats these see each
lease tea me eel lee read cheap reach fear legal
week people leave team keep meal teach league
thief beer gear sheer if bill simple wish finance
building instead little milk pity rich big live ring
inch image easy easily coffee policy money body
lady valley rocky

Third-place vowels – dashes

The vowels heard in the words *food* and *book* are represented by a heavy dash and a light dash respectively. They are placed as described in the preceding paragraph, as in:

ooze zoo book look

Note again that when the first vowel in a word is a third-place vowel the first upward or downward stroke is written through the line. Also note that a third-place vowel occurring between two consonants is written in the third place before the second consonant:

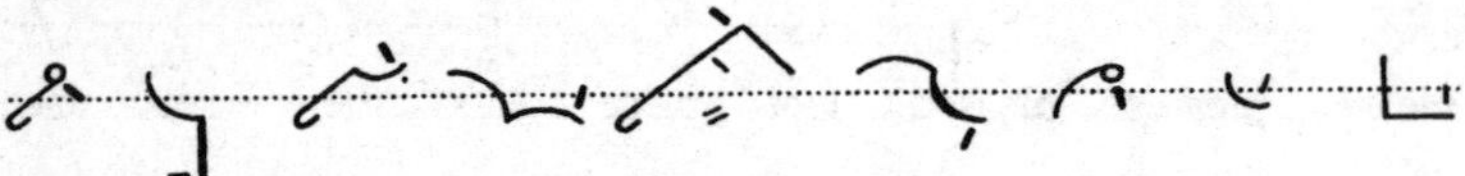

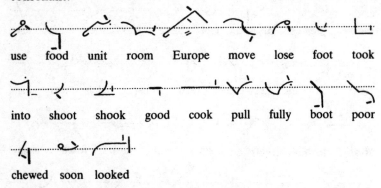

use food unit room Europe move lose foot took

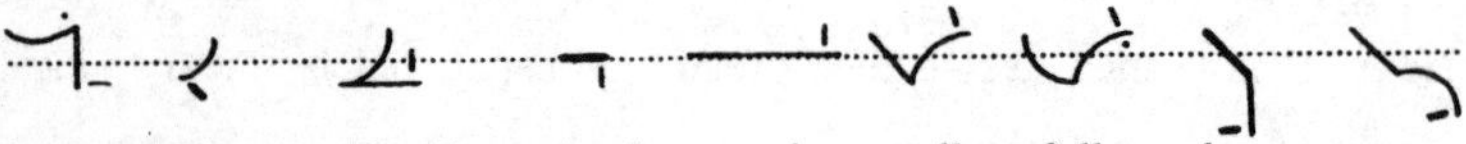

into shoot shook good cook pull fully boot poor

chewed soon looked

Remember that when the first vowel in the word is a third-place vowel, and the outline has no upward or downward strokes, then the outline is written on the line:

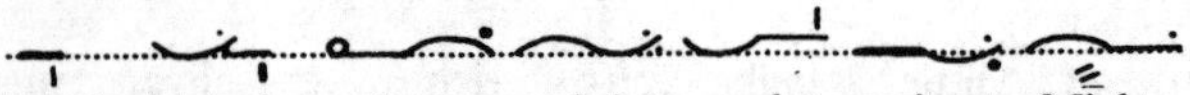

good include scheme mini nook guinea Mick

Writing note Notice how a dash vowel is always written at right angles to the stroke at the point at which it is written, for example:

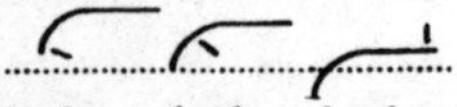

lock luck look

EXERCISE 17

(*a*) 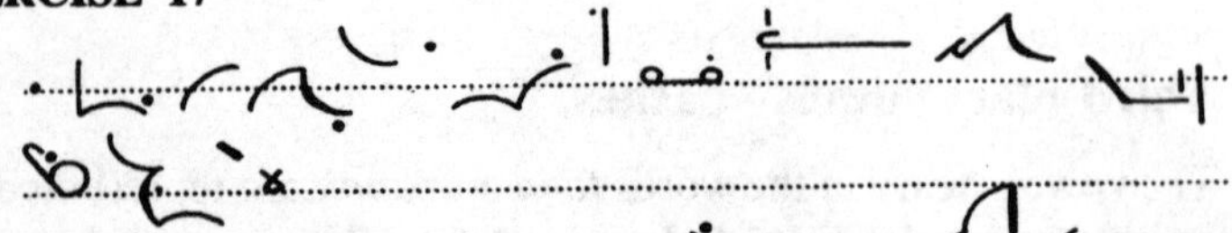

(*b*) 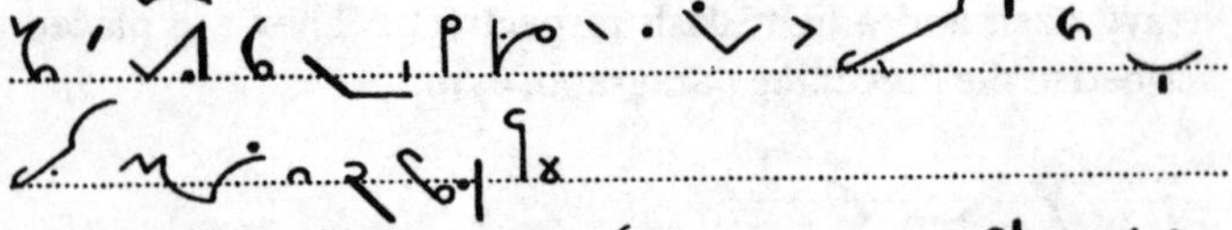

(c) 

(*d*) 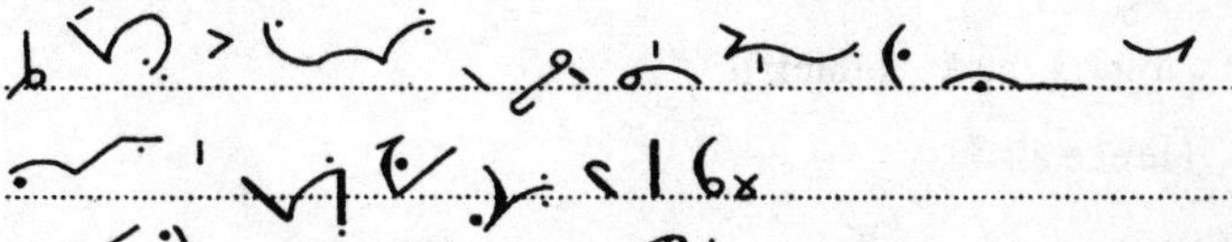

(*e*) 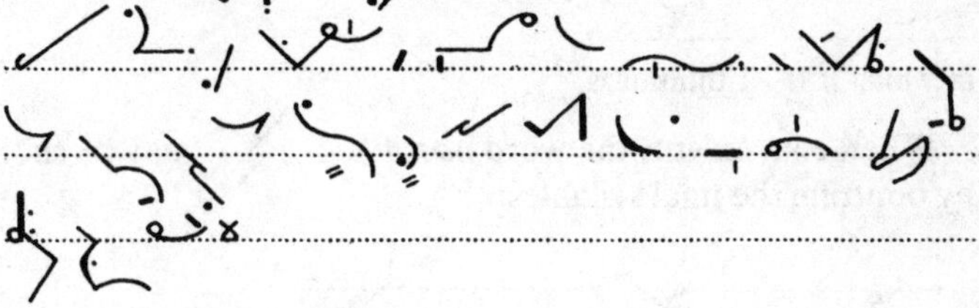

Short forms and intersections

year Mrs

The word *business* may, when convenient, be represented by striking a stroke B circle S through the last stroke of an outline, thus indicating that the next word is *business*, as in:

export business your business tomorrow's business

It is also possible for this or any other intersection to strike the stroke through at the beginning and thus indicate that the intersecting word comes first, as in:

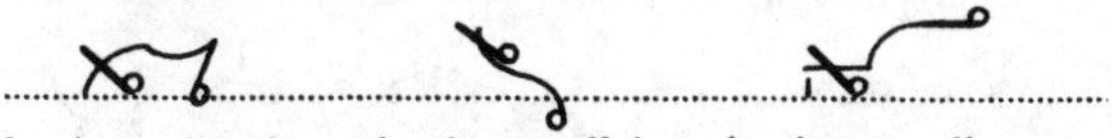

business lunches business affairs business colleagues

This is also true of any other intersection, as in:

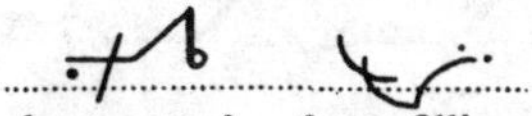

charge cards form-filling

Phrasing

The phrase *to be* is represented by the single stroke for B written through the line: *to be.*

Halving is used in various ways in phrasing. This is the first way. A stroke halved may add the word *it*, for example:

if   if it   I think   I think it

Hence also:

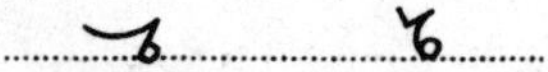

in which it is   I think it is

When convenient, the word *possible*  may be shortened by omitting the final syllables:

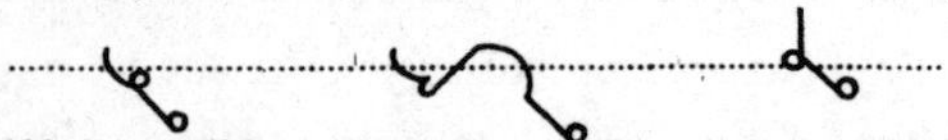

if it is possible   if it were possible   it is possible

Omission of a word or of a syllable or of one sound is a common method used in phrasing and we shall meet many other examples.

EXERCISE 18

(*a*) 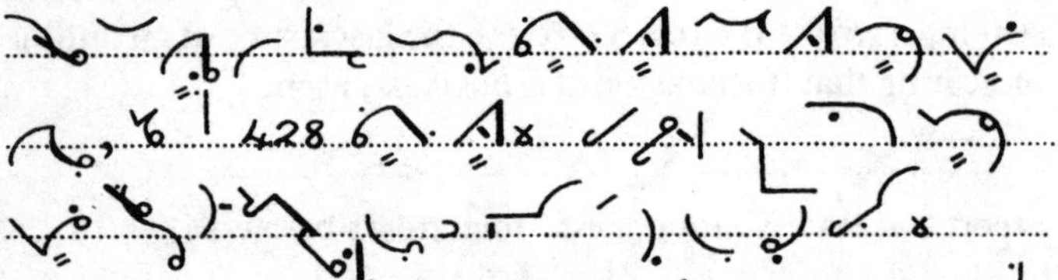

(*b*) 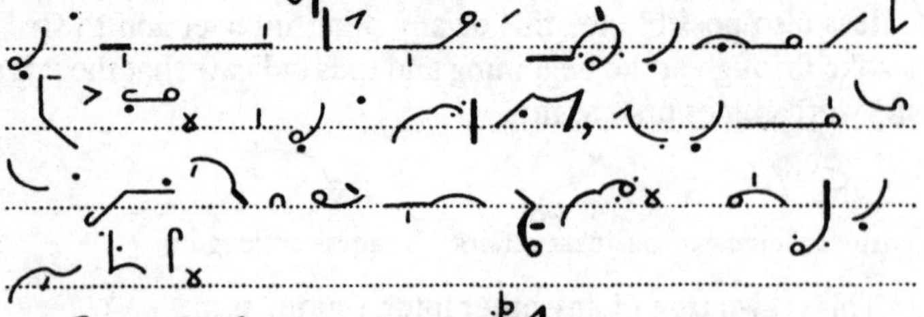

(*c*) 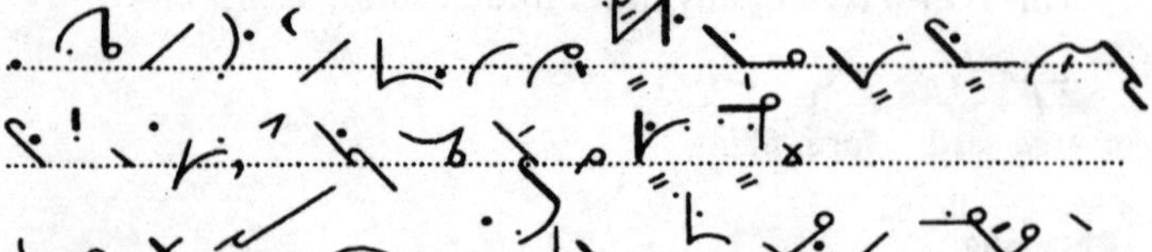

(*d*) 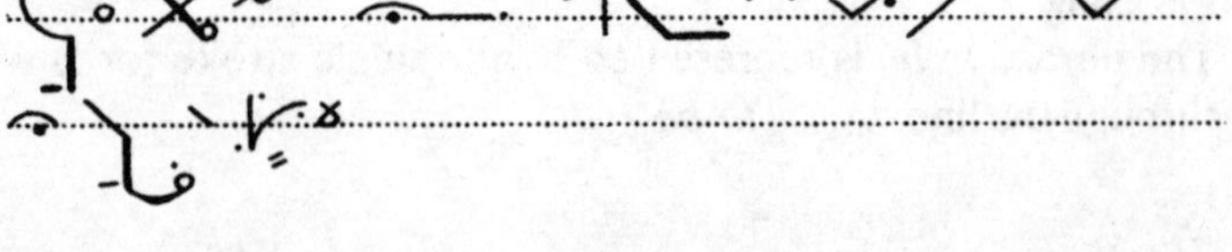

EXERCISE 19 Write the following exercise in shorthand. Check your notes from the key and then re-write the exercise (phrasing is indicated by hyphenation):

(*a*) This year we-shall-be publishing two books on Kenya, and-they-will both include articles on coffee, tea and cashew nuts, and, of-course, on safaris and-the game that roam in-the parks.

(*b*) We-have managed to-get Sea Cottage on lease for a year and-we-are-pleased with-it. It-has ample space for-the six of-us and-the rooms are sunny and welcoming. It-has all-the facilities that-we-could wish for.

(*c*) I-have a scheme to-sell this mini this year and purchase an MG instead. But I-shall-have to-save to-get-the necessary money.

(*d*) This shop sells clothes and food, both of-them good, and it-has built up a large-business in four years.

(*e*) We-are asking Mrs Cody to-go into Europe to build up our export-business in Italy and Germany.

Section 7

Diphthongs

1 There are four diphthongs. These are the run-on combinations of two vowel sounds heard in the words of this sentence:

I enj*oy* l*ou*d m*u*sic

The first two of these four are represented by first-place symbols, as in:

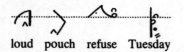

time by joy toil

The second two are represented by third-place symbols, as in:

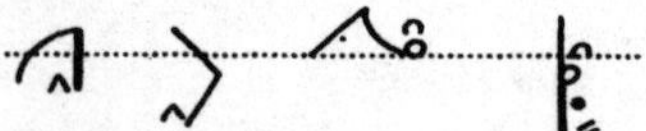

loud pouch refuse Tuesday

Writing note Three of these symbols are small 'arrowheads' pointing down, to the right and up. The fourth is a small complete semicircle just like the *you* short-form.

2 An initial sign for I  , if immediately followed by a downstroke, is joined to it, writing the two together without a lift of the pen. An I sound following the consonant N is attached at the end of the N stroke:

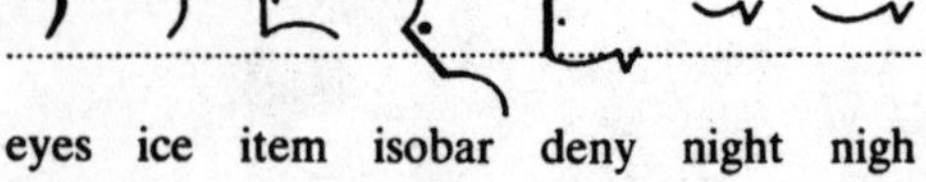

eyes ice item isobar deny night nigh

3 An initial OI preceding an L is joined to it, as in:

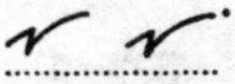

oil oiling

4 A diphthong OW (as in *loud*) following a downstroke is joined to it, if the diphthong is the final sound in the word. If circle S follows, then the diphthong sign cannot be joined:

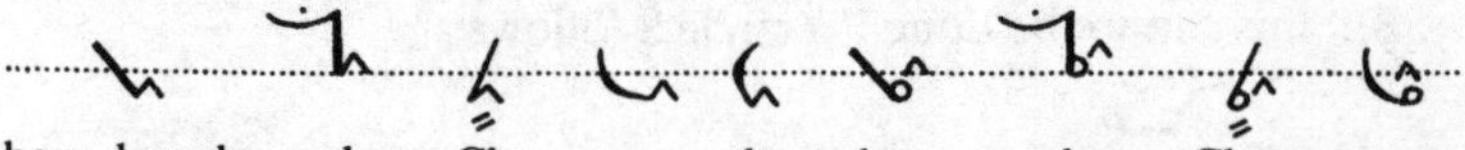

bow, bough endow Chow vow thou bows endows Chows vows

Straight downstrokes to which an OW can be joined may be halved for T or D. When a circle S follows, however, the normal halving rules hold (remember that in words of one syllable, light strokes may be halved for T and heavy strokes for D):

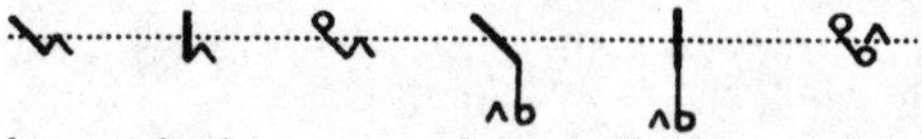

bout doubt spout bouts doubts spouts

5 Similarly, if YU occurs at the end of a word the sign may be joined to downstrokes:

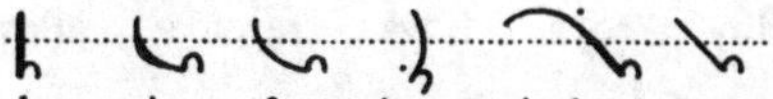

due view few issue imbue pew

This cannot be done if a circle S follows:

dues views fuse etc

6 Single stroke outlines to which a YU can be joined may be halved for T or D, but normal halving rules apply when a circle S follows:

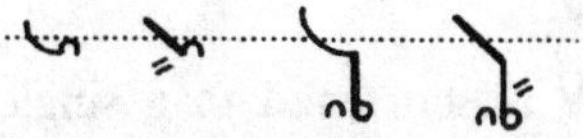

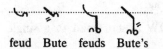

feud Bute feuds Bute's

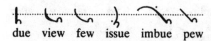

7 Following the consonants K, G, M, N and L the YU diphthong may be turned and written anticlockwise as shown:

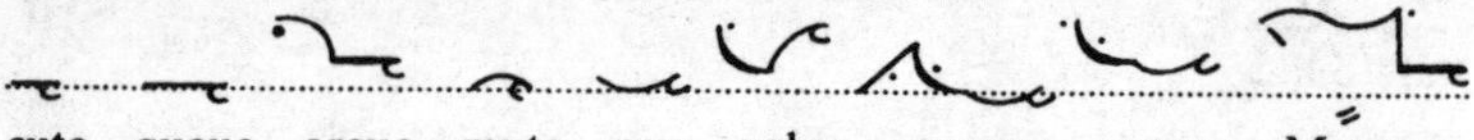

cute queue argue mute new value revenue avenue Montagu

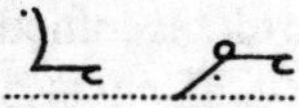

askew rescue

But this cannot be done if a circle S follows:

queues argues etc

I diphthong:

time type miles might light apply like sight reply

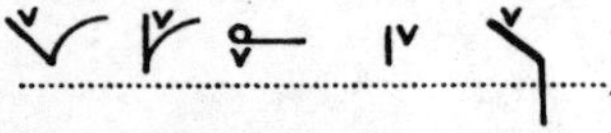

pile tile sky tight bite

OI diphthong:

voice invoice enjoy employ toys boys rejoice alloy

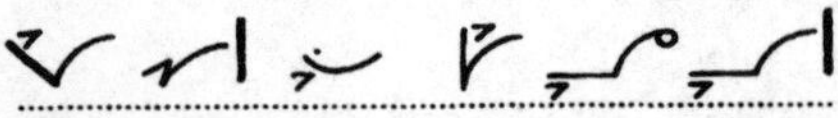

boil oiled annoy toil coils coiled

OW diphthong:

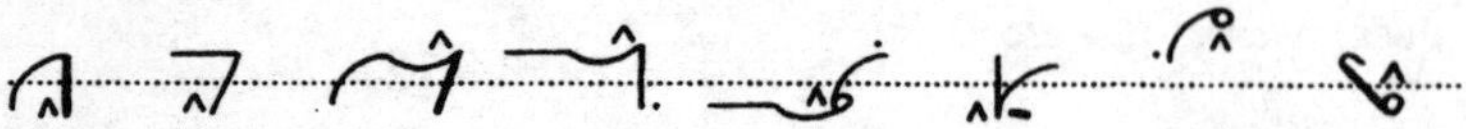

loud couch lounge county council outlaw allows blouse

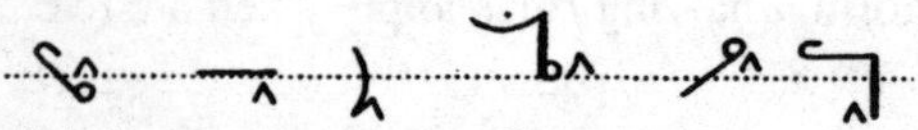

ploughs cow sow endows rouse cloud

(Note  *now*, in which the OW is shortened to a single stroke.)

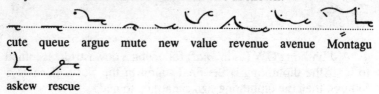

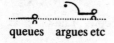

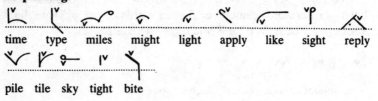

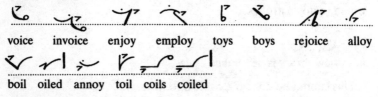

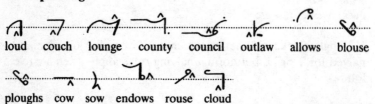

YU diphthong:

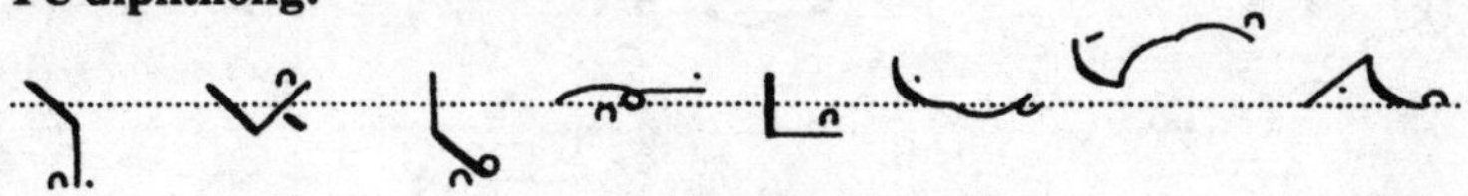

beauty bureau tubes music duke venue volume review

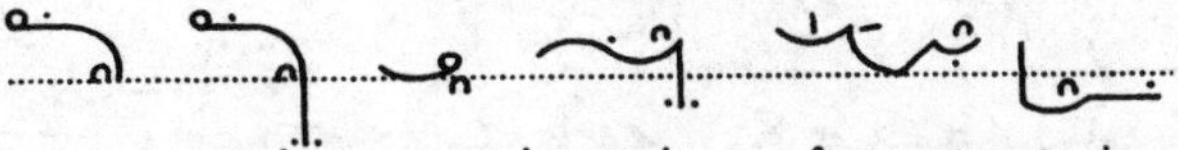

secure security news immunity unfortunate tunic

Triphones

Sometimes a further vowel is added to a diphthong. The sound is then called a *triphone*. It is shown by adding a tick to the diphthong:

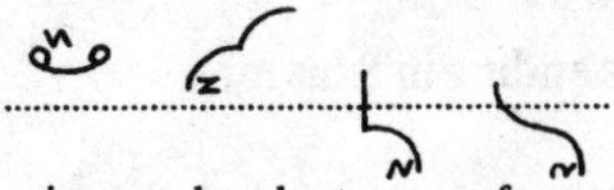

science loyal tower fewer

EXERCISE 20

(*a*) 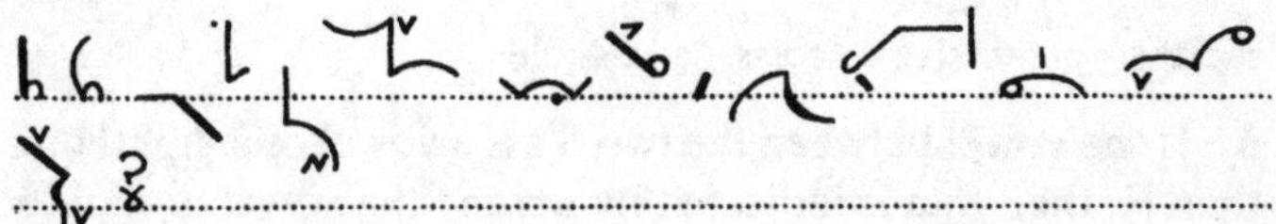

(*b*) 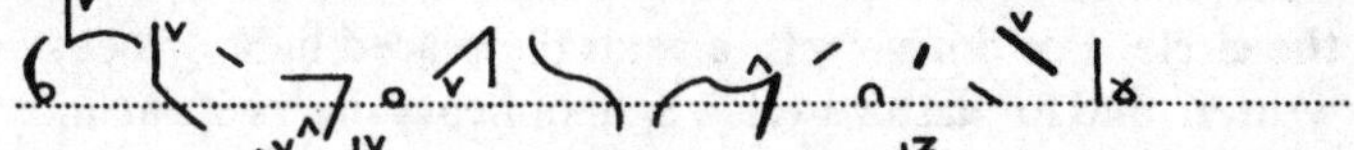

(*c*) 

(*d*) 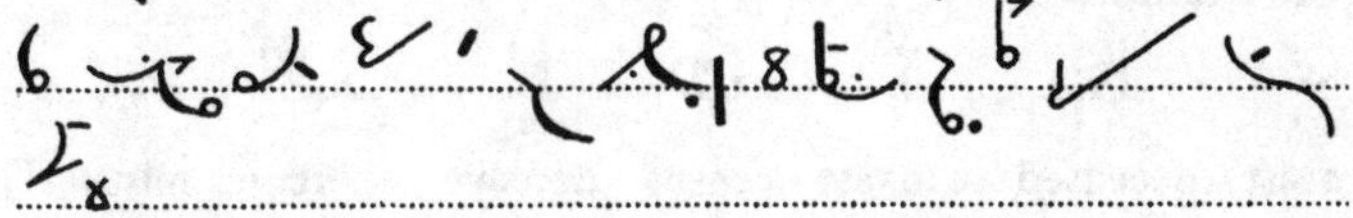

(*e*) 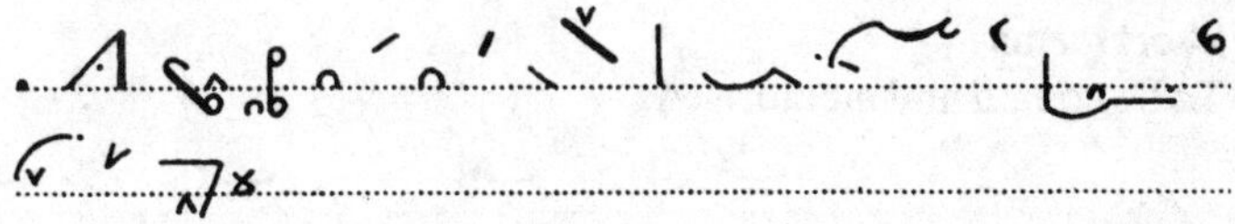

(*f*) 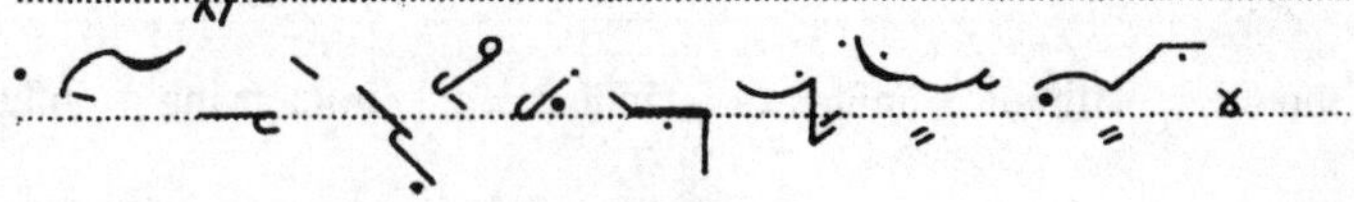

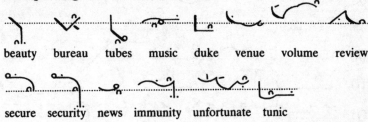

(g)
(h)
(i)
(j)

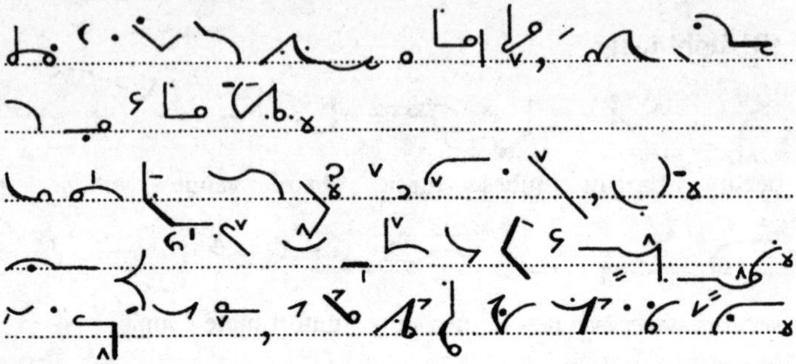

SES circle

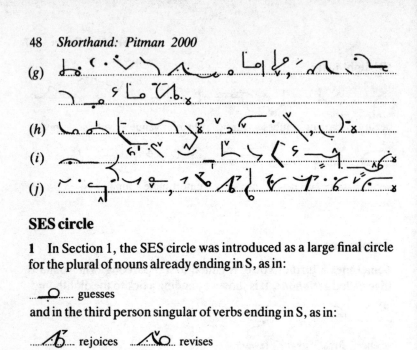

1 In Section 1, the SES circle was introduced as a large final circle for the plural of nouns already ending in S, as in:

 guesses

and in the third person singular of verbs ending in S, as in:

 rejoices  revises

2 This large circle is often used in the middle or at the end of an outline, as in:

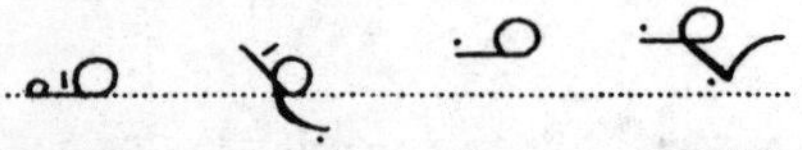

success possessive access accessible

3 If the vowel between the two S's is a vowel or a diphthong other than E, then that is indicated by writing the vowel or diphthong in the circle. For dot vowels, a centrally placed light or heavy dot is written, and for dash vowels a light or heavy dash with an indication of the place of the vowel by sloping the inserted vowel as shown in the examples:

insist deceased exhaust census decisive exercise misuse

Short forms

To be copied and memorised:

should without influence influenced influencing influences

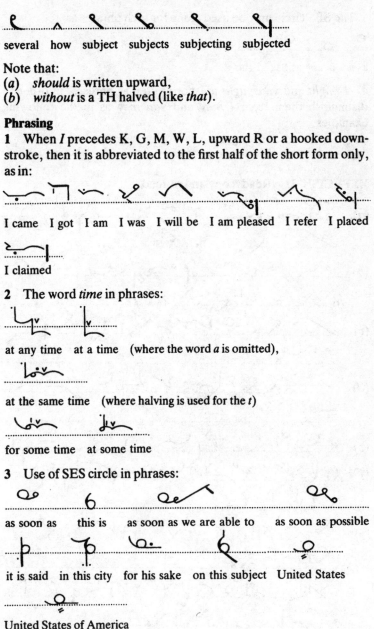

several how subject subjects subjecting subjected

Note that:
(*a*) *should* is written upward,
(*b*) *without* is a TH halved (like *that*).

Phrasing

1 When *I* precedes K, G, M, W, L, upward R or a hooked down-stroke, then it is abbreviated to the first half of the short form only, as in:

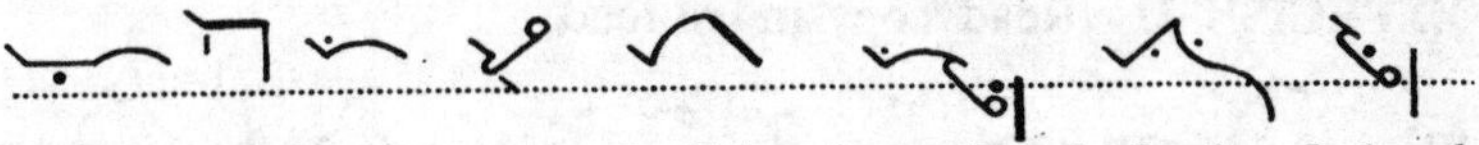

I came I got I am I was I will be I am pleased I refer I placed

I claimed

2 The word *time* in phrases:

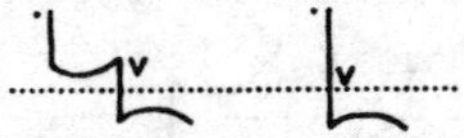

at any time at a time (where the word *a* is omitted),

at the same time (where halving is used for the *t*)

for some time at some time

3 Use of SES circle in phrases:

as soon as this is as soon as we are able to as soon as possible

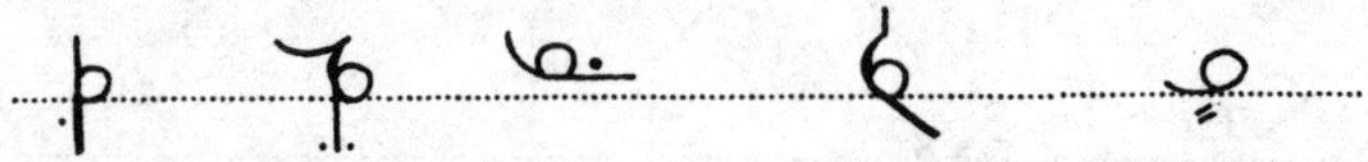

it is said in this city for his sake on this subject United States

United States of America

The SES circle may be used alone for such phrases as:

as is   is as   as has   is his

4 *I might* and *you might* are not written as phrases, in order to distinguish them from *I may* and *you may* as in the following examples:

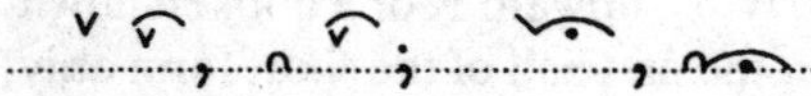

EXERCISE 21 Read, copy and re-read.

(*a*)
(*b*)
(*c*)
(*d*)
(*e*)
(*f*)
(*g*)
(*h*)

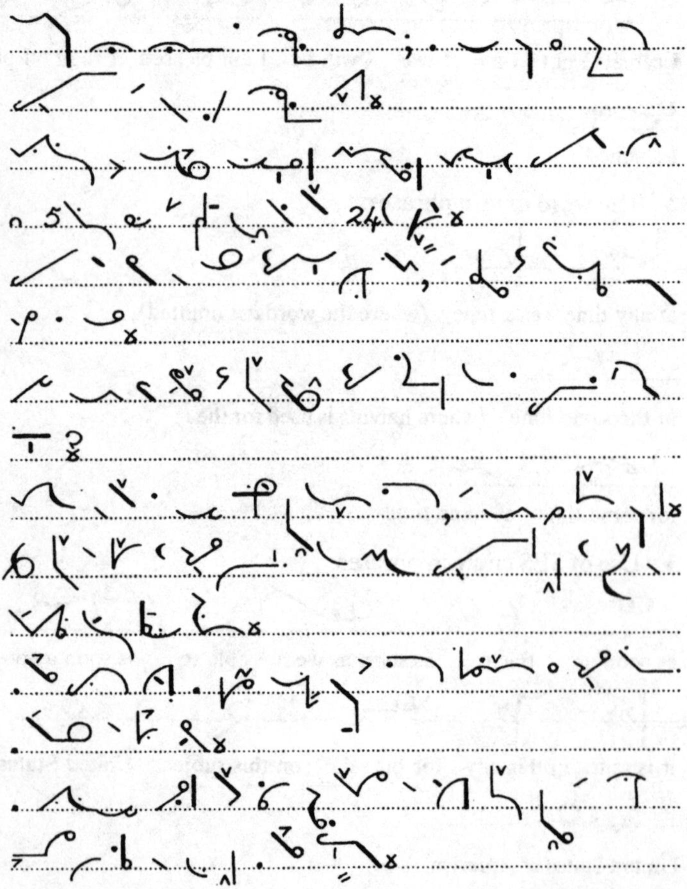

EXERCISE 22 Write the following exercise in shorthand. Check your notes from the key, and then re-write the exercise (phrasing is indicated by hyphenation):

(*a*) I-have-no-doubt that at-some-time we ought to-meet to-discuss-the replies we-have received as a result of-our county survey.

(*b*) I-think-we should decide on-the venue of-the meeting right now, and discuss nothing else till that subject is settled.

(*c*) Joyce Lloyd has bought some space in-the local gazette to-tell people about-the beauty bureau she now has in-the market place.

(*d*) It-is-said that in-this-city about eight per cent of-the people are unemployed, but-we-are told that no boys or girls are among them.

(*e*) Sue Boyd has worked at-this job till she-is exhausted, and-is now lying on-the couch in-the lounge for an hour or-so.

Section 8

The ST loop

1 The consonant combination ST is frequent in English, initially, finally, and medially as in words like *stock*, *last*, and *elastic*.

2 The sound of the ST combination is represented by a flat loop which is half the length of the stroke to which it is written. The direction of writing the ST loop is the same as for circle S: left motion anticlockwise to straight strokes, and always inside curves:

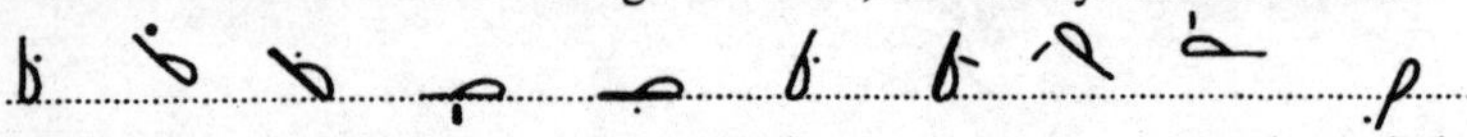

test past best coast guest chest just stop stock stitch

state study story stage most nest last vast assist stores

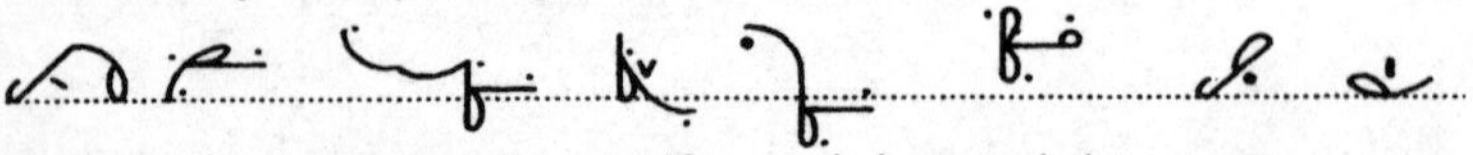

worst elastic fantastic testify artistic statistics waste stone

3 Circle S may be added to an ST loop as shown:

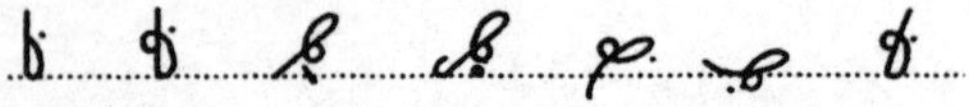

test tests rusts wastes lists nests chests

4 Notice that in words like *worst* and *bursts*, a final R followed by a simple ST is written downwards:

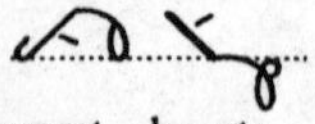

worst bursts

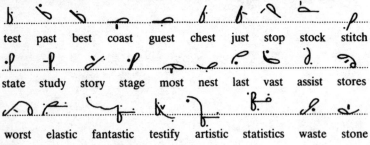

5 If a vowel precedes an initial ST as in *astute* or if a vowel follows a final ST, as in *bestow*, then the ST loop cannot be used:

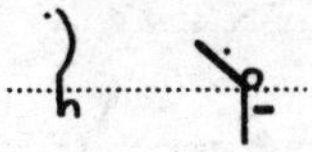

astute bestow

6 If a vowel separates the S and the T then circle S and stroke T are used:

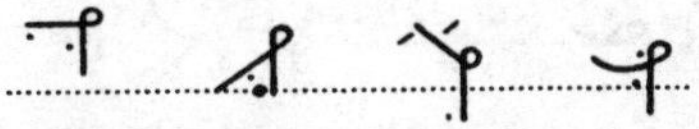

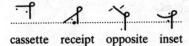

cassette receipt opposite inset

The -STER loop

The final and medial sound combination of -STER is written with a loop similar to ST but much larger, two-thirds of the length of the stroke to which it is written.

-STER cannot be used initially. Circle S can be added to -STER as shown:

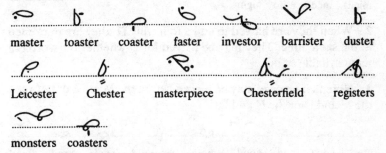

master toaster coaster faster investor barrister duster

Leicester Chester masterpiece Chesterfield registers

monsters coasters

Writing note The ST loop must be kept small and flat. The -STER loop may be large, even slightly bulbous, as long as its size does not affect the length of the stroke to which it is written.

EXERCISE 23

(*a*) 

(*b*) 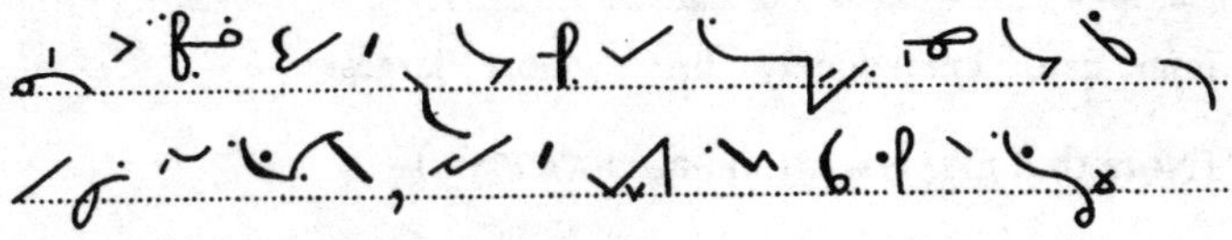

(c)

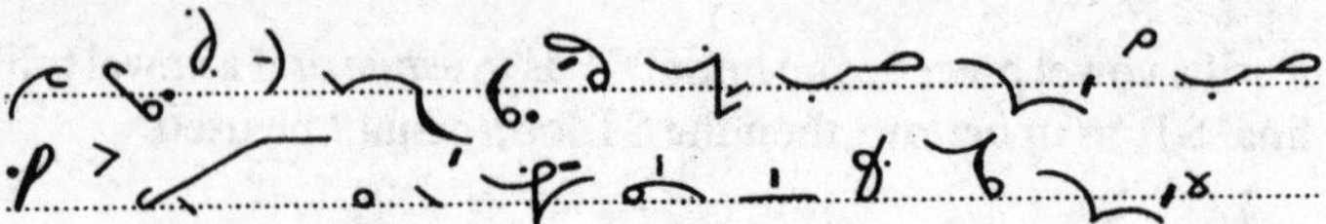

(d)

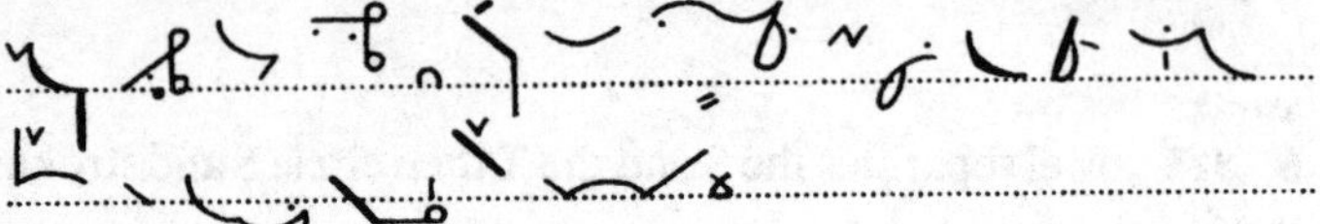

(e)

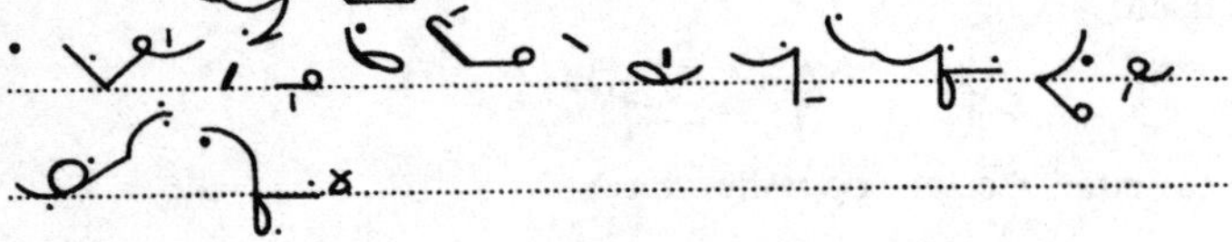

M and N halved and thickened

1 The consonants M and N are halved in the usual way to add a following T, as in:

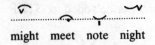

might meet note night

2 When they are halved to add a following D, they are thickened at the same time. They may be halved for D whether the word is a monosyllable or not.

3 Note that a vowel may be placed before the M or N, or between the M and D or the N and D:

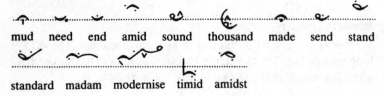

mud need end amid sound thousand made send stand

standard madam modernise timid amidst

Short forms

To be copied and memorised:

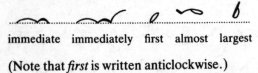

immediate immediately first almost largest

(Note that *first* is written anticlockwise.)

Phrasing

1 We use the ST loop in phrases as follows:

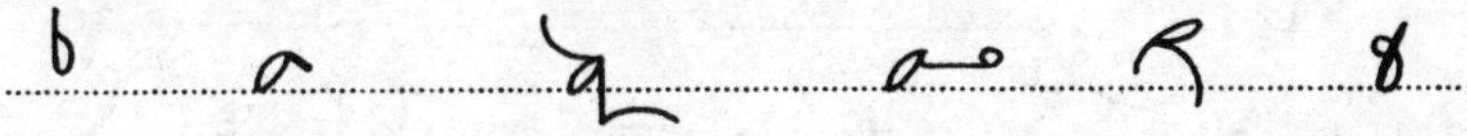

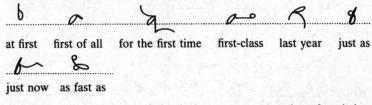

at first first of all for the first time first-class last year just as

just now as fast as

(Note that the second and third phrases are examples of omitting a word.)

2 By omitting the T and writing just a circle S we have a useful group of phrases:

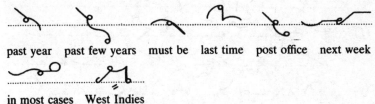

past year past few years must be last time post office next week

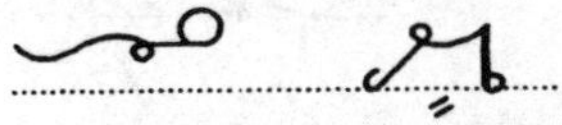

in most cases West Indies

3 Other useful 'time' phrases (*see* Phrasing 2 in Section 7) are:

lunch time spare time

4 The word *out* can be shown in some phrases by halving the stroke that precedes *out* and adding the diphthong OU, as in:

set set out brought brought out carried carried out

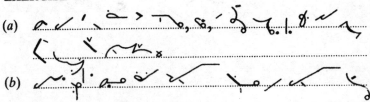

EXERCISE 24

(*a*) 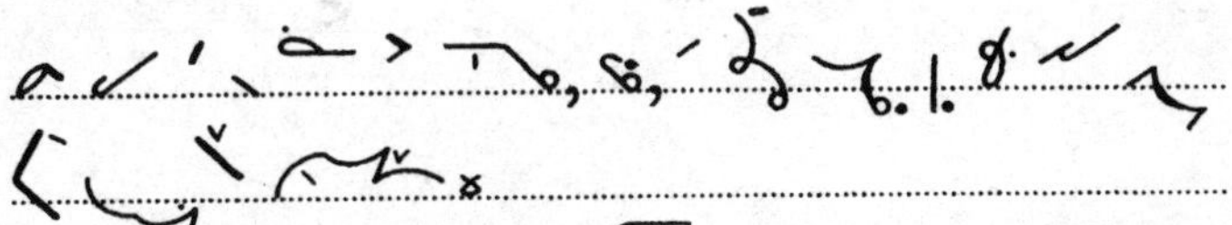

(*b*) 

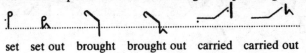

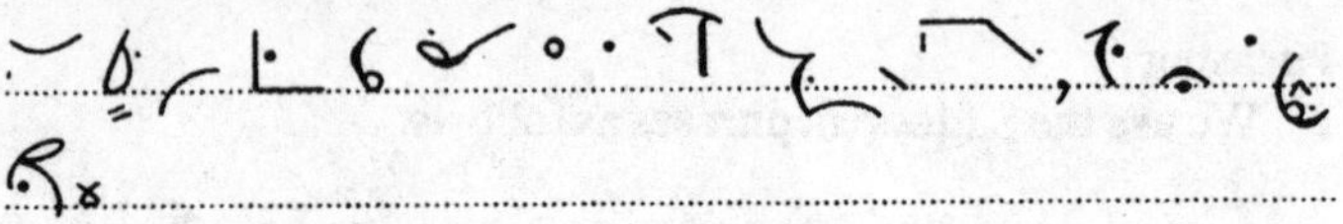

(c)

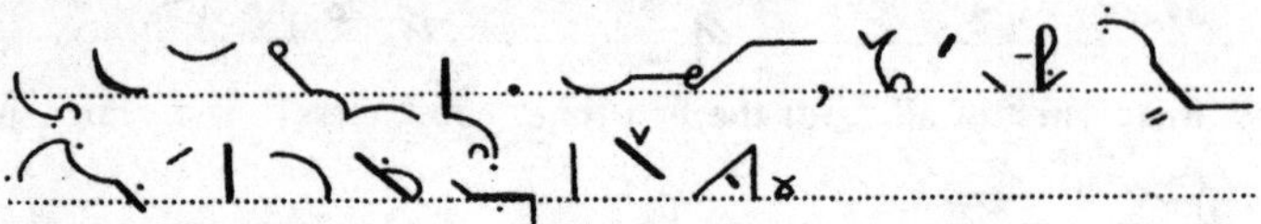

(d)

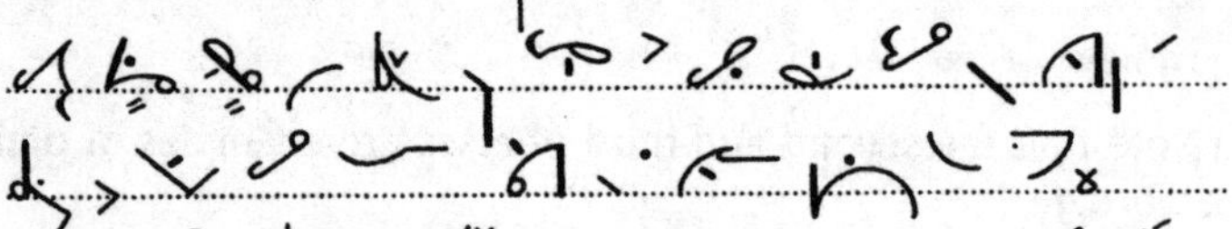

(e)

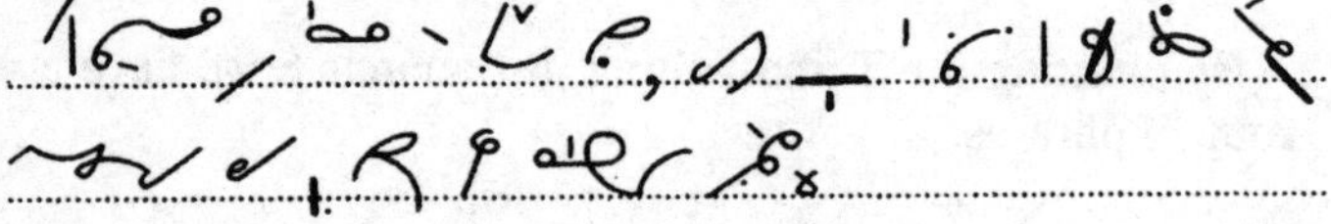

(f)

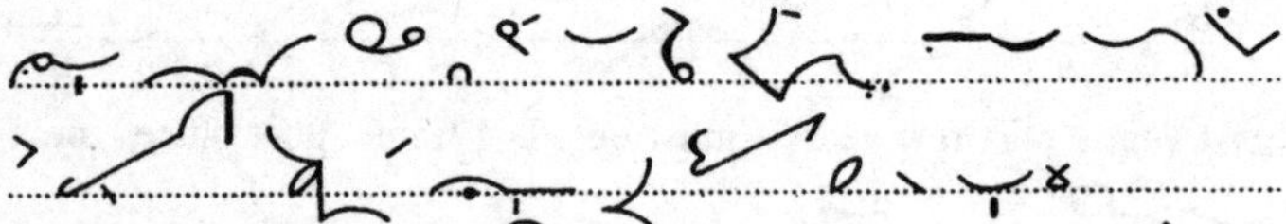

(g)

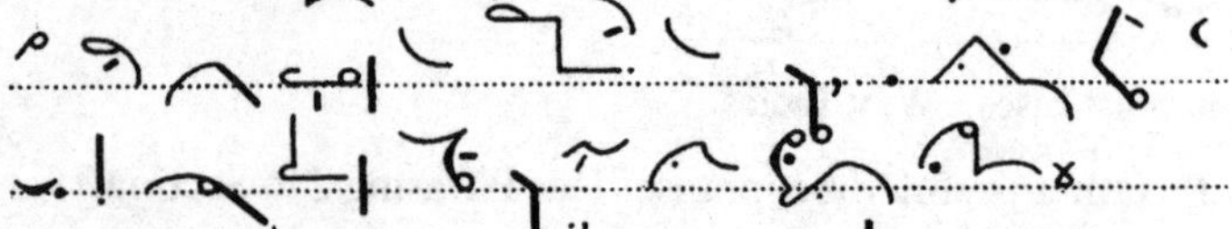

(h)

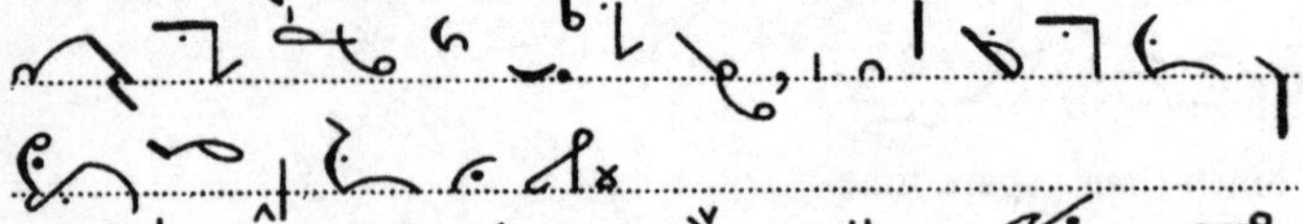

(i)

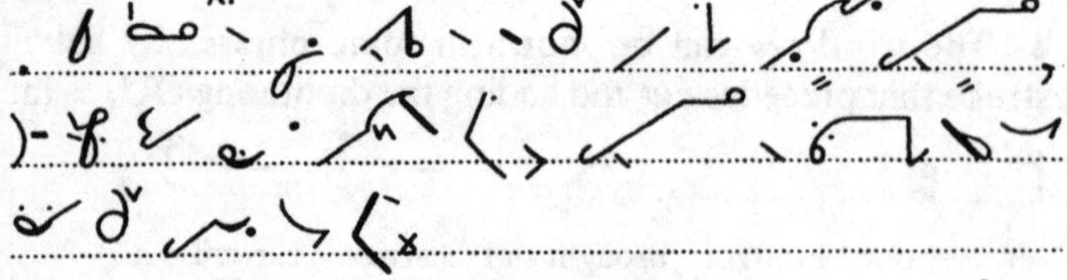

(j)

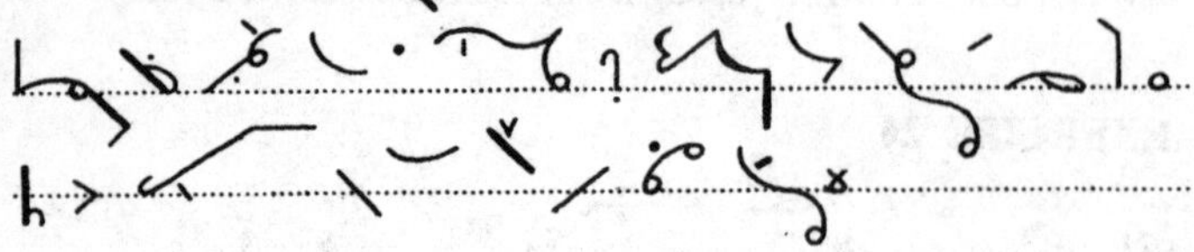

Section 9

S and Z

1 There are two ways of representing the sound of S in shorthand – by the small circle S and by the stroke, as in:

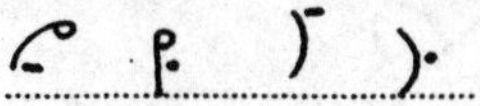

laws stay saw say

2 The small circle is used for the sound of S when it is the first sound in the word. When the initial sound in a word is Z (the voiced consonant) then the stroke  is used:

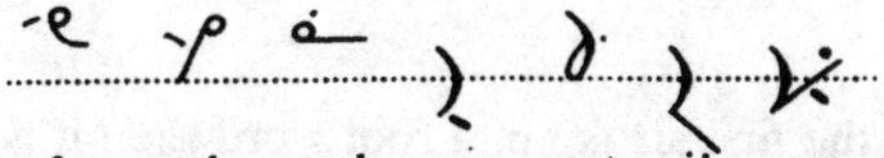

soft such sack zoo zest zip zero

3 Medially and finally, the circle S represents either the S or the Z sound:

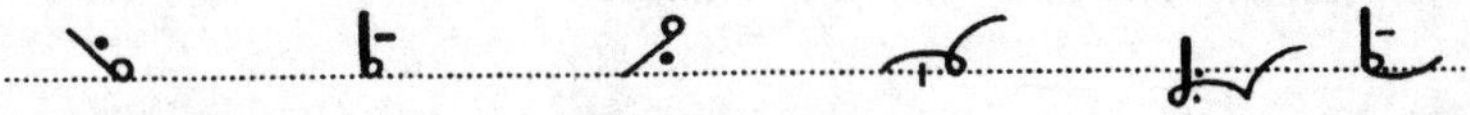

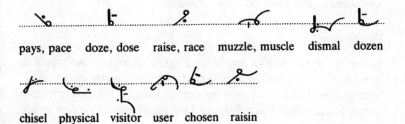

pays, pace doze, dose raise, race muzzle, muscle dismal dozen

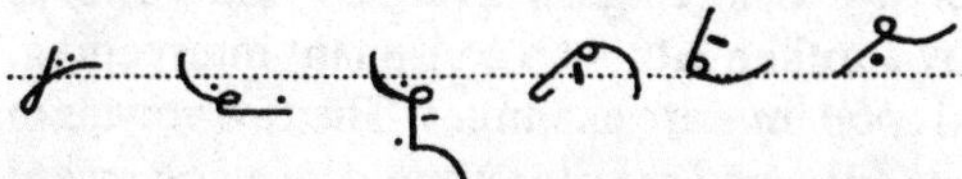

chisel physical visitor user chosen raisin

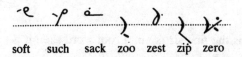

4 When S or Z is the only consonant in the word then the S or Z stroke is used according to whether the sibilant sound is voiced or unvoiced, as in:

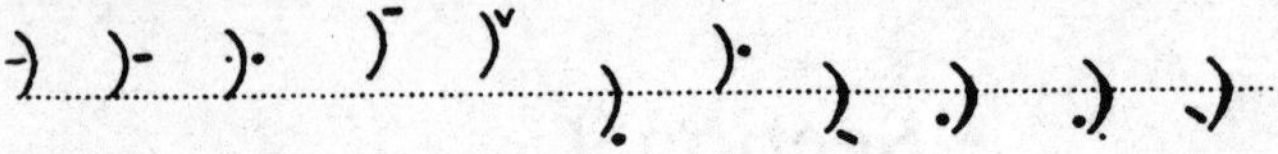

us so essay saw sigh see say zoo ease easy ooze

5 When S or Z is the first consonant in a word and is preceded by a vowel then the stroke is used:

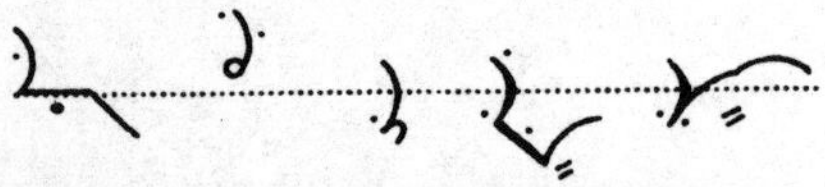

escape assess issue Isabel Islam

6 When S or Z is the last consonant in a word and is followed by a vowel then the stroke is used:

legacy lazy accuracy daisy agency rosy policy

Note that the rules defined in 5 and 6 give us a way of indicating the presence or absence of a vowel without the need to write it in, as in:

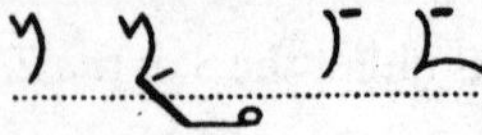

ask sack lass lasso

7 If the stroke S or Z is the first stroke in a root word then it is retained in derived words, as in:

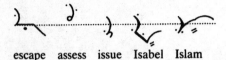

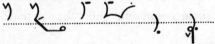

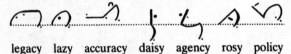

ice icebox saw sawmill sea seaside

Diphones

There are a number of words in English in which one vowel is immediately followed by another without a consonant intervening. Such words as *radio* and *cooperate* are examples. The two vowels in succession are called *diphones*, and are represented by a downward pointing sign as shown, which is placed in the position of the first of the two vowels in the pair. The use of this sign is often very helpful in making words instantly readable:

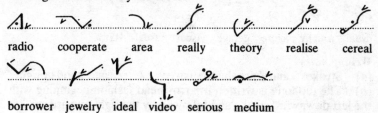

radio cooperate area really theory realise cereal

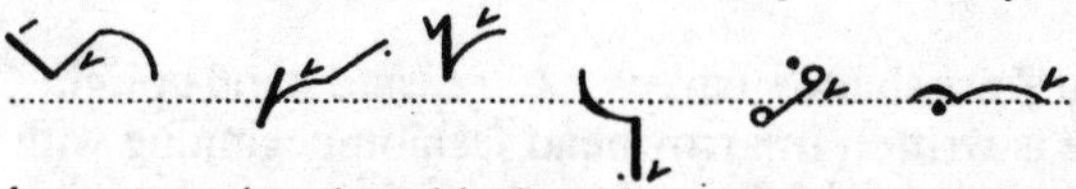

borrower jewelry ideal video serious medium

EXERCISE 25

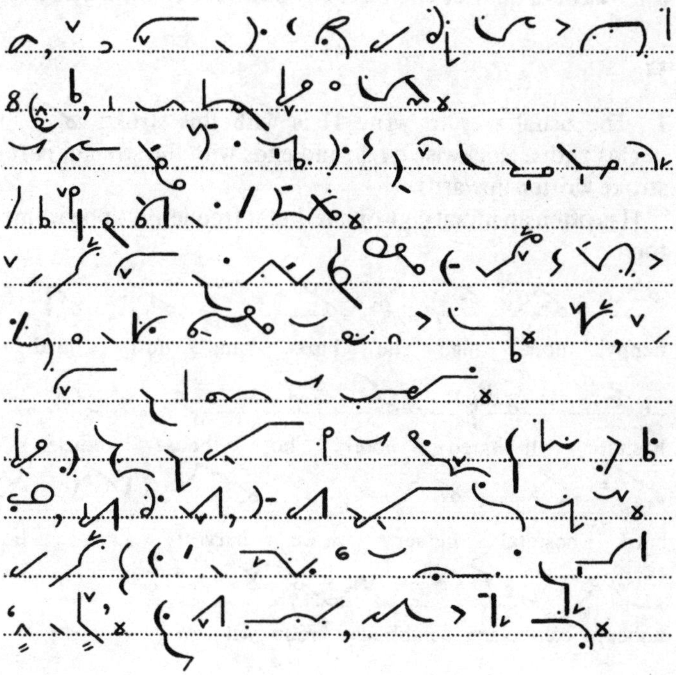

(*a*)
(*b*)
(*c*)
(*d*)
(*e*)

ZH

This spelling is conventionally used for the sound heard in such words as *garage*, *usual*, *visual*, *azure*, etc. The sound is the voiced form of SH, and is written in the same way, except that it is written with a heavier line:

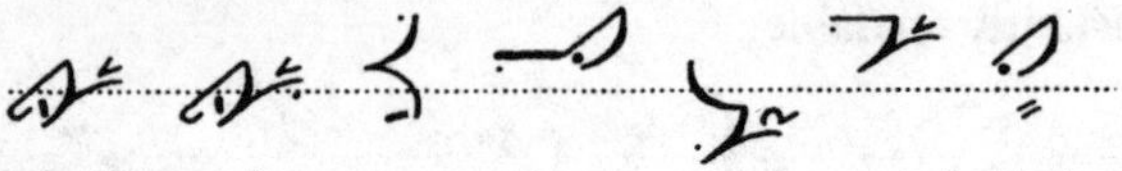

usual usually azure garage visual casual Raj

Writing notes

(*a*) Strokes S and Z are shallow curves)) and stand upright.

(*b*) The diphone is written in arrowhead fashion beginning with the left downward stroke and followed by the right upward stroke:

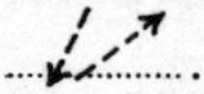

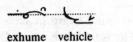

(*c*) ZH is a quarter circle exactly like SH only with a heavier line.

H

1 The usual way to write H is with this stroke ..., which begins with a clockwise circle and ends with the straight part of the stroke written upwards.

H is often an initial consonant, but it frequently appears medially too:

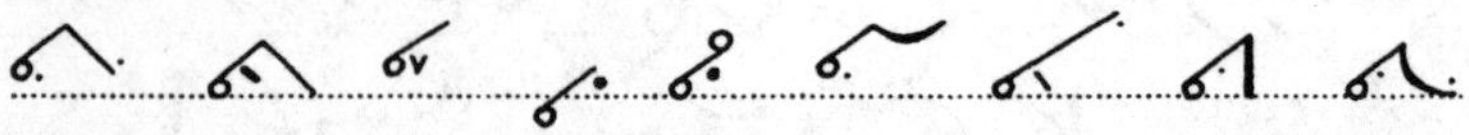

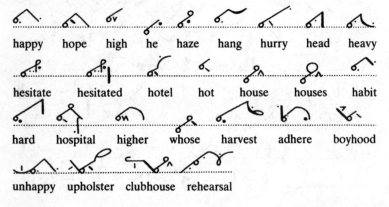

happy hope high he haze hang hurry head heavy

hesitate hesitated hotel hot house houses habit

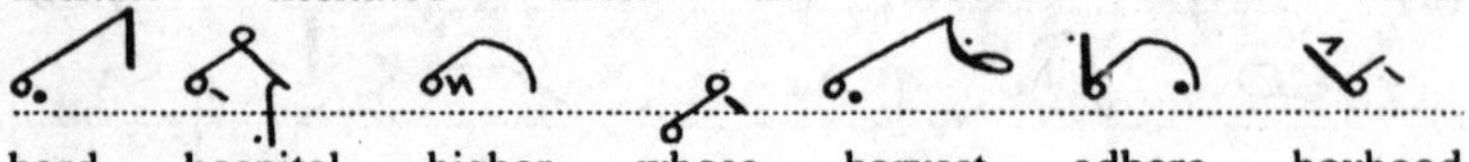

hard hospital higher whose harvest adhere boyhood

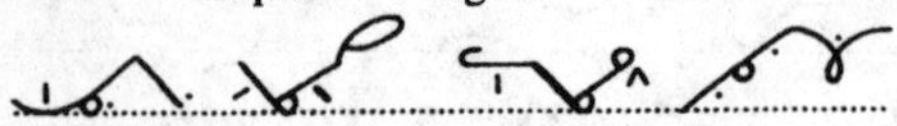

unhappy upholster clubhouse rehearsal

2 When a medial H is not sounded, then it is omitted from the shorthand, as in:

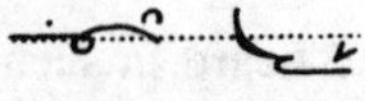

exhume vehicle

3 When H immediately follows an S medially, it is omitted:

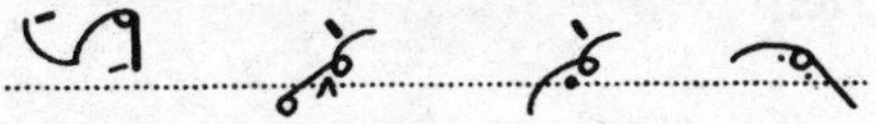

falsehood household leasehold mishap

Note the way these last words are written:

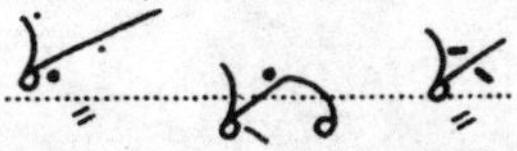

Sahara seahorse Soho

4 When H is initial and the next consonant is an M or an L or an R downwards, then H is written by a short downward tick from right to left known as tick H, as in:

ham home him her hair harm horse homicide humble

hall holiday hills heal healthy hear heard

5 Monosyllabic H-RT words are written with tick H and downward R halved:

heart hurt

6 Remember that if a downward R is used in a root word, it is retained in words derived from it (see page 19):

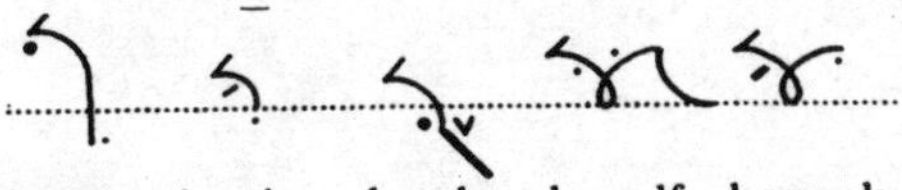

hearty hurting hereby herself hoarsely

Writing notes

(*a*) It is important to note the clear distinction between H and S plus R up, and between H and CH plus circle S:

hoe sorry hay chase

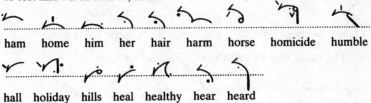

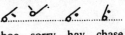

(*b*) The tick H used initially before M, L and R down is short and slopes slightly from right to left:

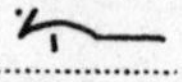

hammock

Short form

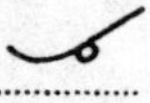

anyhow

Phrasing

1 In suitable phrases, the word *hope*  may be represented by the stroke P alone, omitting the H:

I hope we hope we hope that you will we hope you are

2 The usual way to write *he is*  So we have:

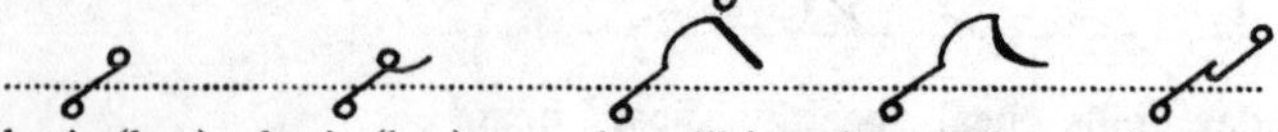

he is (has) he is (has) not he will be he will have he was

However, when *he* is medial or final, it is written, when convenient to do so, with a short heavy vertical downstroke, as in:

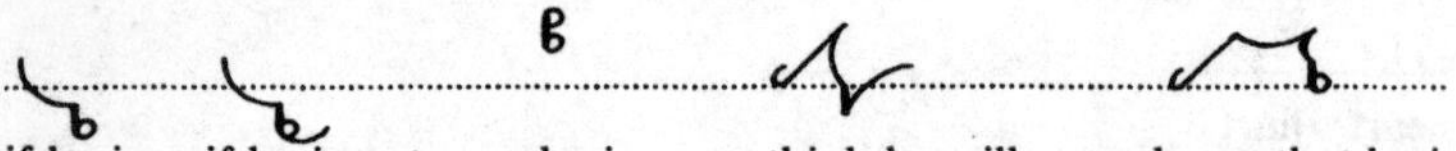

if he is if he is not as he is we think he will we know that he is

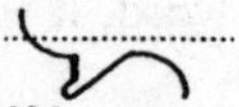

if he were

3 Note the useful phrase:

how much

4  is the short way of writing *New York*.

5 The tick H may be used medially in such phrases as:

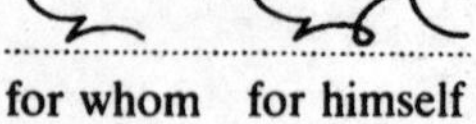

for whom for himself

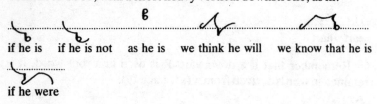

EXERCISE 26

(*a*)

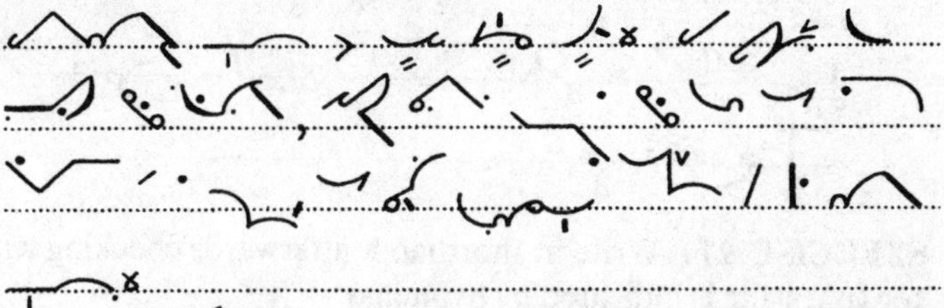

(*b*)

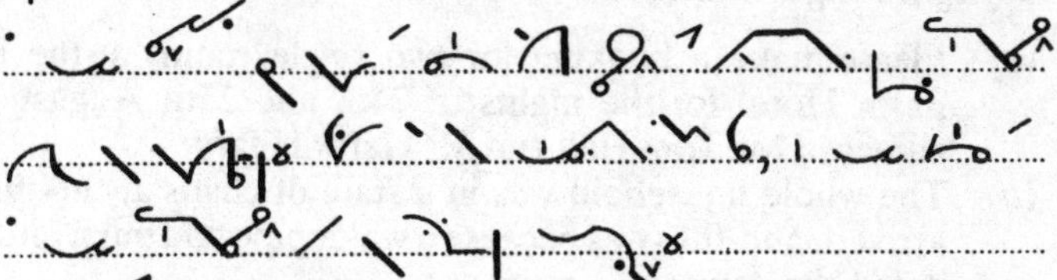

(*c*)

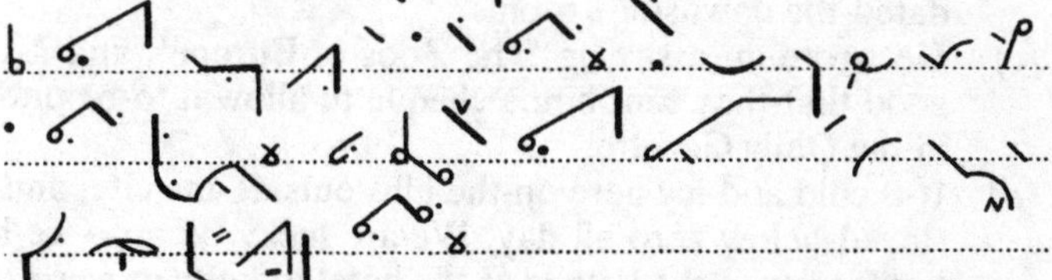

(*d*)

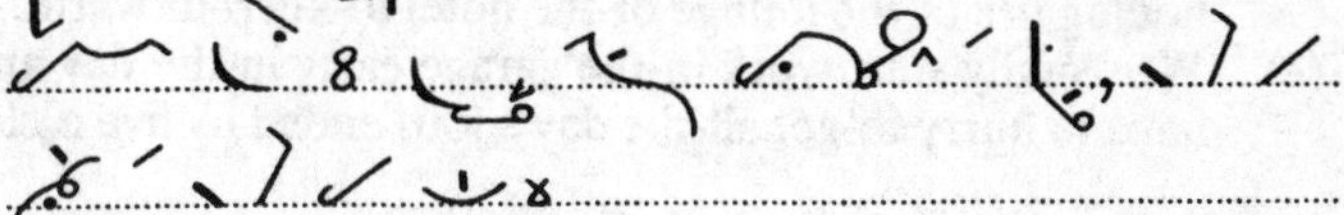

(*e*)

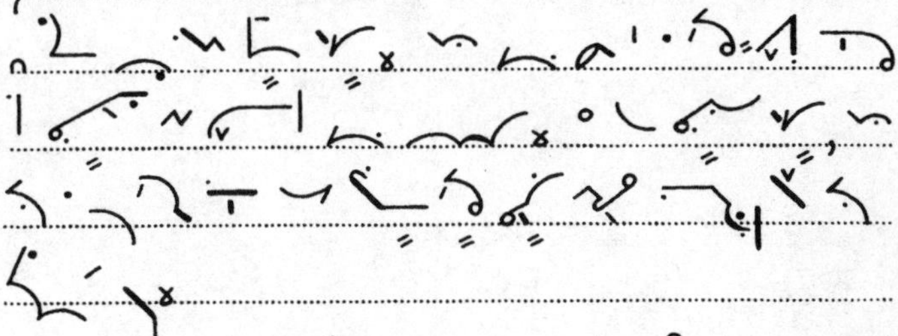

(*f*)

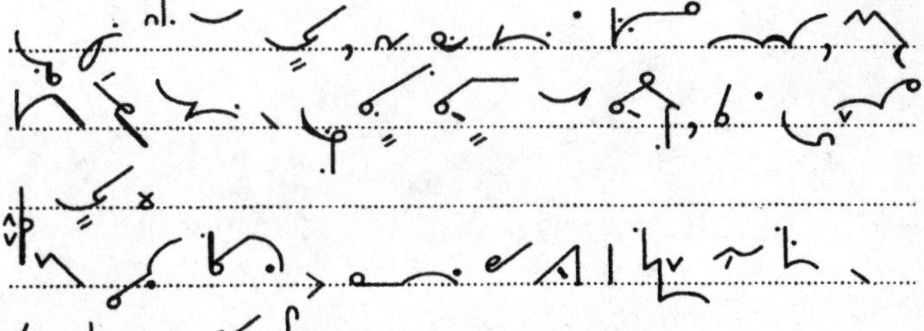

(*g*)

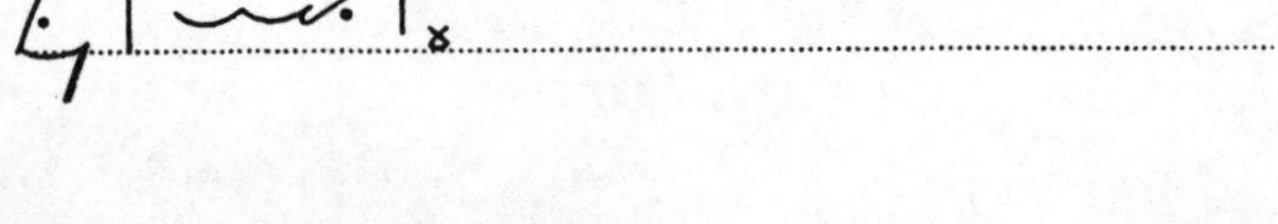

(*h*) 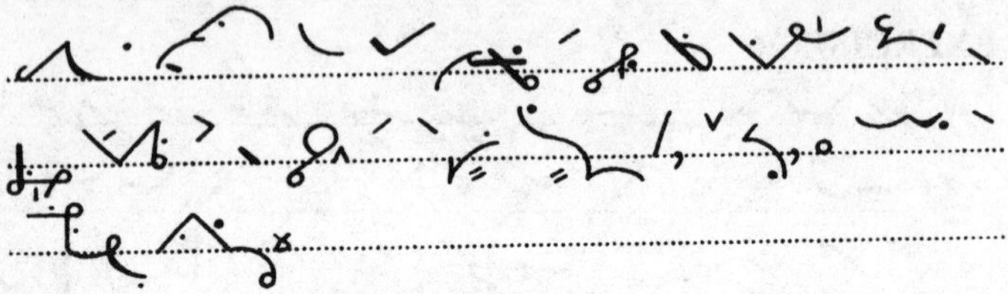

EXERCISE 27 Write in shorthand, afterwards checking with the key (phrasing is indicated by hyphens):

(*a*) Please-make a booking for two single rooms at-the Home Farm Hotel for-the nights of 24th and 25th August in-the names of Mr Tom Hall and Mr Harry Hilary.

(*b*) The whole household was in a state of chaos at-the-time we arrived, and-this-was because a water pipe had burst and inundated-the downstairs rooms.

(*c*) He wrote an essay on 'The Zoos of-Europe', and it-was so good that-they sent him a cheque to allow it to-be published in-the Daily Gazette.

(*d*) It-is cold and-icy here on-the hills outside-the city, and it-has stayed below zero all day. We-are lucky because-we-have a hot log fire in-the lounge of-the hotel to-keep-us warm.

(*e*) We usually start work in-the garage early in-the day and-we-have to hurry to-get all-the day's jobs ended by five o'clock.

Section 10

Initial R hook to straight strokes

1 Each of the simple straight strokes

P B T D CH J K G

may be written with a small round hook at the beginning in a clockwise direction. This adds R to the stroke:

PR BR TR DR CHR JR KR GR

The consonant combinations PR, BR, etc., are very common in English, not only at the beginning of words, but also medially:

Initially:

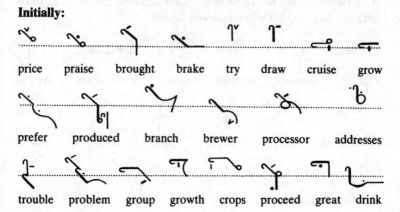

price praise brought brake try draw cruise grow

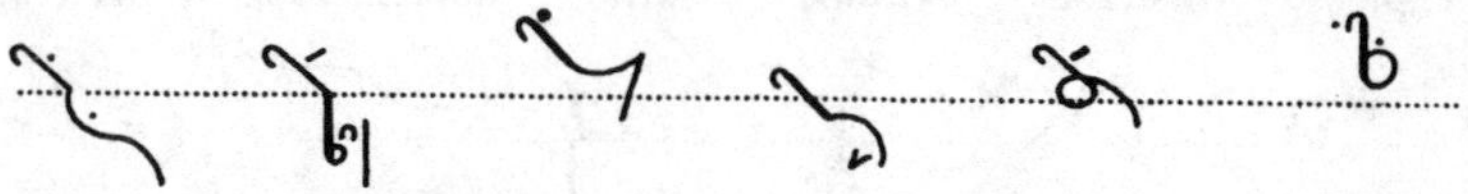

prefer produced branch brewer processor addresses

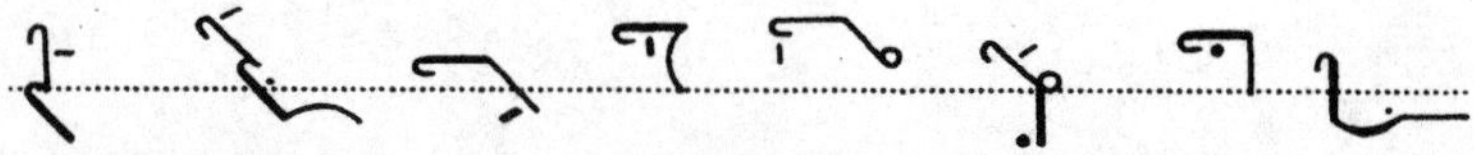

trouble problem group growth crops proceed great drink

Medially:

depress entry interest impressive increased fabric petrol

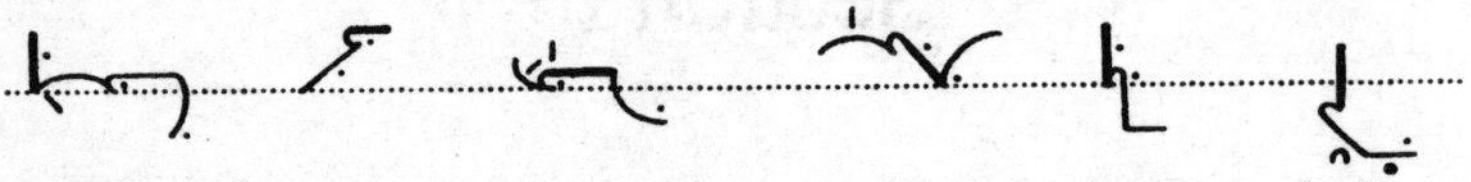

democracy regret photography umbrella detract duplicate

replace

2 The R hook is also used syllabically:

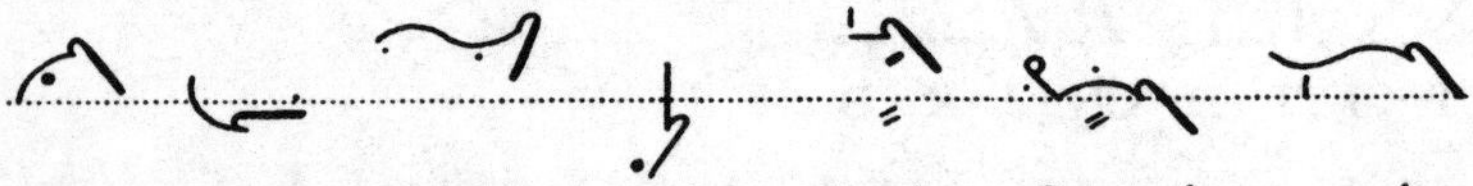

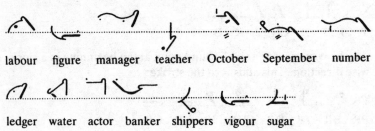

labour figure manager teacher October September number

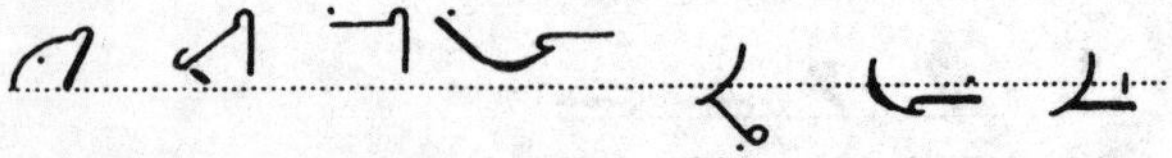

ledger water actor banker shippers vigour sugar

3 If a circle S precedes an R hook to a straight stroke in the middle of an outline, then the circle is written clockwise too, so as to show both the circle and the hook clearly, as in:

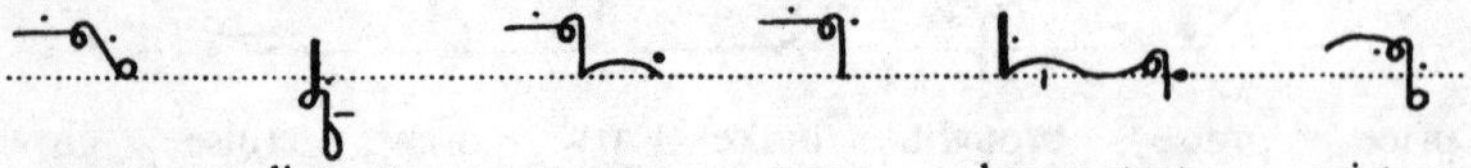

express distrust extreme extra demonstrate mistress

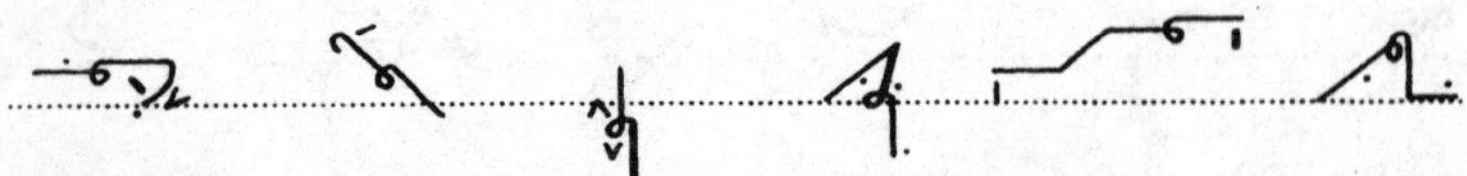

excruciating prosper outsider registry corkscrew restrict

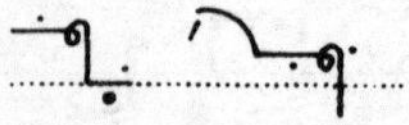

extricate orchestra

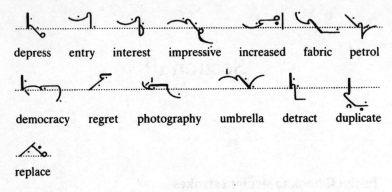

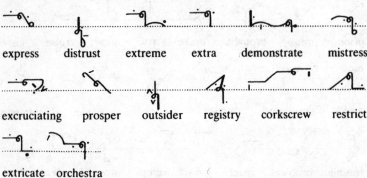

EXERCISE 28

(*a*)

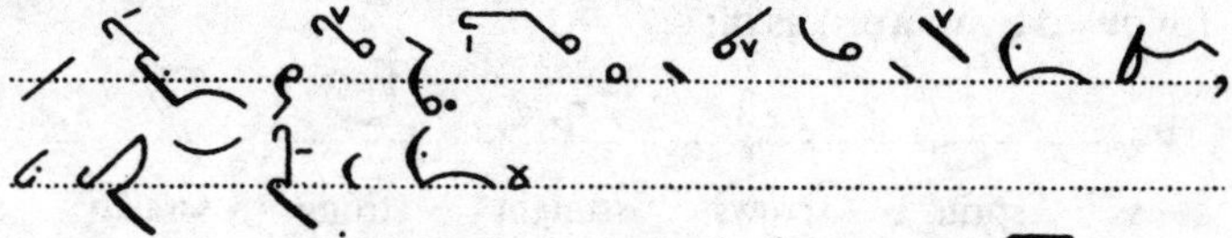

(*b*)

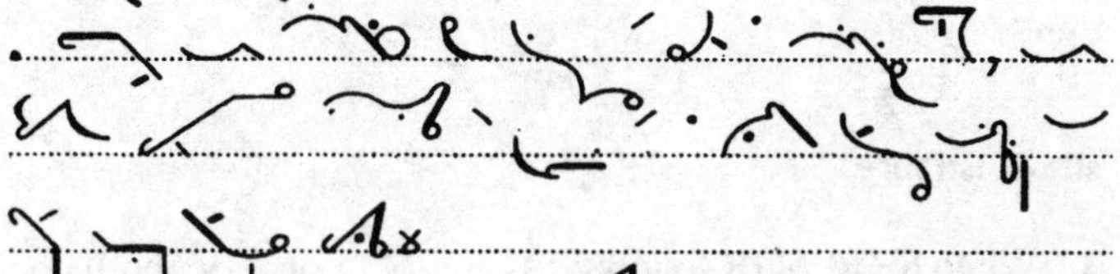

(*c*)

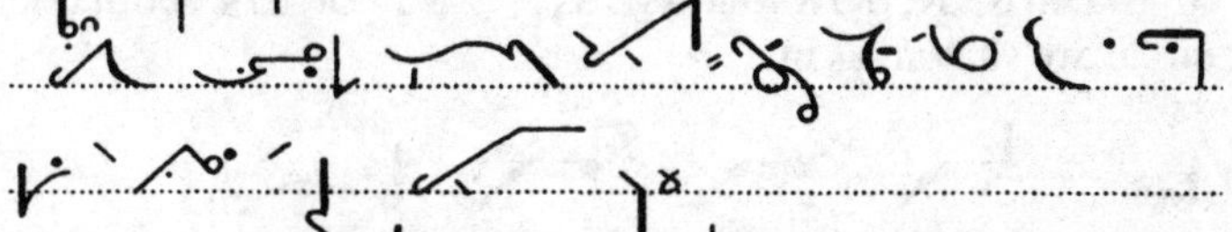

(*d*)

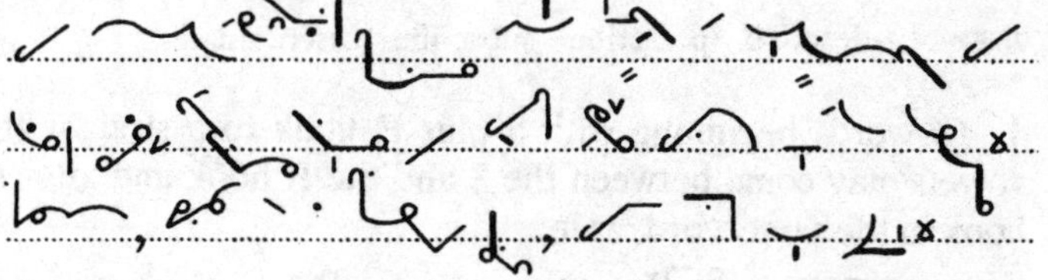

(*e*)

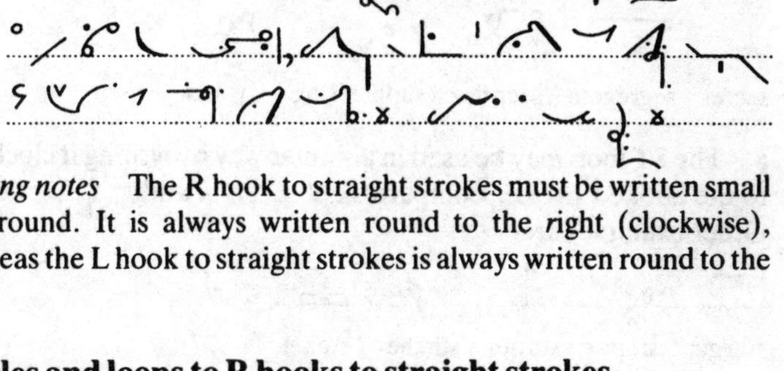

Writing notes The R hook to straight strokes must be written small and round. It is always written round to the *r*ight (clockwise), whereas the L hook to straight strokes is always written round to the *l*eft.

Circles and loops to R hooks to straight strokes

1 A circle S is written to an R hook to a straight stroke merely by closing the hook, as in:

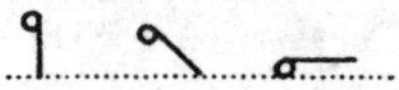

STR SPR SKR

2 Vowels may come between the S and the initial hook, as in:

setter sober cider seeker

or the STR, SPR, SKR combinations of consonants may be followed by vowels, as in:

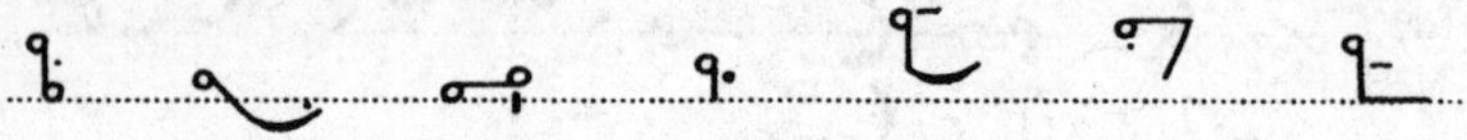

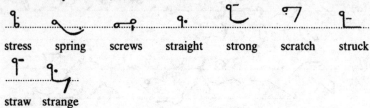

stress spring screws straight strong scratch struck

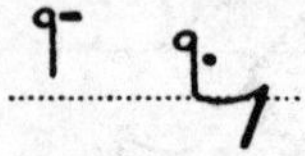

straw strange

3 When SKR, SGR follows 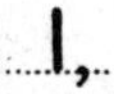 or  both hook and circle are shown, as in:

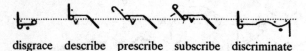

disgrace describe prescribe subscribe discriminate

4 In words beginning with S plus R hook to a straight stroke, vowels may come between the S and the R hook and after the R hook in the same word, as in:

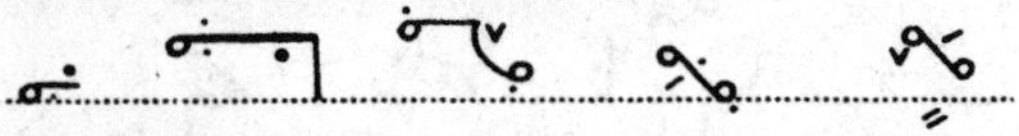

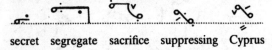

secret segregate sacrifice suppressing Cyprus

5 The ST loop may be used in a similar way by writing it clockwise to the hooked stroke. Compare 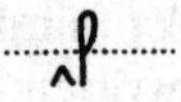 *stout* and 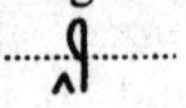 *stouter*. Other examples are:

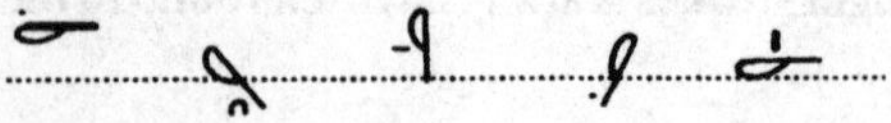

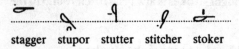

stagger stupor stutter stitcher stoker

EXERCISE 29

(*a*) 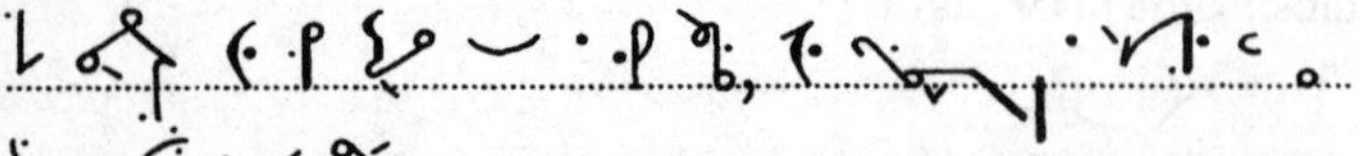

(*b*) 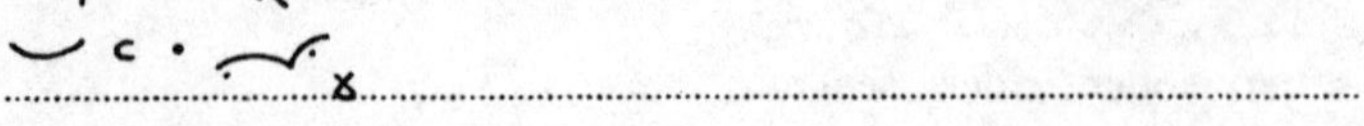

(c) 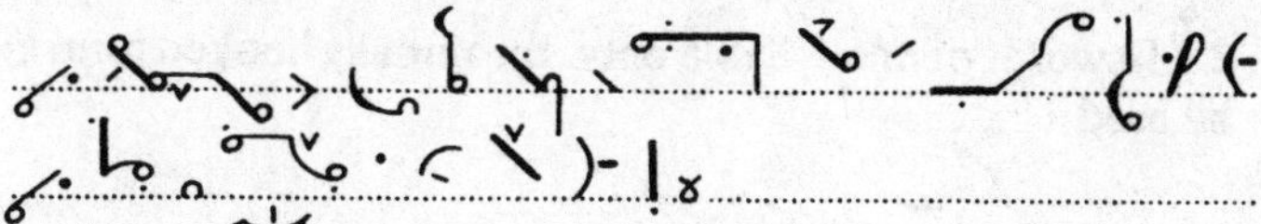

(d) 

Stress rules

You will have noted that we now have two initial hooks to straight strokes, the L hook and the R hook. Both of these hooks may be used consonantally, as in 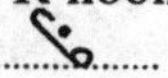 *place* and  *press*, or syllabically, as in  *people* and  *papers*.

The stress rules are concerned with the occasions when hooks may be used syllabically and when they may not.

Almost every English word that has two syllables or more has a firm stress on one syllable. That is to say that one syllable is spoken more firmly and loudly than the rest. For example in the word *paralyse* the stress is on the first of the three syllables. In the word *informer* the stress is on the second syllable, and in *engineer* it is on the third syllable.

1 The rule is that any initially hooked stroke may be used to represent syllables, no matter what vowel comes between stroke and hook, in words of more than one syllable as long as the syllable is an unstressed one.

For example, in the words *perform*, *portray*, *collect* and *curtail*, the hooked forms may be used for all the first syllables of these words because these syllables are *unstressed*, and so we write:

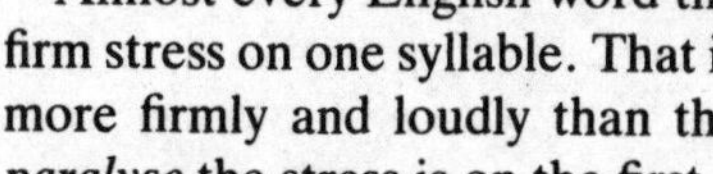

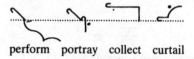

perform portray collect curtail

On the other hand, in the words *purpose*, *barley*, *calorie* and *corridor* the first syllable is stressed in each case, so that the initially hooked form may not be used, and so we write:

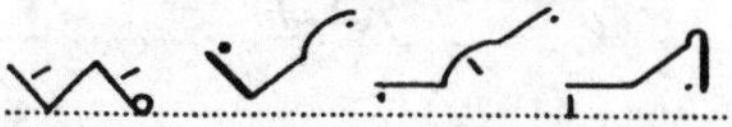

purpose barley calorie corridor

2 In words of one syllable only, the initially hooked form may *not* be used:

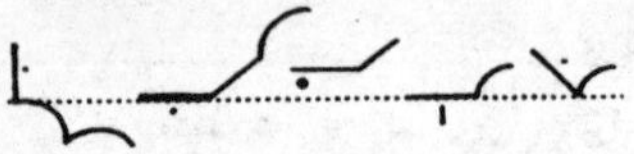

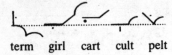

term girl cart cult pelt

3 If an initially hooked form is used in a root word, that form is retained in derivatives even though the stressed syllable may change in the derived word, as in:

territory terri**tor**ial **par**ticiple parti**cip**ial

These stress rules are generally followed, although in a few words – in order to achieve a more readable or more easily written outline – they are not, as in:

collapse collide

Short forms

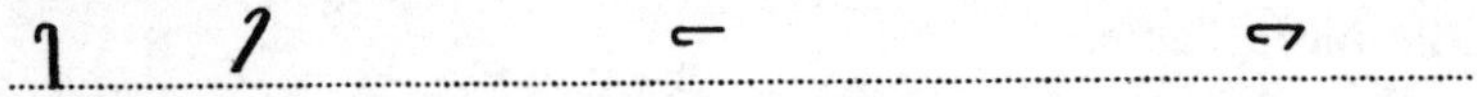

dear larger accord, according, according to according to the

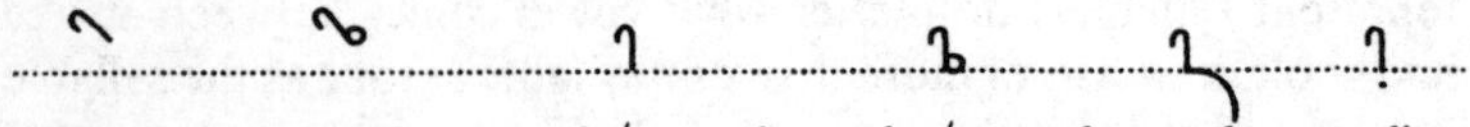

particular particulars trade/toward trades/towards trader trading

Intersections

A consonant K may be struck through another stroke to indicate the word *company*:

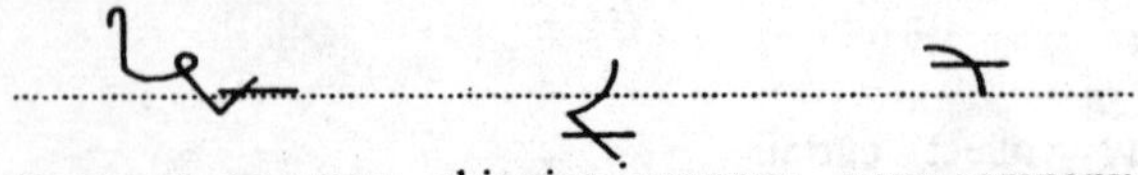

transport company shipping company your company

Consonants K, L may be struck through another stroke to indicate *company limited*:

The Paper Company Limited The Wholemeal Loaf Company Limited

Phrasing

Dear Sir Dear Madam yours faithfully yours truly yours sincerely

of course in due course

(The word *course* being a monosyllable is written  – the initial hook may not be used because of the stress rule above. In a phrase, however, the hooked form is used.)

EXERCISE 30

(*a*) 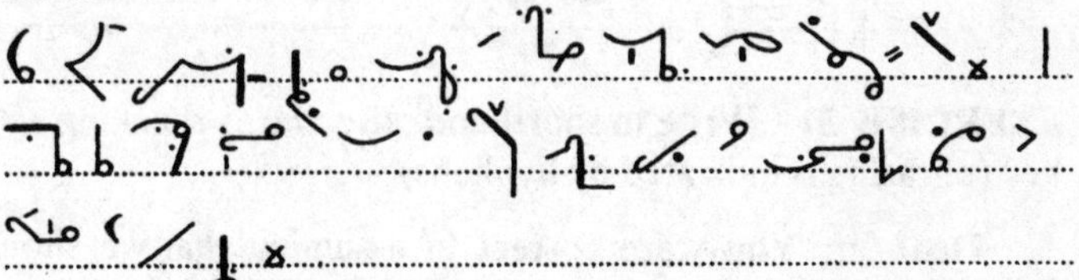

(*b*) 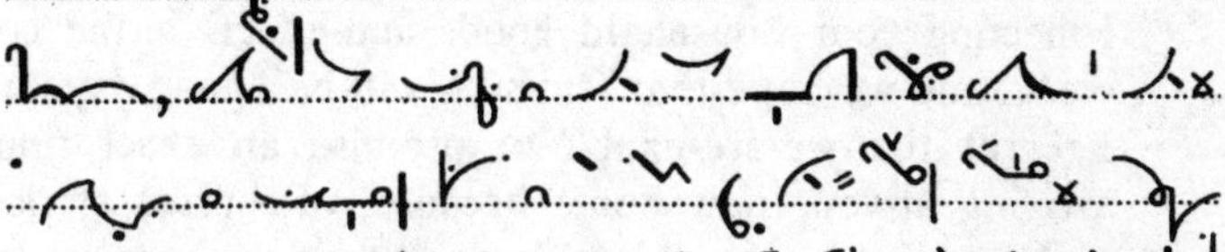

(*c*) 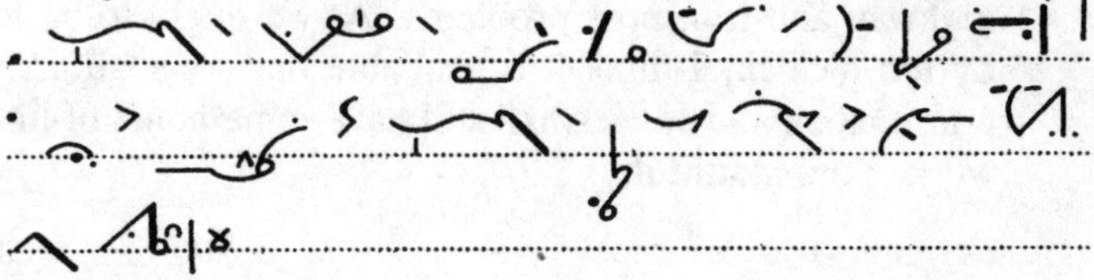

(*d*) 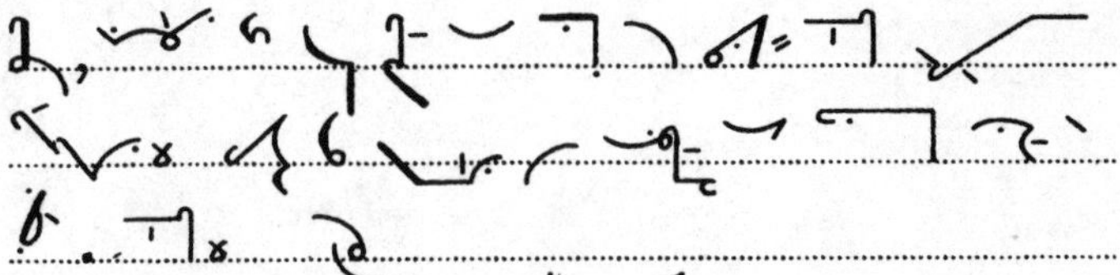

(*e*) 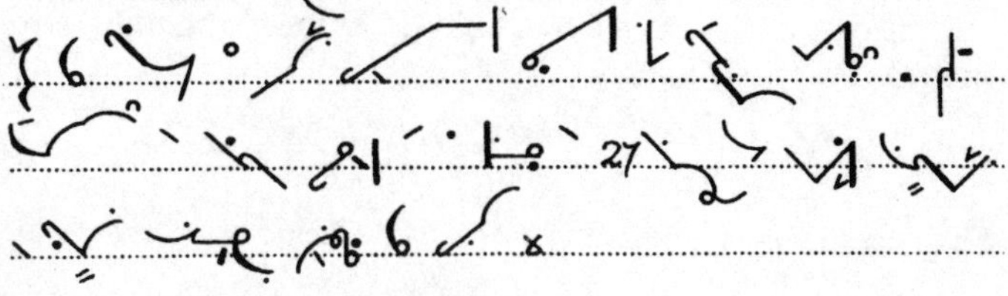

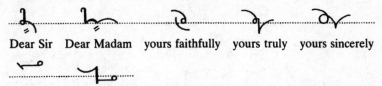

(*f*)

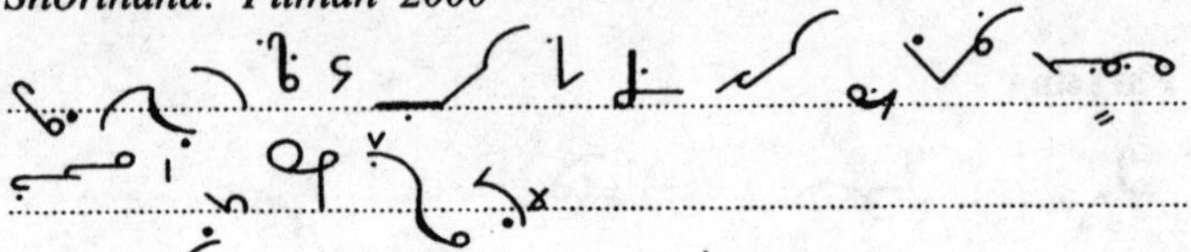

(*g*)

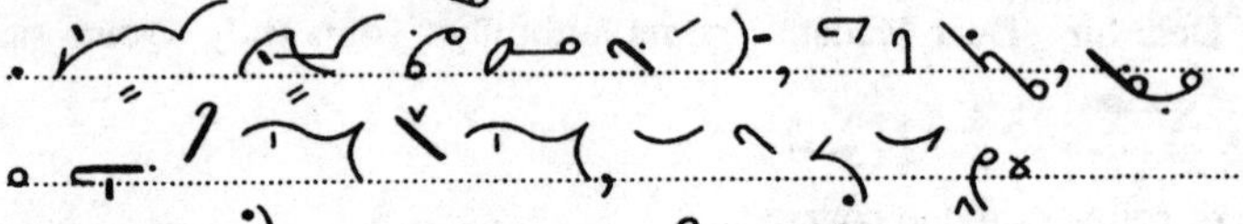

(*h*)

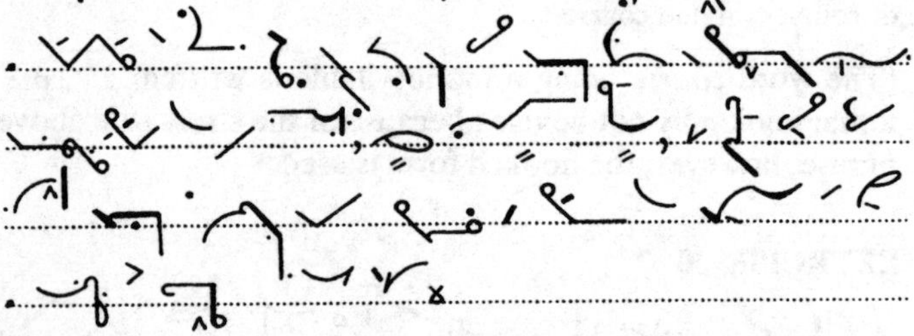

EXERCISE 31 Write in shorthand, afterwards checking with the key (phrasing is indicated by hyphens):

Dear-Sir, You were correct in assuming that-we should-be collecting your household goods and-effects in-the coming week, and-we-hope-that Thursday will-be a good day for-you. I-regret that-we-are-unable-to promise an exact time for arriving at-your new home because, of-course, of possible highway and-transport problems. As-we ought-to-be loaded by ten o'clock, I-think-it-is probable that-we-shall arrive by four o'clock and so we-shall still have some hours of-light for work. Yours-faithfully,

Section 11

Review

Read, copy, and then re-read from your own copy each of the four passages that follow. Then re-transcribe them back into the shorthand from the key without reference to your original shorthand.

1

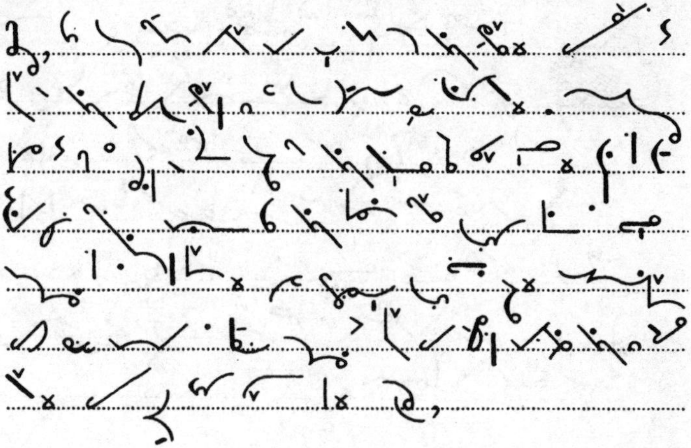

2

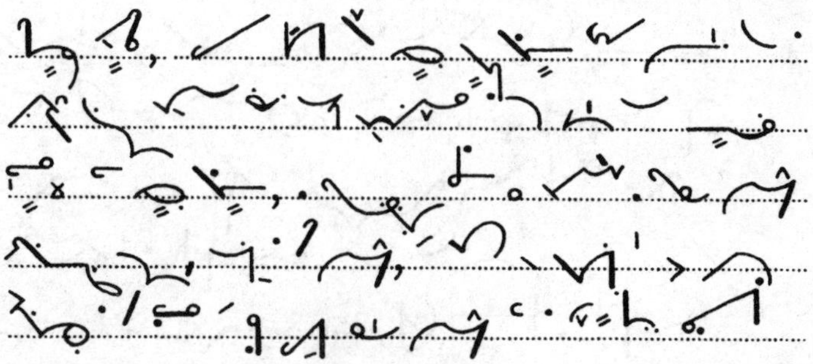

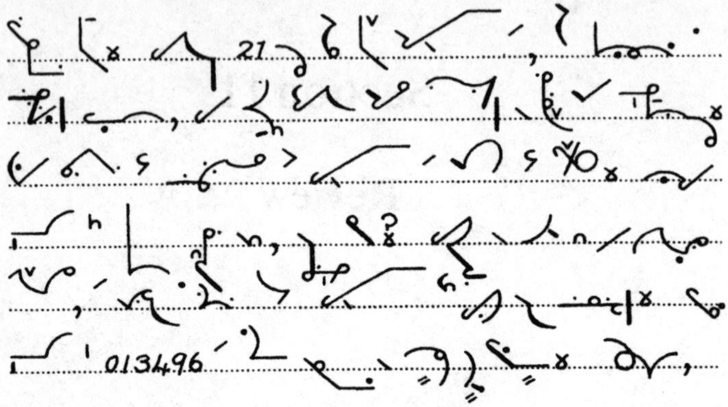

3

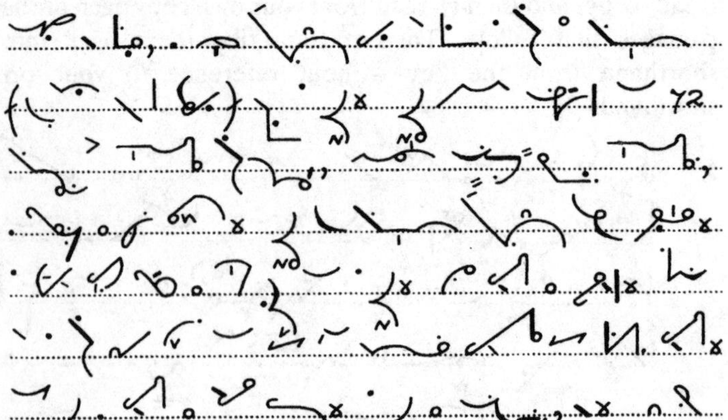

4

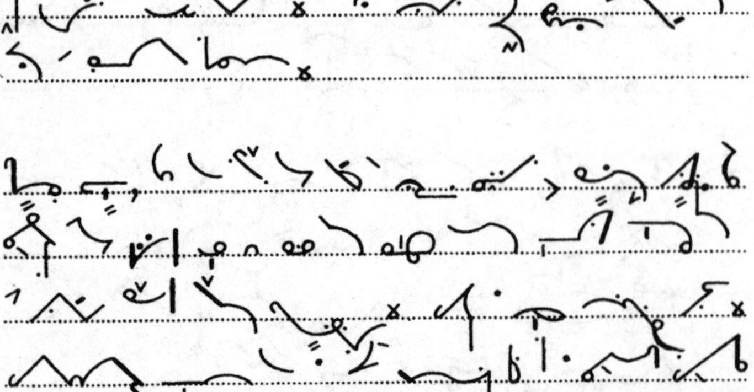

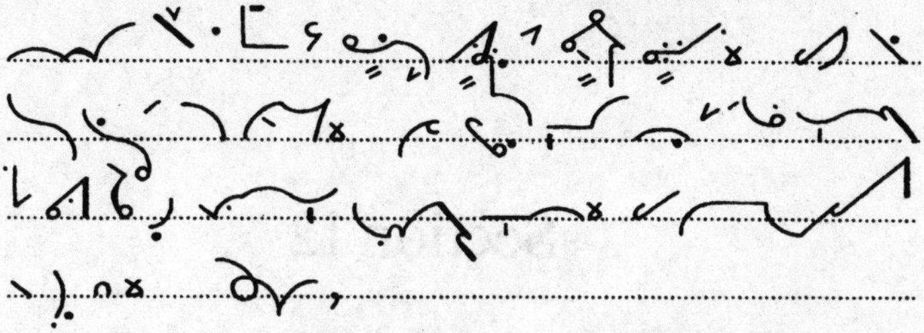

Note The number of words in each review section now appears in the Key to the Exercises at the back of this book (see page 170).

Section 12

Final hook N to curved strokes

1 The sound of N at the end of a word is very common in English. When N is the last sound in a word and is not followed by a vowel, a small round hook is used to represent it. This small round hook can be written to every one of the 24 consonants.

2 When it is written at the end of a curved stroke, it is written *inside* the curve. Here are some examples of N hook written to curves:

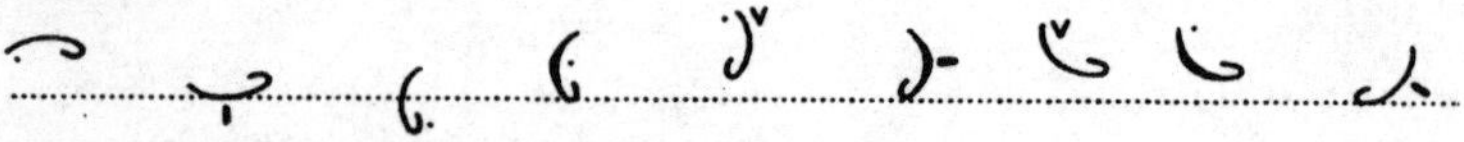

man known thin then assign zone fine van shown

shine loan lane earn iron gammon gallon

3 When it is written at the end of a straight stroke, it is written clockwise. Here are some examples of final N hook to straight strokes:

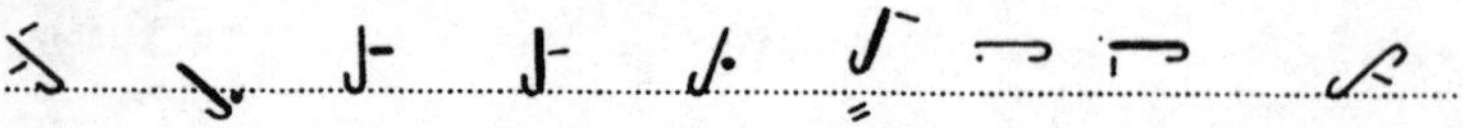

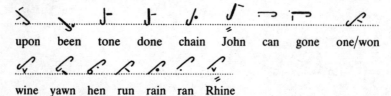

upon been tone done chain John can gone one/won

wine yawn hen run rain ran Rhine

In this section we shall discuss final N to curved strokes and in Section 13 final N to straight strokes.

Writing Notes The final hook N must be written small and round. It is in fact a small semicircle.

4 A circle S may be tucked inside the final hook N when the final sounds are -NZ, as in:

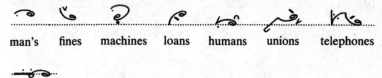

man's fines machines loans humans unions telephones

examines

5 When the final sounds after a curved stroke are -NS or -NSES, then a stroke and a circle are used:

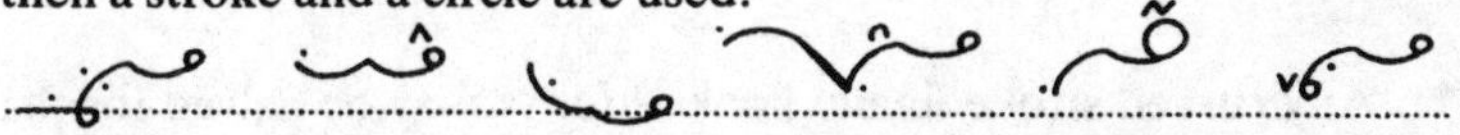

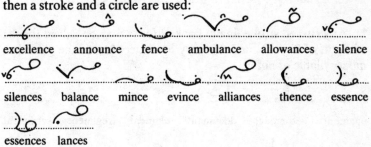

excellence announce fence ambulance allowances silence

silences balance mince evince alliances thence essence

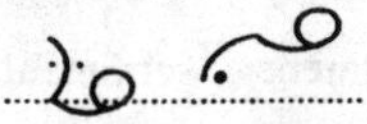

essences lances

6 When a vowel occurs between final N and S or Z *or* when a vowel follows a final N, then a stroke and not the hook is used:

minus Venice illness money many avenue funny lino

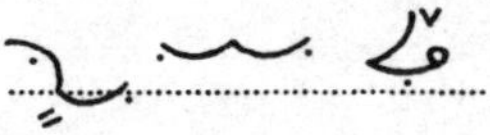

Ernie nanny shyness

A final vowel must always have a final stroke.

EXERCISE 32

(*a*) 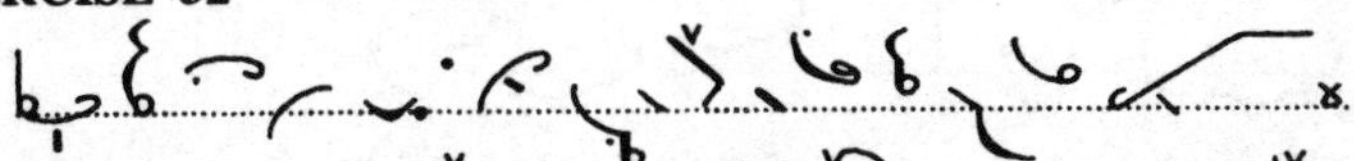

(*b*) 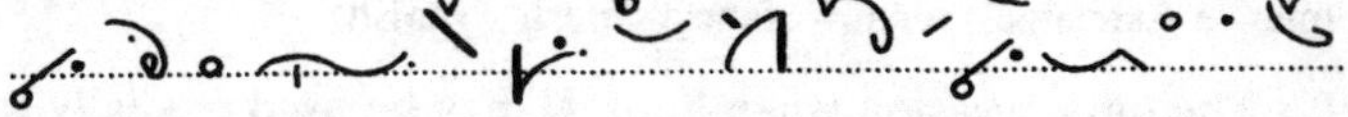

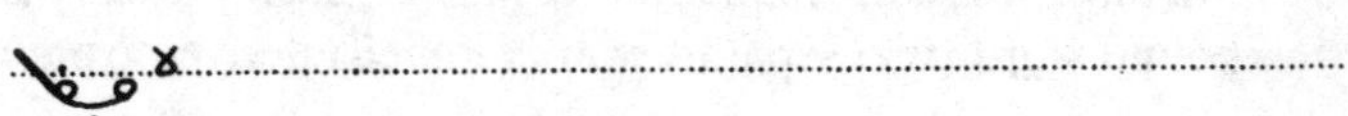

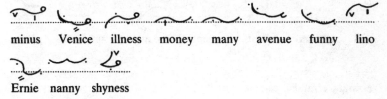

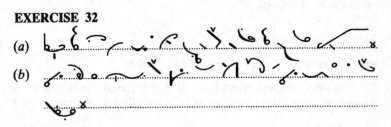

(*c*) 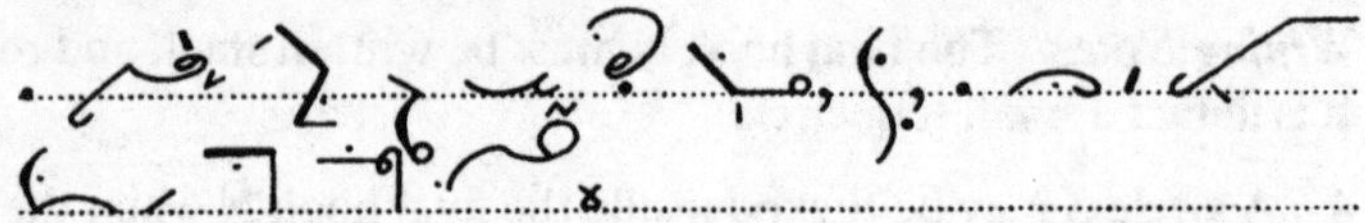

(*d*) 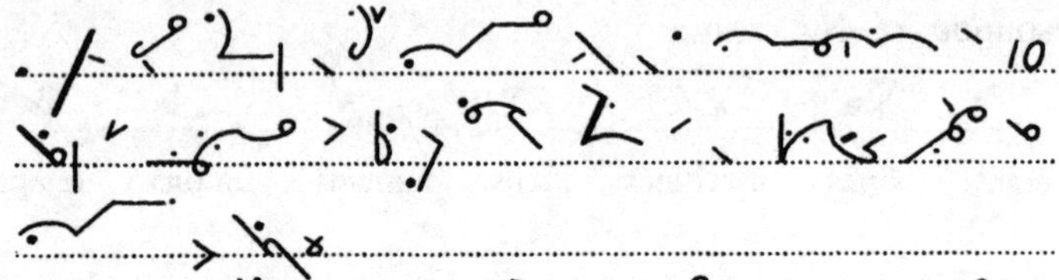

(*e*) 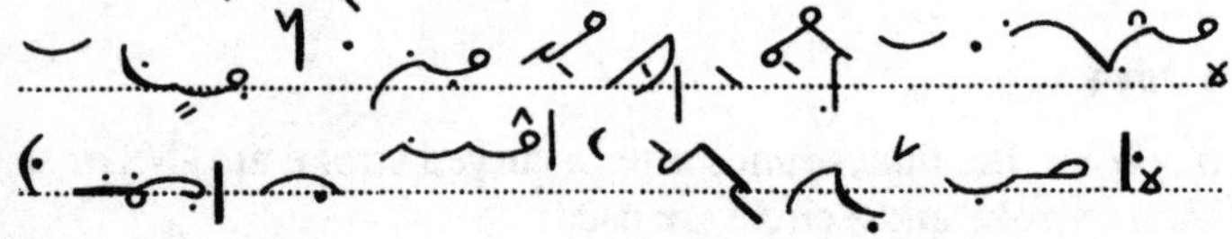

7 Any curved stroke finally hooked for N may be halved for the addition of T or D, and this may be done whether the word is a monosyllable or not:

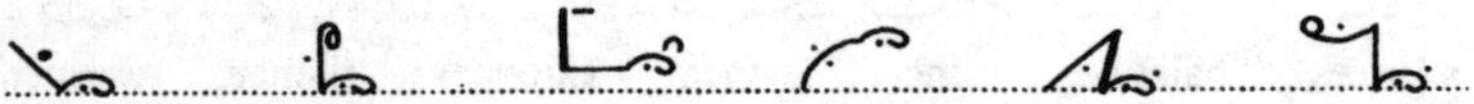

payment settlement document element regiment sentiment

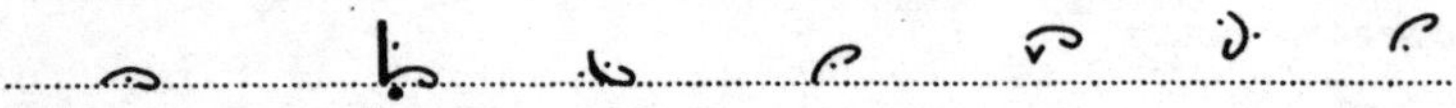

meant/mend demand event lent/lend mind assent land

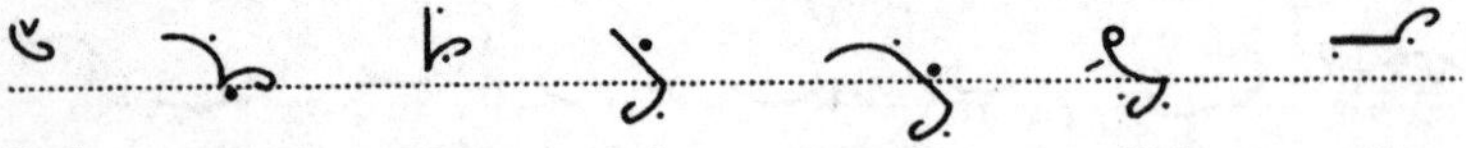

find remand talent patient impatient sufficient gallant

errand errands cement

8 Note that when N occurs medially, the hook is not used but the stroke is used instead, as in:

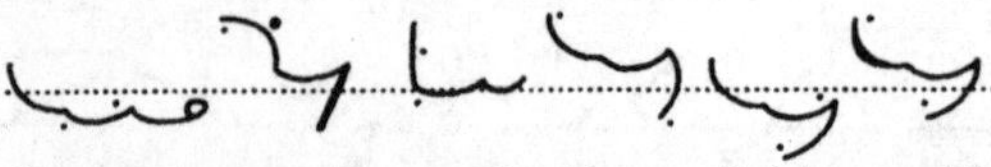

finance arrange tenant fancy finish vanish

9 The only occasion when hook N may be used medially is for a compound word (two separate words joined) derived from a root word, the outline for which is written with a final hook N. Examples are:

Root Word: 

man land moon mind

Compound Word: 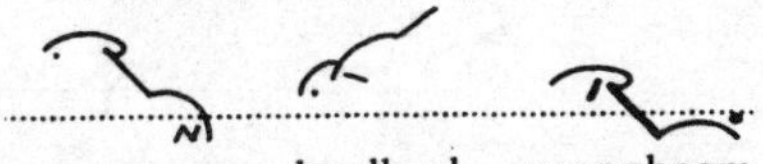

manpower landlord moonbeam

EXERCISE 33

(*a*) 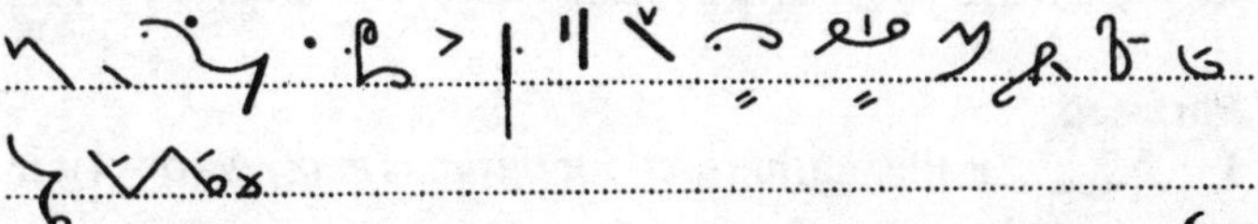

(*b*) 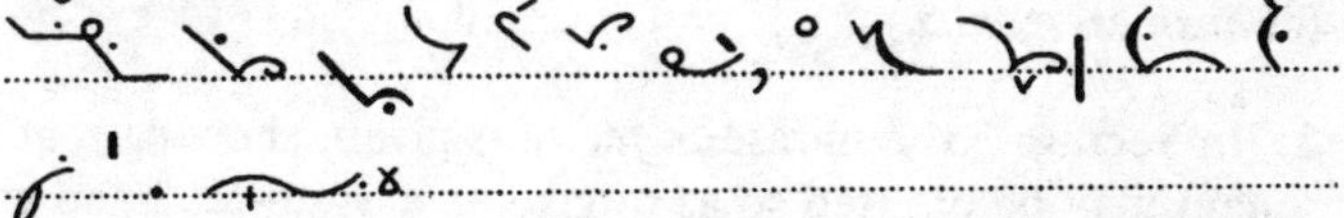

(*c*) 

(*d*) 

(*e*) 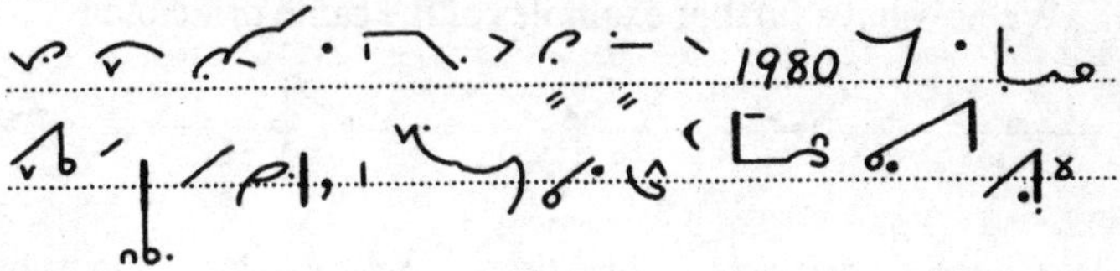

Short forms

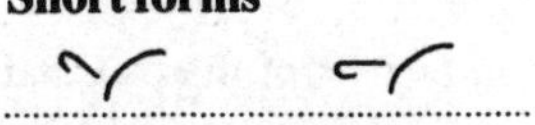

particularly accordingly

The reason for the disjoining of -LY is to make it unmistakable that these are short forms to which -LY has been added.

Intersections

A downward R struck through a stroke represents *arrange* or *arranged* or *arrangement*. A circle S added represents *arrangements*; a dot -ING added represents *arranging*:

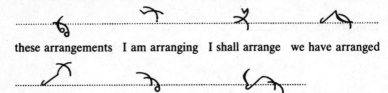

these arrangements   I am arranging   I shall arrange   we have arranged

we will arrange   your arrangements   they were arranged

Phrasing

1  is the outline used for *business man*. A vowel is inserted for *business men* .

2 In Section 3 the phrase *in fact* was given, showing that a consonant may be omitted so as to give an easy-to-read and easy-to-write outline. Again, in Section 8 we showed the same method of consonant omission in such phrases as:

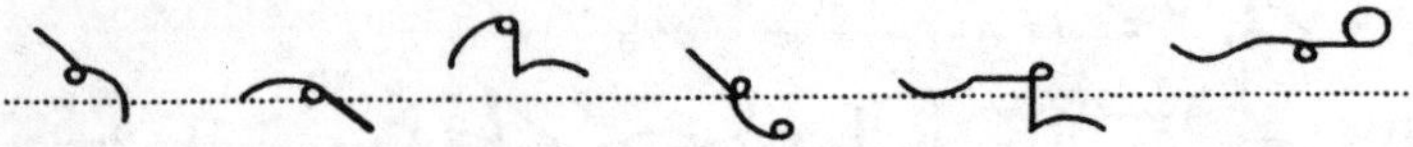

past year   must be   last time   post office   next time   in most cases

We now have further examples of the same principle:

take steps   best way   best time   we trust that   most probably

take care   family life   Prime Minister   in fact   of the fact that

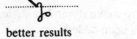

better results

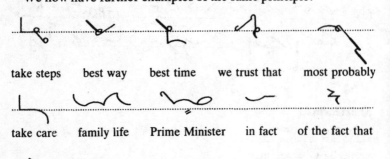

EXERCISE 34

(*a*)
(*b*)
(*c*)
(*d*)
(*e*)
(*f*)
(*g*)
(*h*)

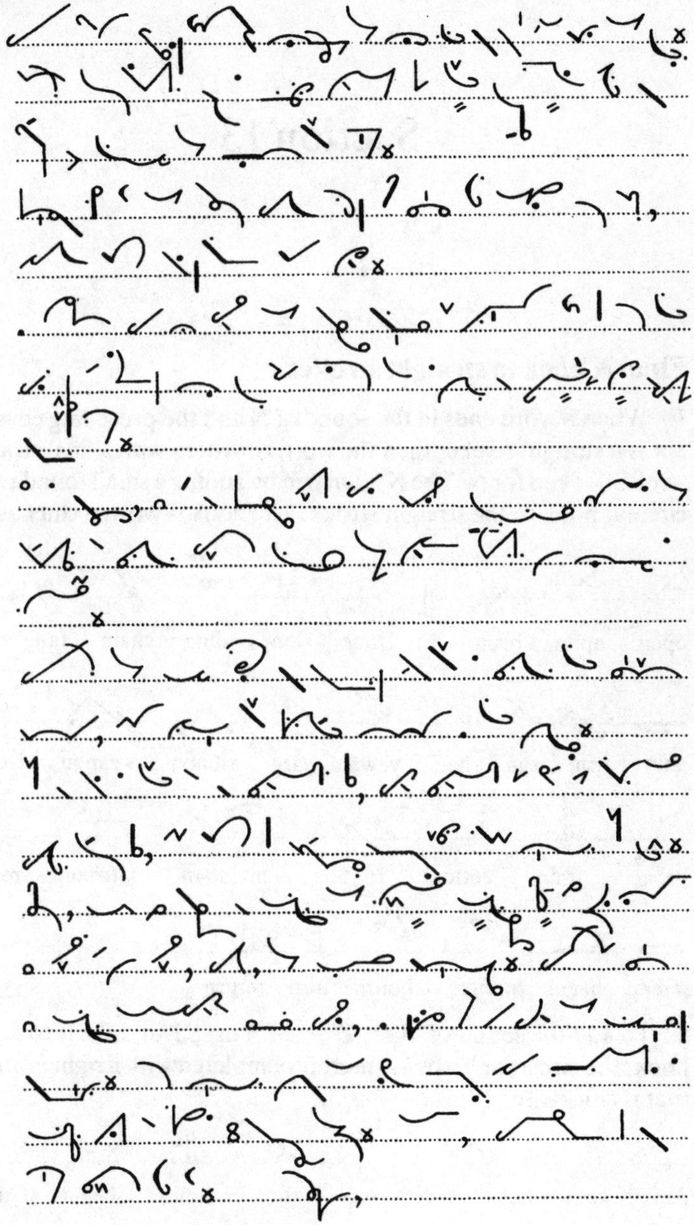

Section 13

Final N hook to straight strokes

1 When a word ends in the sound of N and the preceding consonant is a straight stroke, then the word is written with a final straight stroke hooked for N. The N is written by adding a small round semicircular hook to the straight stroke. The hook is written clockwise:

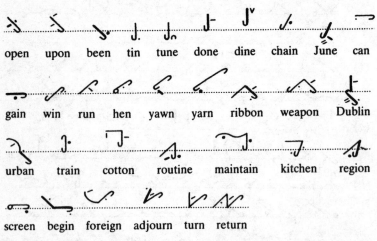

open upon been tin tune done dine chain June can

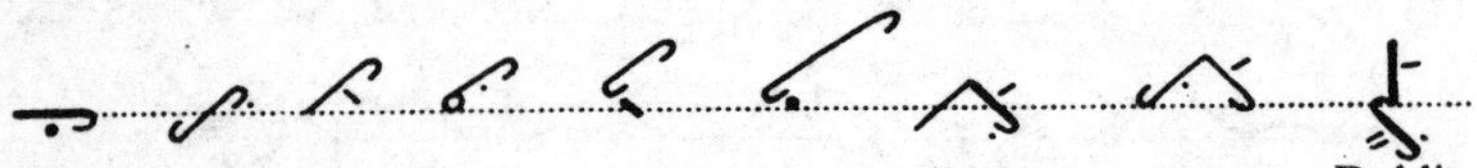

gain win run hen yawn yarn ribbon weapon Dublin

urban train cotton routine maintain kitchen region

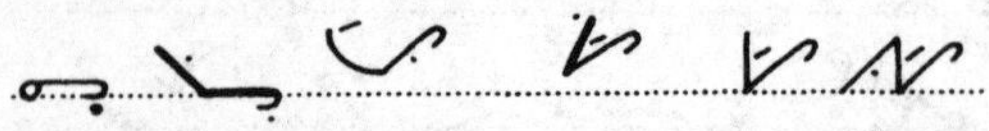

screen begin foreign adjourn turn return

2 To add the sound of -S or -Z or -SES or -ST or -STER to the N hook, the circles or loops are merely completed with a right motion, that is clockwise:

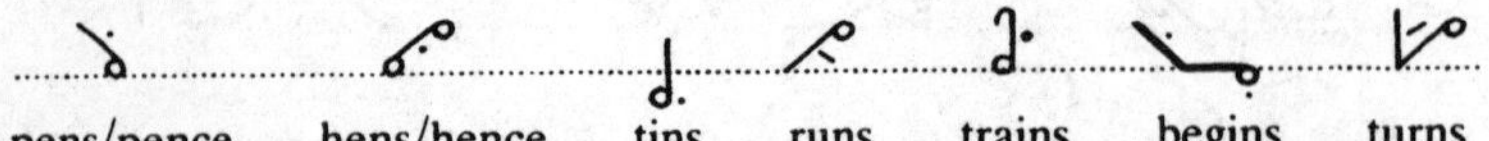

pens/pence hens/hence tins runs trains begins turns

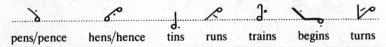

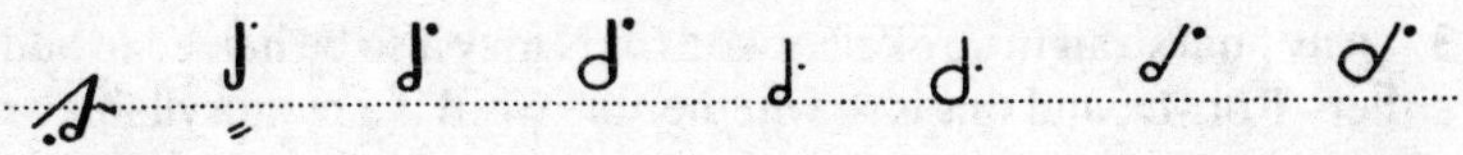

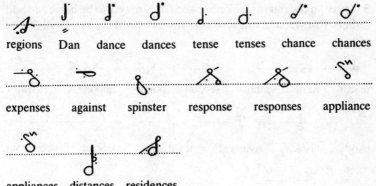

regions Dan dance dances tense tenses chance chances

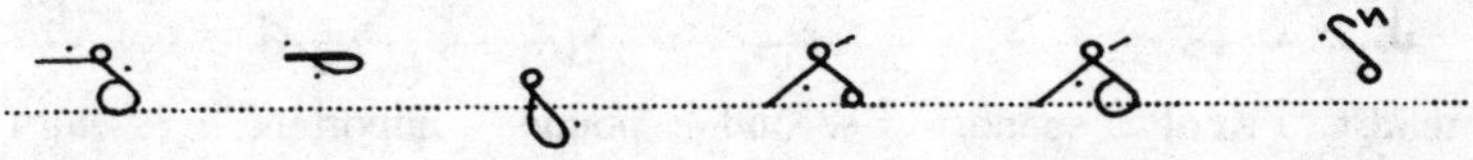

expenses against spinster response responses appliance

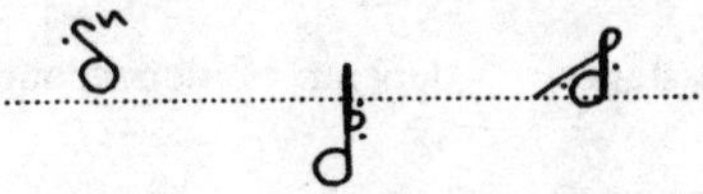

appliances distances residences

The *direction* of the circles or loops includes the N hook. Compare:

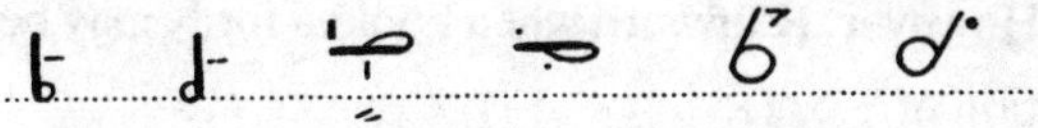

does dunce August against choices chances

These examples make the difference clear.

EXERCISE 35

(*a*)

(*b*)

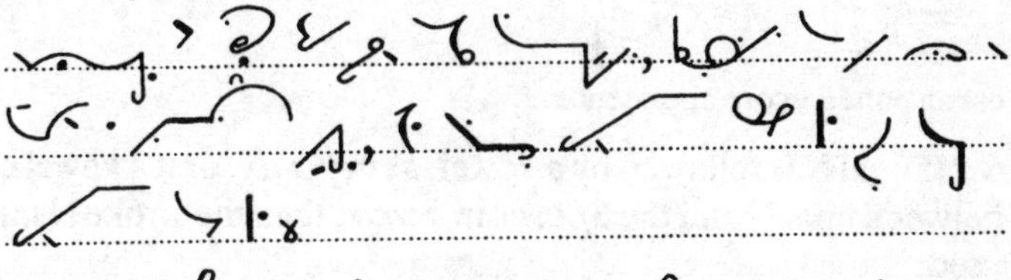

(*c*)

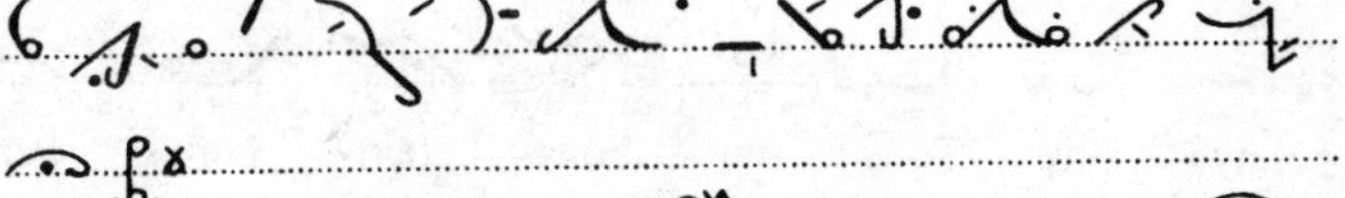

(*d*)

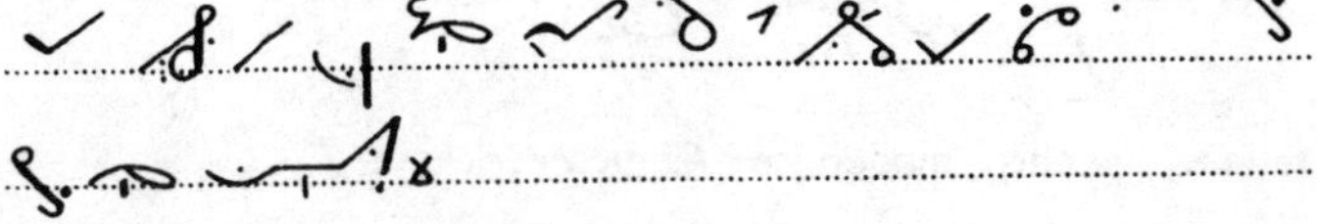

3 Any final straight stroke hooked for N may also be halved to add either -T or -D, and this is so whether the word is a monosyllable or not:

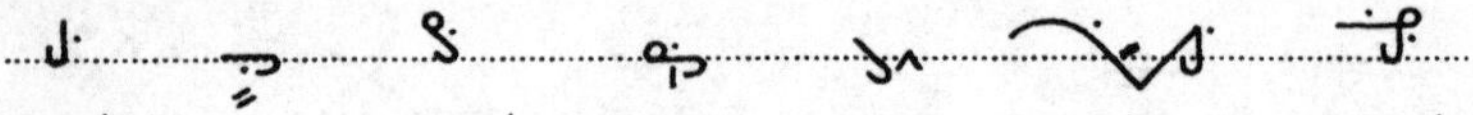

tend/t Kent spend/t second pound important extend/t

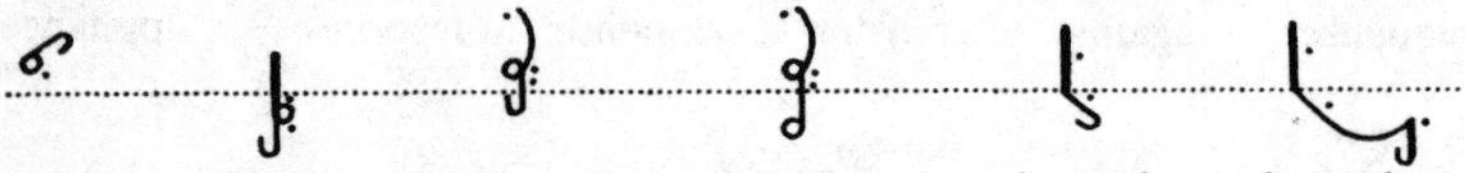

hand distant assistant assistance depend dependant

accident paint joint

4 R upward, when alone, cannot be halved for T because of possible confusion with *and* or *should*. So we write  *rates*,  *roots* etc. However, R upward when hooked for N may be halved for the addition of T or D:

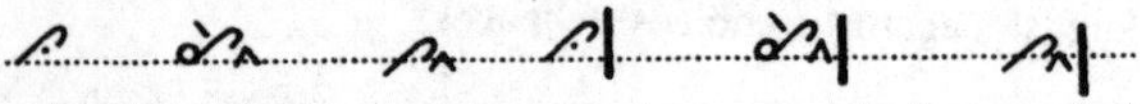

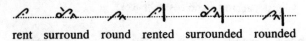

rent surround round rented surrounded rounded

5 A circle S may be added to any of these finally hooked and halved forms:

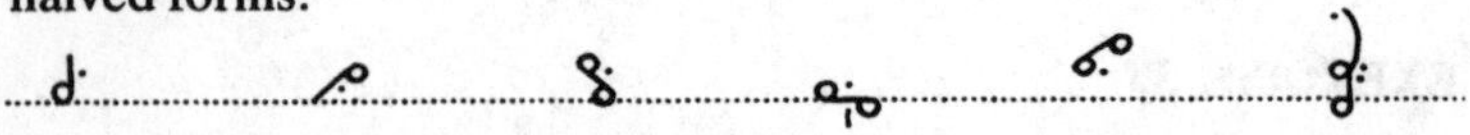

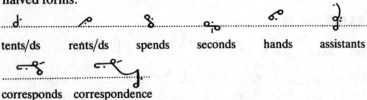

tents/ds rents/ds spends seconds hands assistants

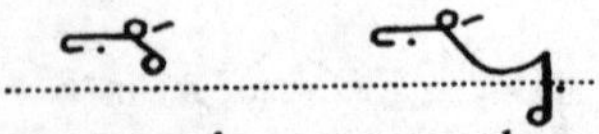

corresponds correspondence

6 If final N is followed by a vowel, as in *penny*, or if a vowel comes between final N and the S/Z, as in *bonus*, then the stroke N must be used:

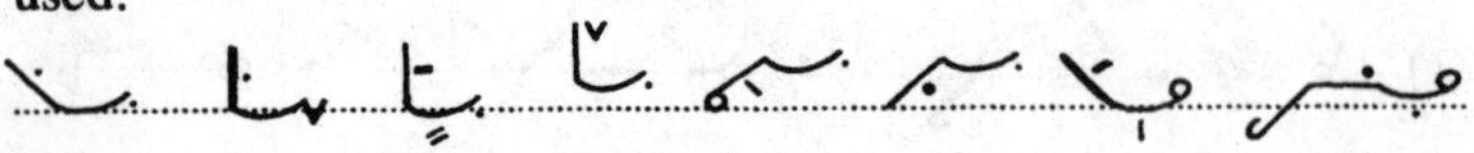

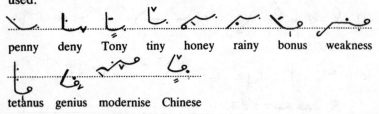

penny deny Tony tiny honey rainy bonus weakness

tetanus genius modernise Chinese

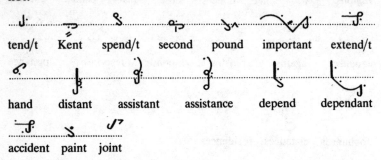

7 An N in the middle of a word is written with a stroke N. The only occasions on which a hook N is written medially are those when a compound word (a word formed of two separate words joined) is written. For example, *bandsaw* is a compound word, made up of two separate words *band* and *saw*. The root word *band* is written with a final N hook,  *band*. This may easily be joined to *saw*, as  *bandsaw*, thus retaining the root word with its final N hook. If the two parts cannot be joined easily, then they are disjoined, the second part being written close up to the first:

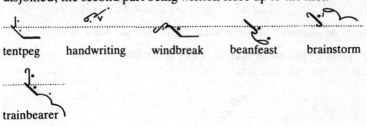

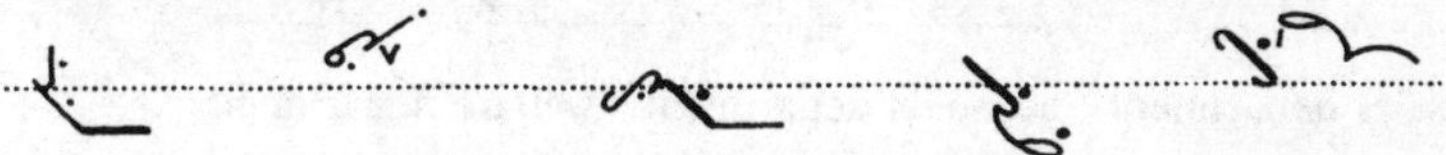

tentpeg handwriting windbreak beanfeast brainstorm

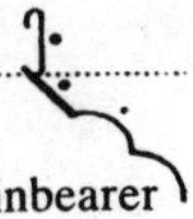

trainbearer

EXERCISE 36

(*a*) 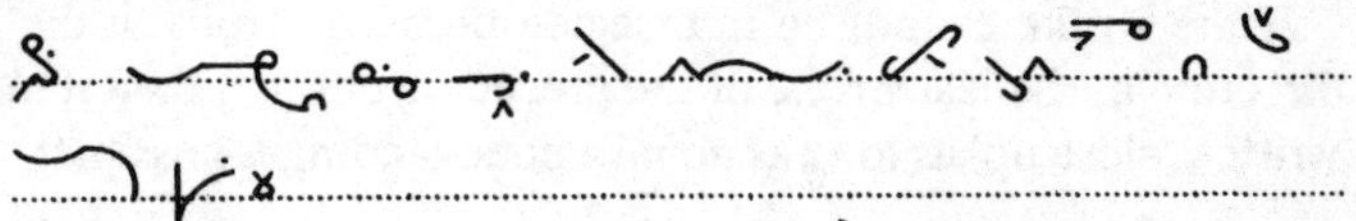

(*b*) 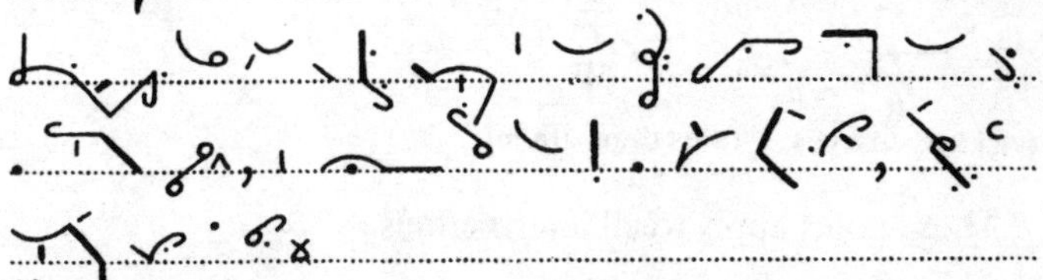

(*c*) 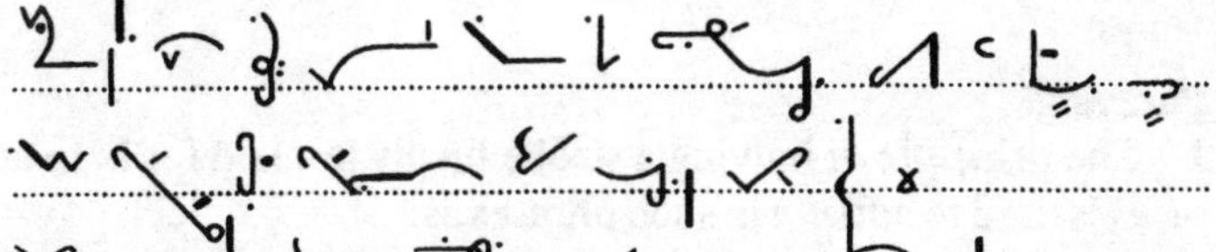

(*d*) 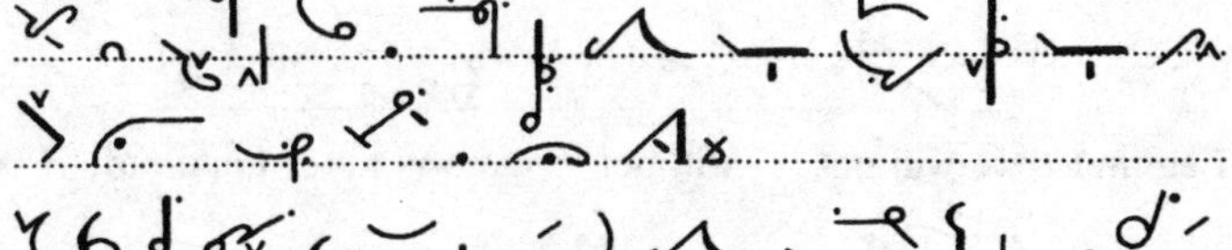

(*e*) 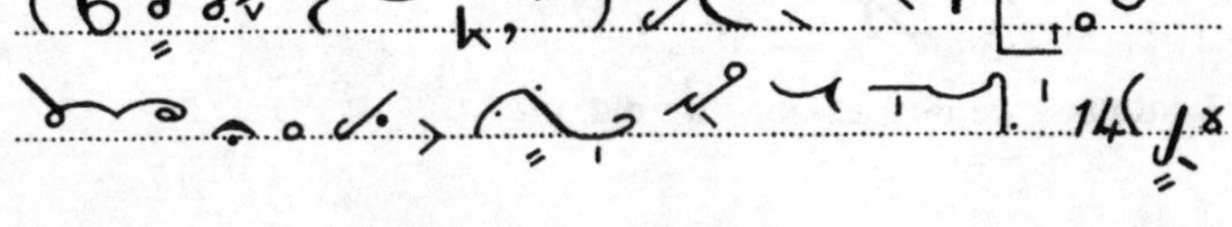

Short forms

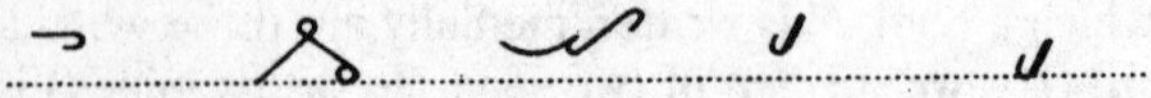

cannot responsibility anyone gentleman gentlemen

Intersections

A stroke D is intersected, when it can be written conveniently, for *department*:

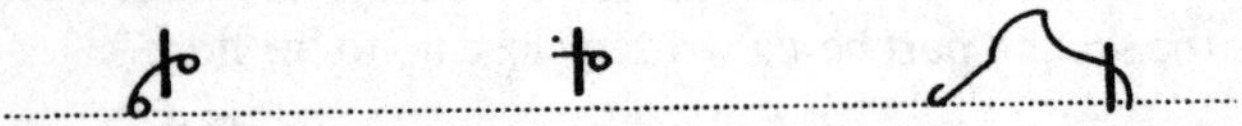

sales department accounts department welfare department

Notice that an intersection can sometimes be made so that the intersection is read first:

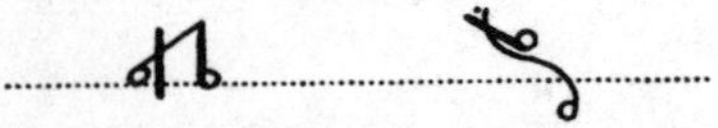

department heads business affairs

If the stroke cannot be intersected because it runs in the same direction as the last stroke of the preceding outline, then it may be written 'close up' as long as no misunderstanding is possible:

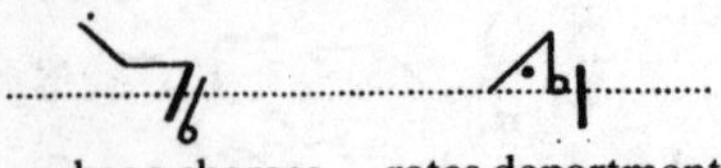

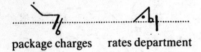

package charges rates department

These notes apply to all intersections.

Phrasing

1 The principle of halving a stroke finally hooked for N to add -T or -D is used to add *not* in such phrases as:

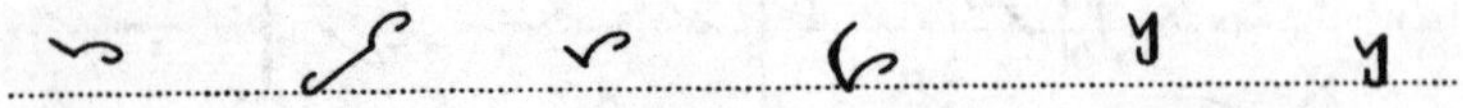

I am not we will not I will not they will not I had not I do not

I did not we do/had not we did not

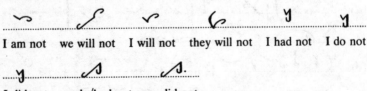

2 If joined to a previous stroke, the same can be done for *are not*, as in: *they are not*, *these are not*, but if not, then *are not* is written .

Note the special – and very useful – phrase *at once*.

3 Other phrases in which a final hook figures are:

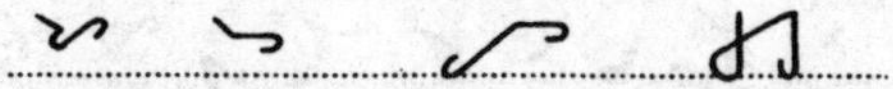

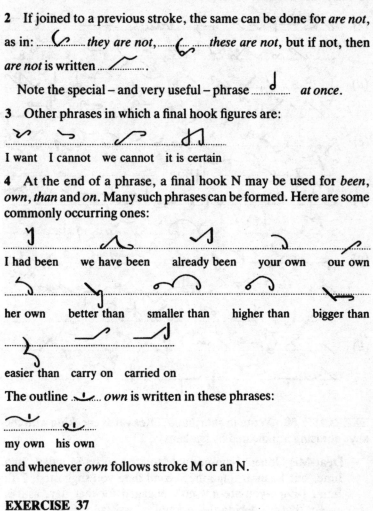

I want   I cannot   we cannot   it is certain

4 At the end of a phrase, a final hook N may be used for *been*, *own*, *than* and *on*. Many such phrases can be formed. Here are some commonly occurring ones:

I had been   we have been   already been   your own   our own

her own   better than   smaller than   higher than   bigger than

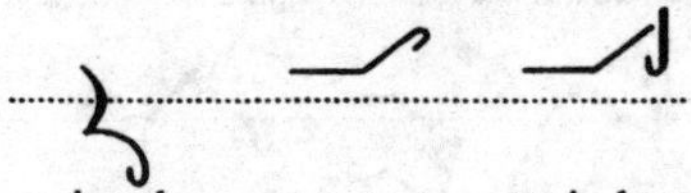

easier than   carry on   carried on

The outline *own* is written in these phrases:

my own   his own

and whenever *own* follows stroke M or an N.

EXERCISE 37

(*a*)

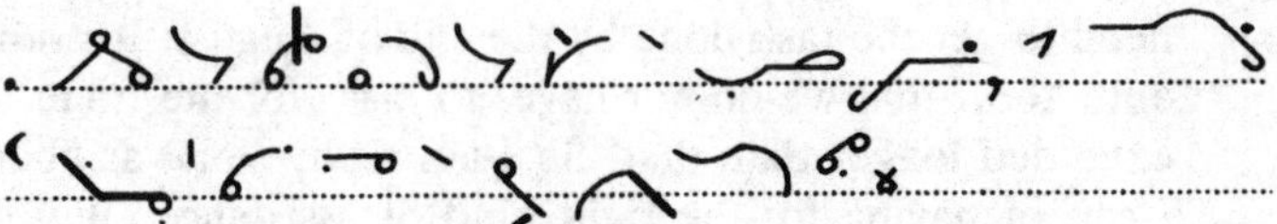

(*b*)

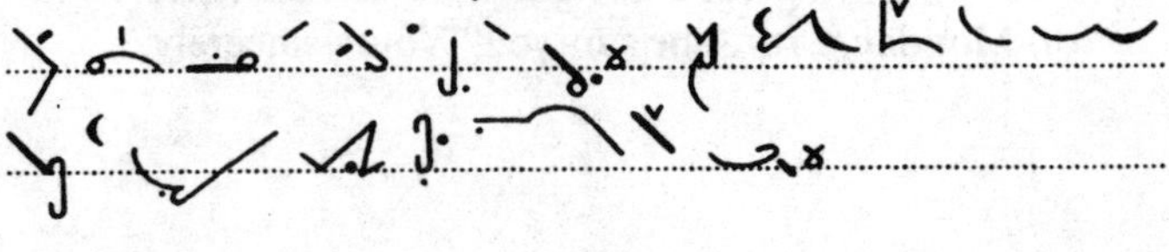

(c) 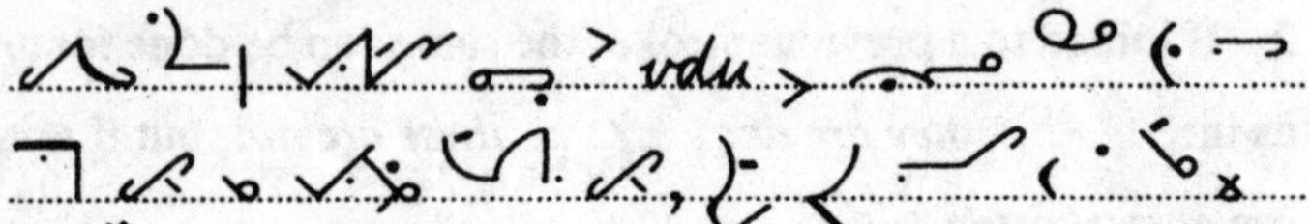

(d) 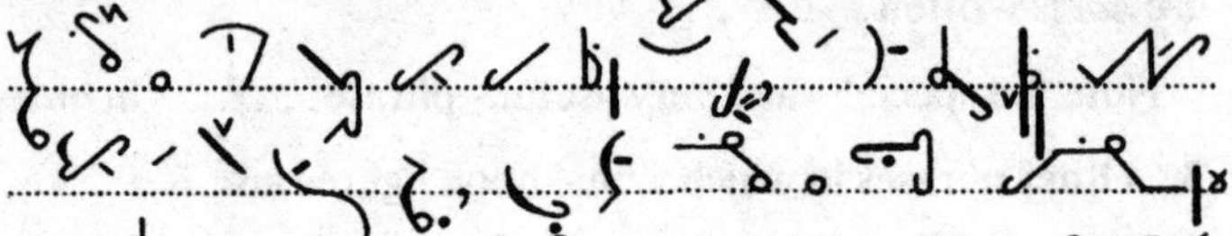

(e) 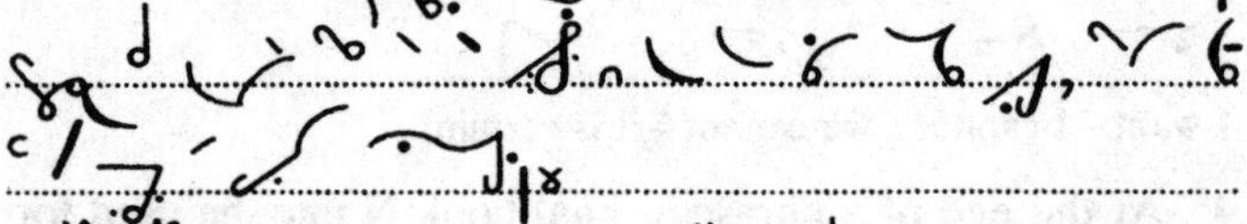

(f) 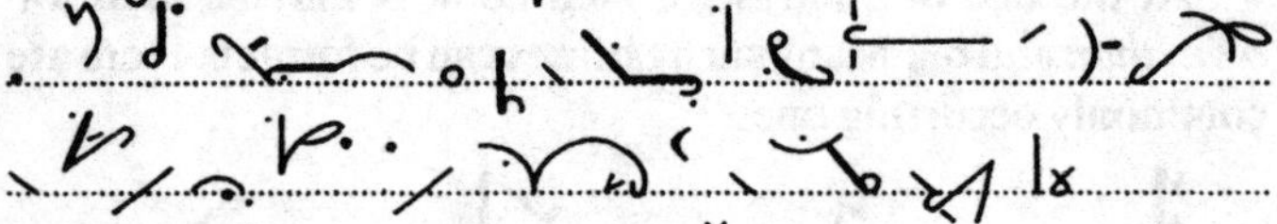

(g) 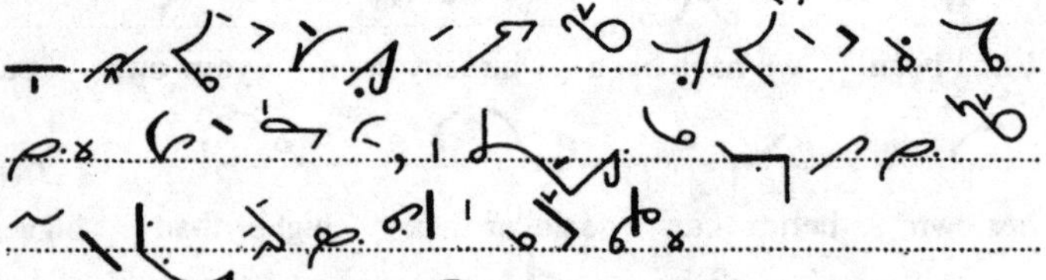

(h) 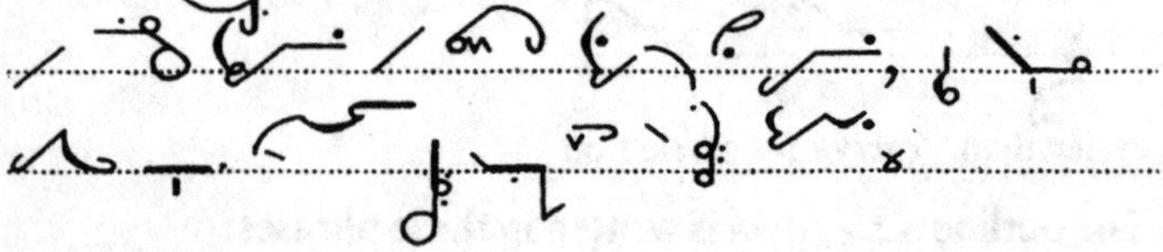

EXERCISE 38 Write in shorthand, afterwards checking with the key (phrasing is indicated by hyphens):

Dear-Miss Jones, I-am-not able-to see-you on-Monday, 20th June, but I-can-arrange-the second date you suggested, 27th June. I-hope-you-are-not now engaged for-that day, as-it-is urgent that-we decide-the amount of assistance that-you-will-need to-get-the task done by-the end of August. It-is-important, too, that-we-do-not-have to ask for-the time to-be extended longer-than that. So I-am ready to-be as liberal as I-can in paying for-the right kind of assistance. Will 11 am on-Monday, 27th June suit-you? Yours-sincerely,

Section 14

Suffixes

1 English has a number of very common suffixes – that is, endings which can be tagged on to a word to add to its meaning or change its function. Examples are:

care, *careless*, *careful*, *carefulness*;
account, *accountable*, *accountability*;
comrade, *comradeship*;
myth, *mythological*;
zoo, *zoological*.

Shorthand treats some of these suffixes in a special way.

2(*a*) A very common suffix is -MENT and that is usually written with M hooked for N and halved for T, as in:

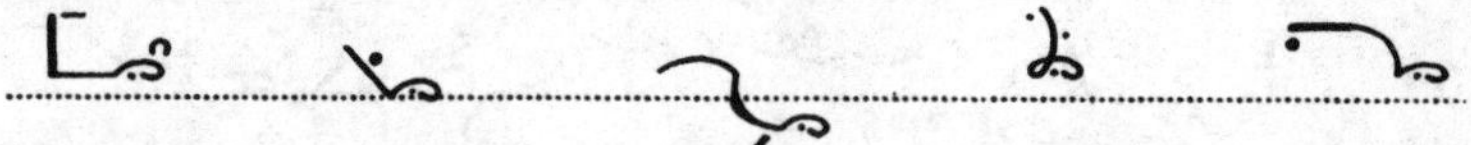

document payment movement assessment garment

cement argument

(*b*) However, when it is difficult or not possible to write -MENT in this way, then a stroke N halved for T represents the ending -MENT, as in:

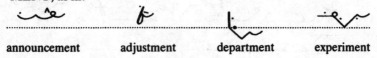

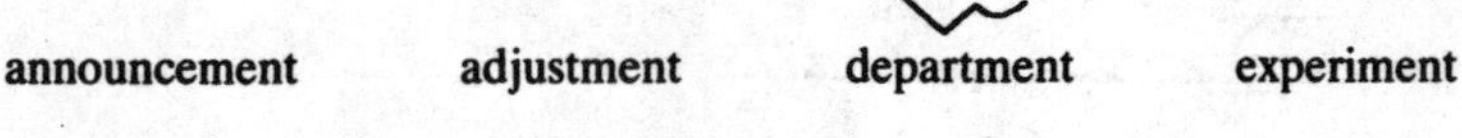

announcement adjustment department experiment

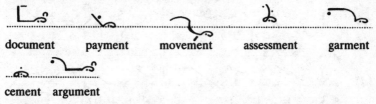

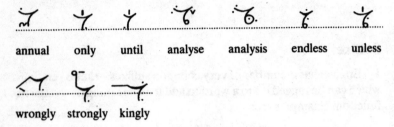

refinement attainment appointment assignment monument

(It will be noted that in words formed from roots written with final N hook, the hook is retained when the -MENT is added.)

3 L is written upward. However, when L immediately follows stroke N, or stroke N halved, or stroke NG then it is always written downward:

annual only until analyse analysis endless unless

wrongly strongly kingly

EXERCISE 39

(a) 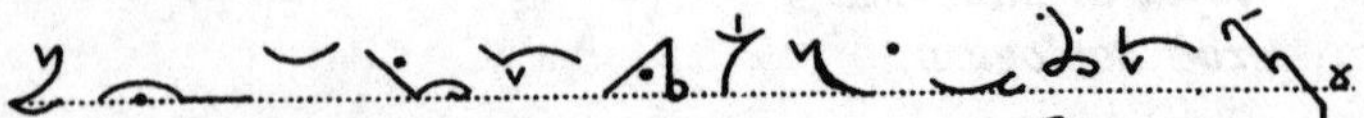

(b) 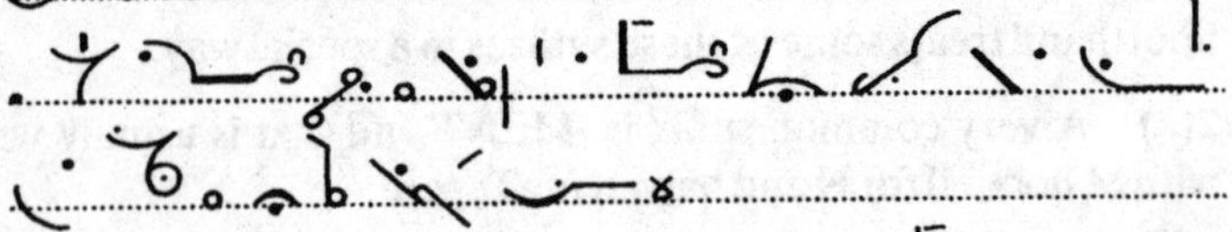

(c) 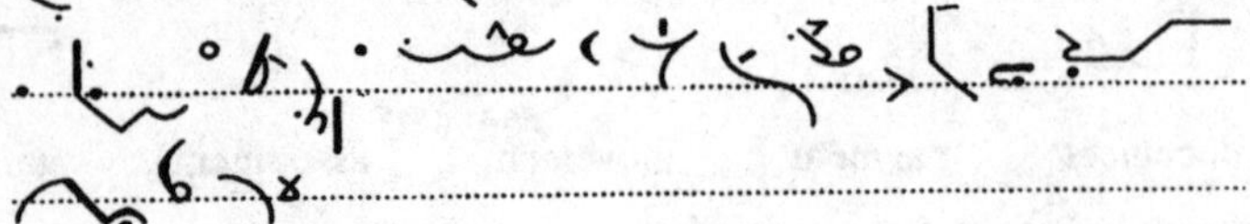

(d) 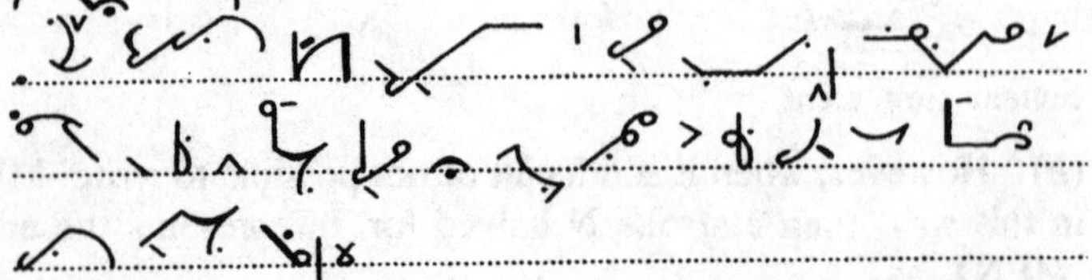

(e) 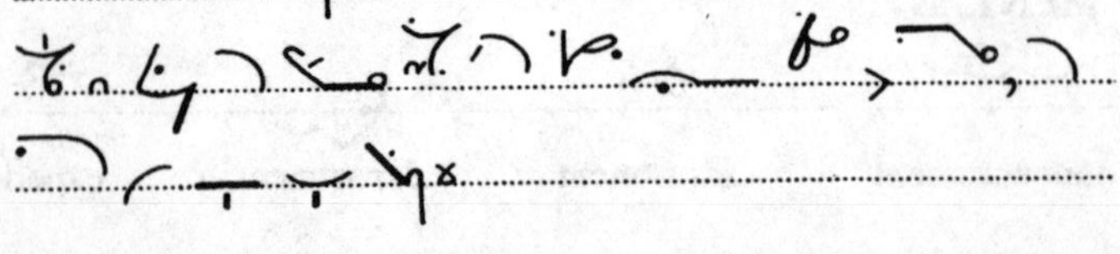

4(*a*) The ending -MENTAL is written as shown in words that use M hooked for N and halved for T:

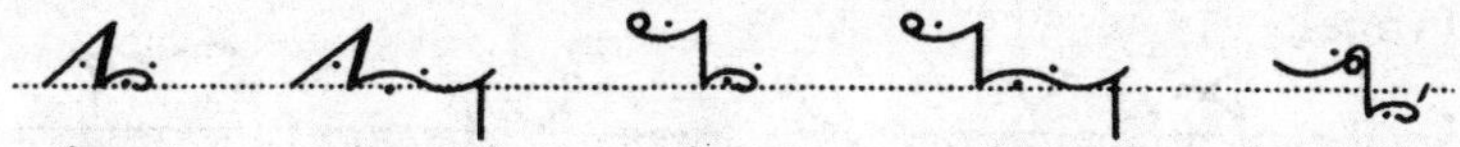

regiment regimental sentiment sentimental instrument

instrumental element elemental

(*b*) If, however, a word is written with N halved to represent -MENT, then downward L is added for the ending -MENTAL:

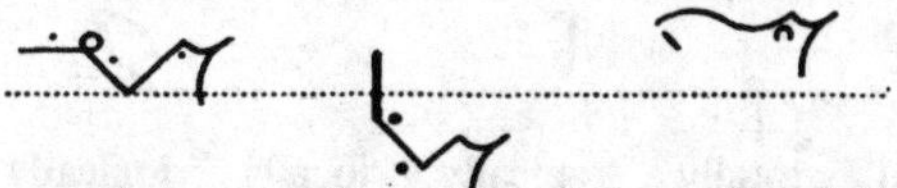

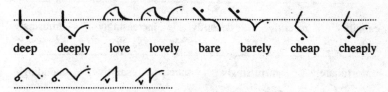

experimental departmental monumental

5(*a*) -LY is a very common ending, either to convert an adjective to an adverb, as in *deep*, *deeply* or *total*, *totally*, or as an integral part of a word, as in *rally* or *holy*.

(*b*) -LY at the end of a word is generally represented by L upward and the third-place short I vowel:

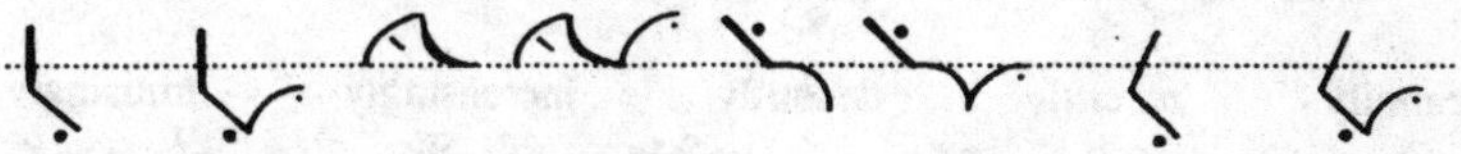

deep deeply love lovely bare barely cheap cheaply

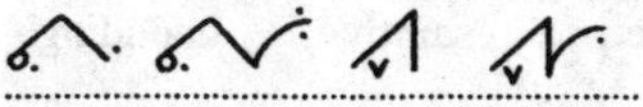

happy happily right rightly

(*c*) When a root outline ends with a hook N, the hook is retained in the -LY word derived from it and, if necessary, the -LY is disjoined as shown:

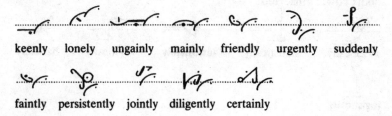

keenly lonely ungainly mainly friendly urgently suddenly

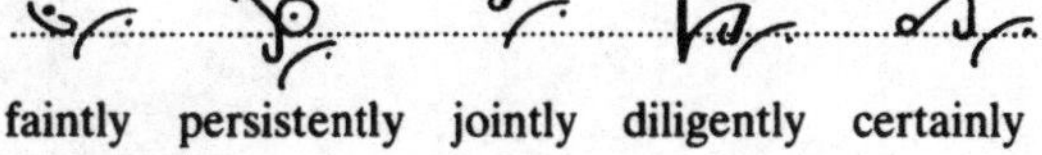

faintly persistently jointly diligently certainly

(*d*) Words that have outlines ending with either an L upward or an L downward, form the -LY ending by inserting the third place short I vowel:

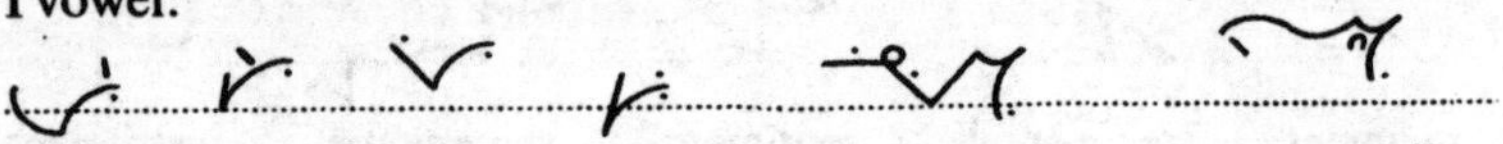

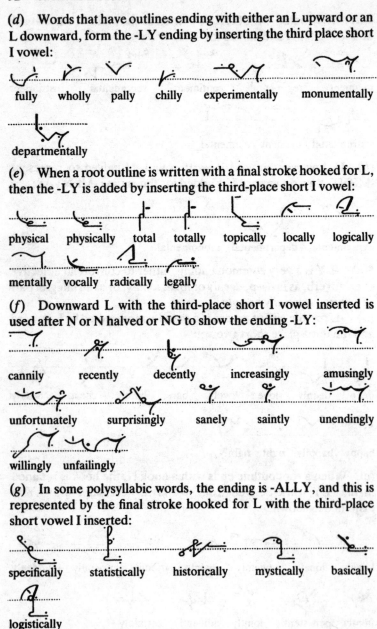

fully wholly pally chilly experimentally monumentally

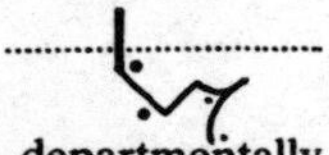

departmentally

(*e*) When a root outline is written with a final stroke hooked for L, then the -LY is added by inserting the third-place short I vowel:

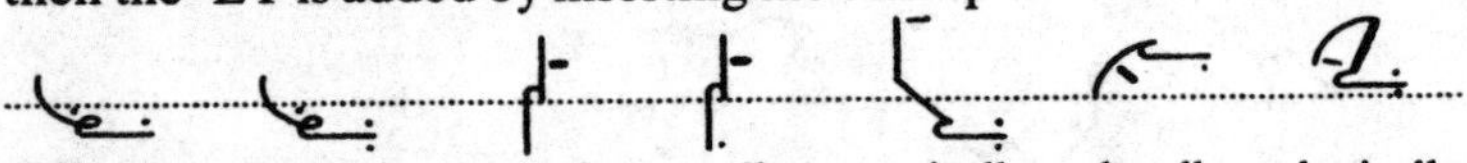

physical physically total totally topically locally logically

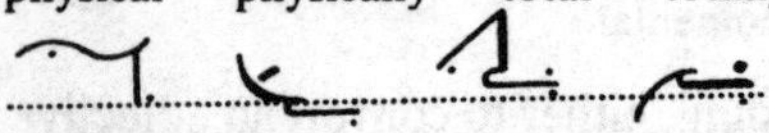

mentally vocally radically legally

(*f*) Downward L with the third-place short I vowel inserted is used after N or N halved or NG to show the ending -LY:

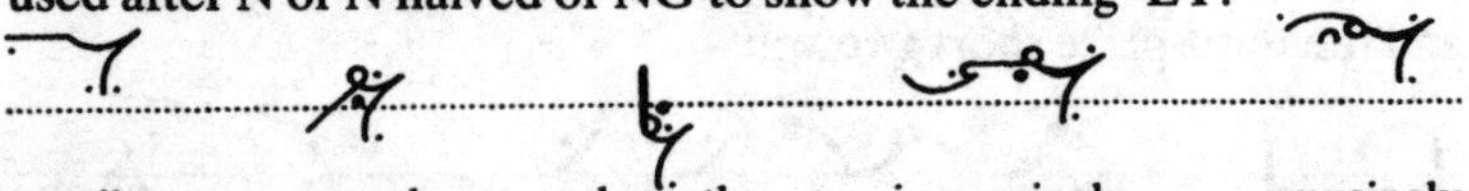

cannily recently decently increasingly amusingly

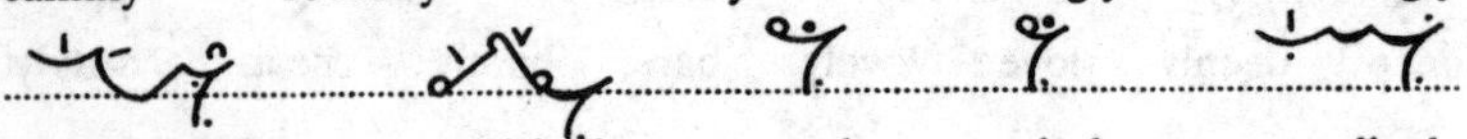

unfortunately surprisingly sanely saintly unendingly

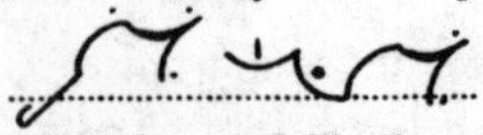

willingly unfailingly

(*g*) In some polysyllabic words, the ending is -ALLY, and this is represented by the final stroke hooked for L with the third-place short vowel I inserted:

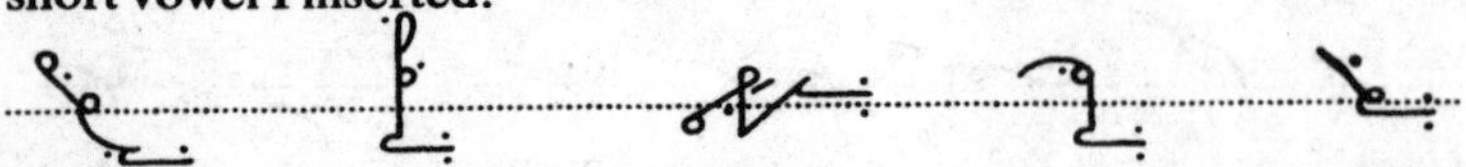

specifically statistically historically mystically basically

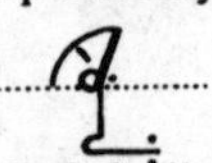

logistically

EXERCISE 40

(*a*) (*b*) (*c*) (*d*) (*e*)

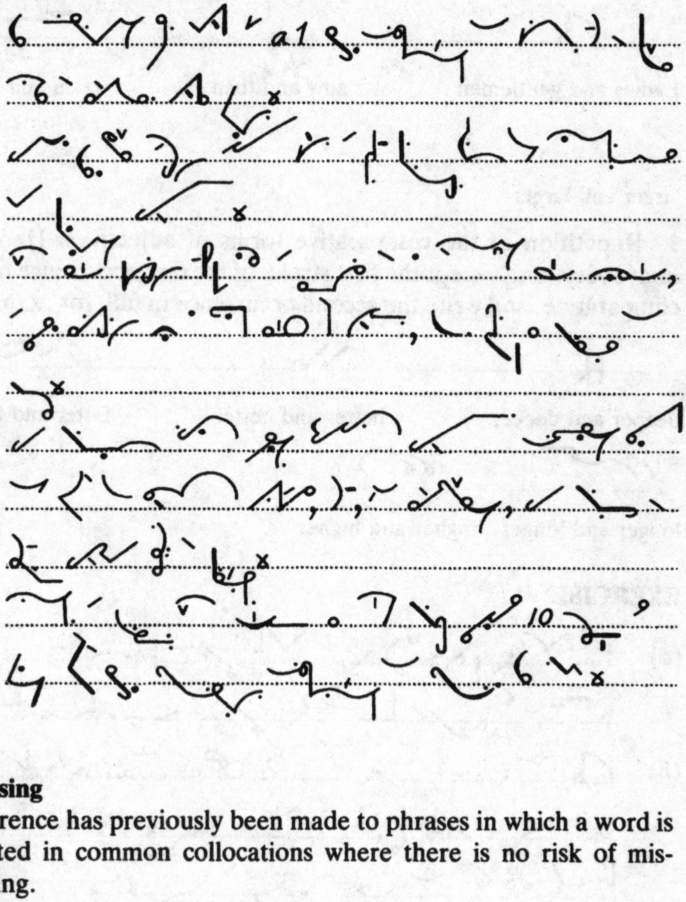

Phrasing

Reference has previously been made to phrases in which a word is omitted in common collocations where there is no risk of misreading.

Here are some further examples:

1 Omitting the word *a*:

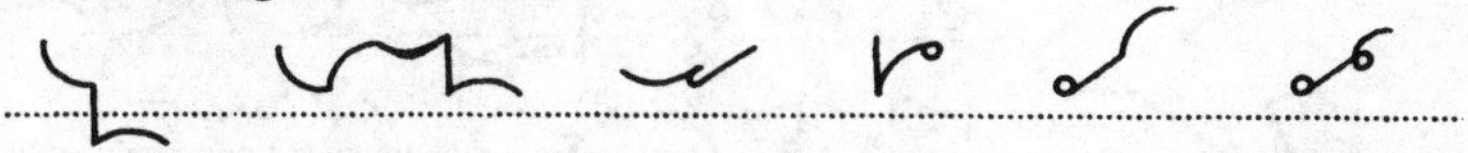

for a time   for a long time   in a way   at a loss   as a rule   as a result

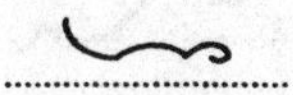

for a moment

2 Omitting the word *and*:

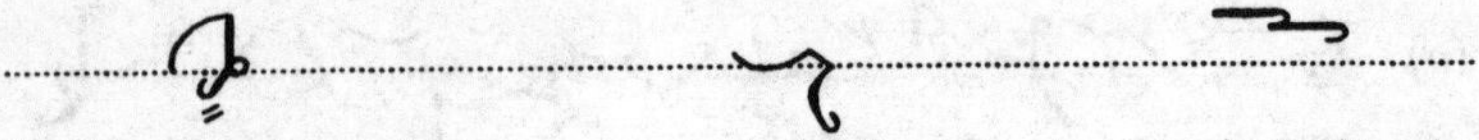

Ladies and gentlemen   now and then   again and again

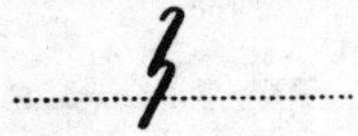

larger and larger

3 Repetition of the comparative forms of adjectives. Here we omit everything except the first stroke of the first occurrence of the comparative, and write the second occurrence in full, for example:

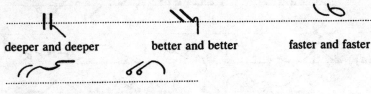

deeper and deeper   better and better   faster and faster

longer and longer   higher and higher

EXERCISE 41

(*a*)

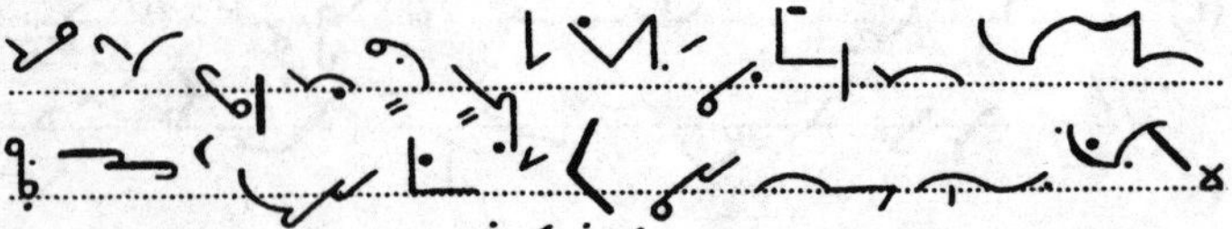

(*b*)

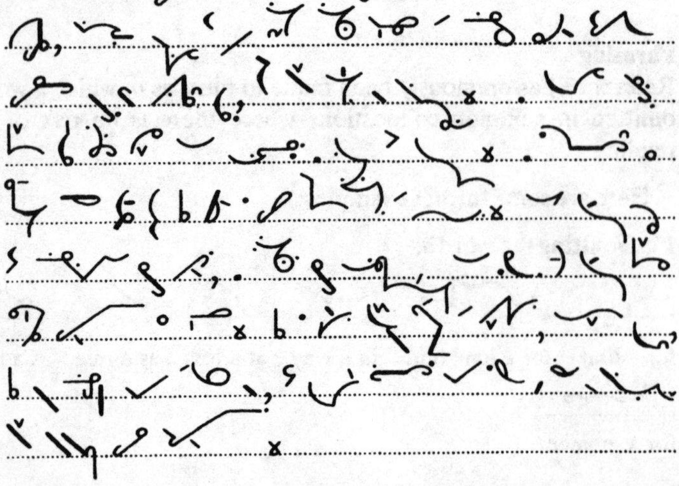

(*c*)

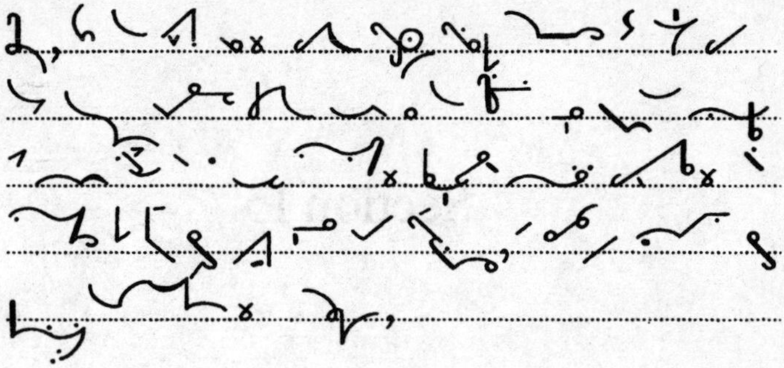

Section 15

Compound consonants

1 Consonants are often pronounced as a group of two or three or even four as in words like *club* (2), *straight* (3) and *twelfths* (4).

When these clusters appear at the beginning of a syllable, then they are called compound consonants. The two initial hooks L and R are, in fact, compound consonants, though it is more practical to call them initial hooks because they have both a syllabic and a consonantal use.

2 We have three other such compounds used initially in syllables.

These are KW, GW, WH and they are written: 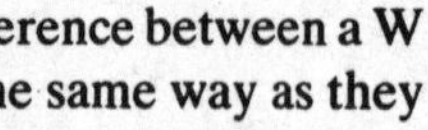 .

Notice that the form for KW is a K with a large initial hook, for GW it is a G with a large initial hook, and for WH it is a W with a similar large hook.

Some people who speak English make no difference between a W and a WH. They pronounce *where* in exactly the same way as they pronounce *wear*. In shorthand the distinction is always made.

Writing note

(*a*) KW begins with a hook twice the size of an L hook written left motion (anticlockwise) just like an L hook. Do *not* allow the writing of a large hook to edge you into writing a longer stroke. The stroke for K stays the same uniform size.

(*b*) GW is exactly the same except for the difference in the weight of the stroke:

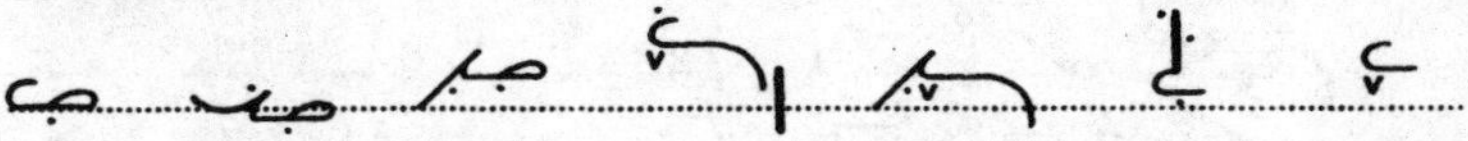

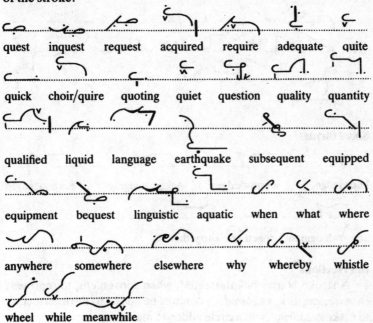

quest inquest request acquired require adequate quite

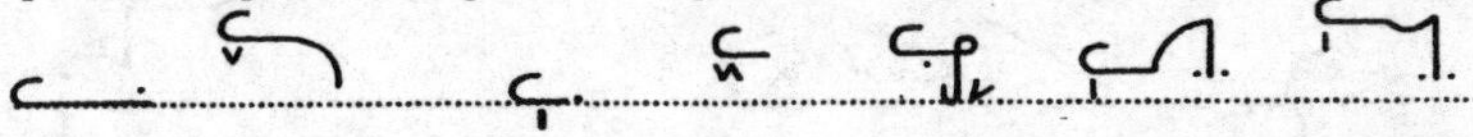

quick choir/quire quoting quiet question quality quantity

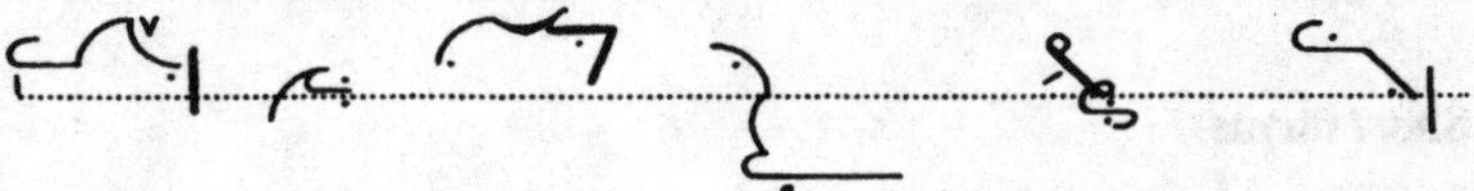

qualified liquid language earthquake subsequent equipped

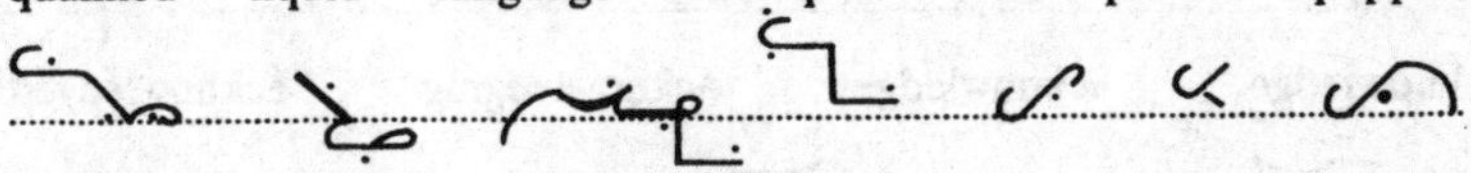

equipment bequest linguistic aquatic when what where

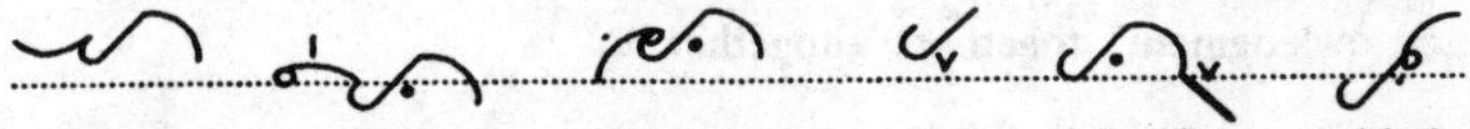

anywhere somewhere elsewhere why whereby whistle

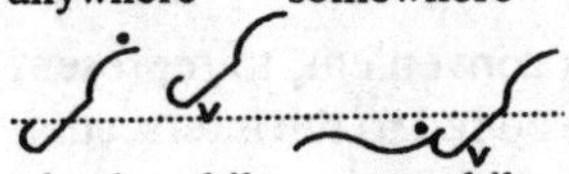

wheel while meanwhile

EXERCISE 42

(*a*) 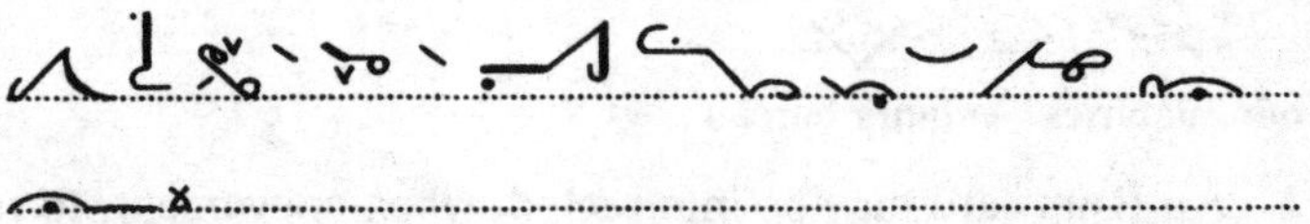

(*b*) 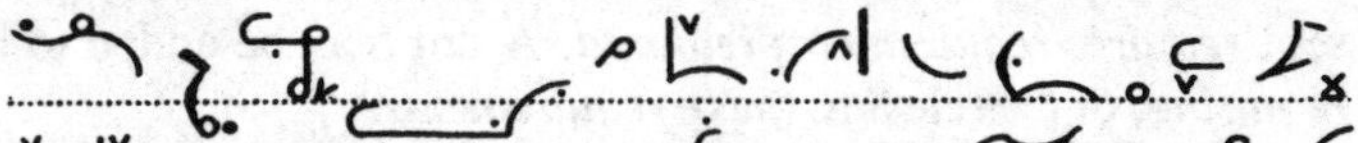

(*c*) 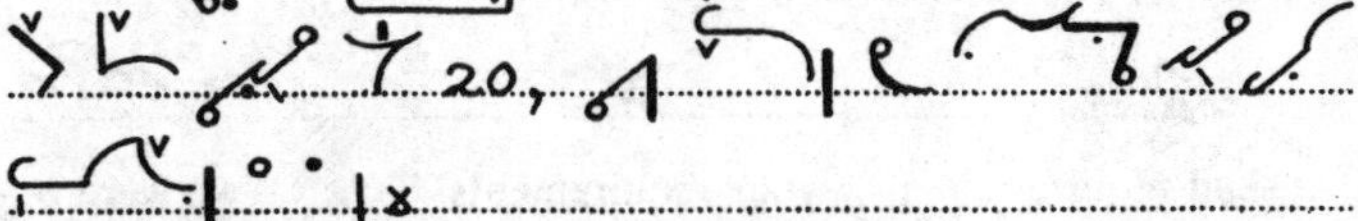

(*d*) 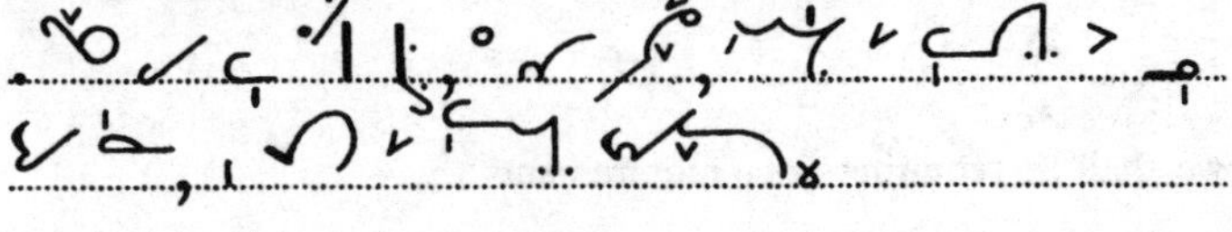

(*e*) 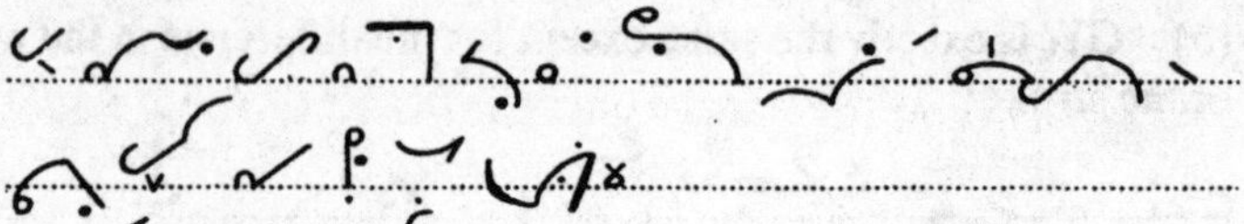

(*f*) 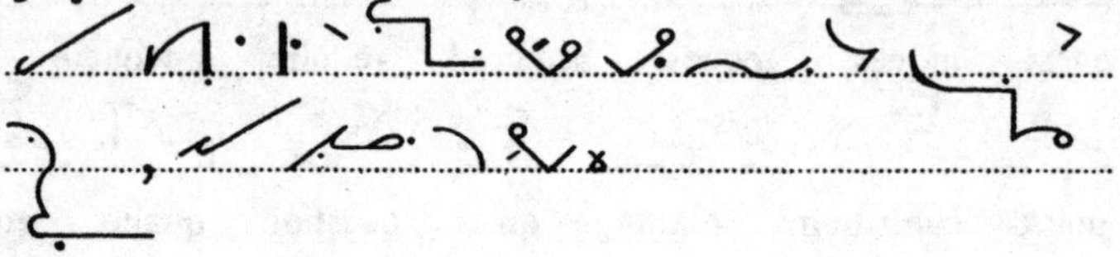

Short forms

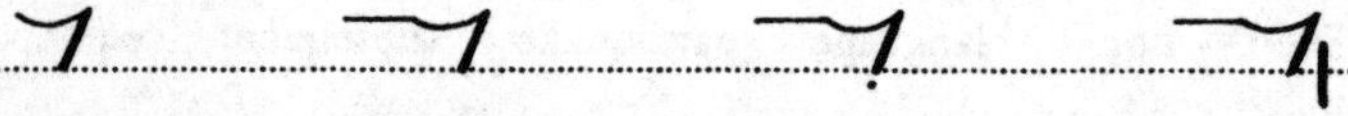

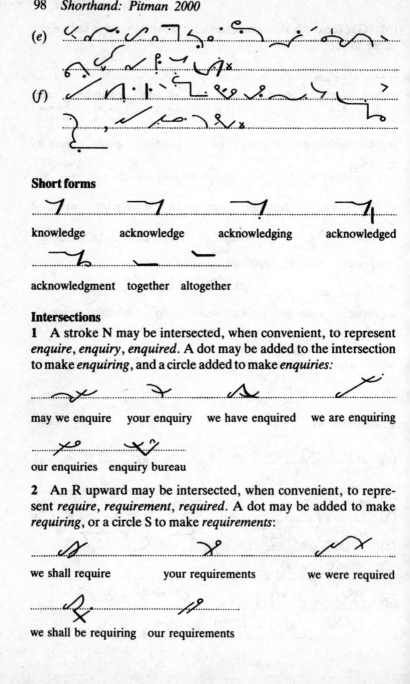

knowledge acknowledge acknowledging acknowledged

acknowledgment together altogether

Intersections

1 A stroke N may be intersected, when convenient, to represent *enquire*, *enquiry*, *enquired*. A dot may be added to the intersection to make *enquiring*, and a circle added to make *enquiries:*

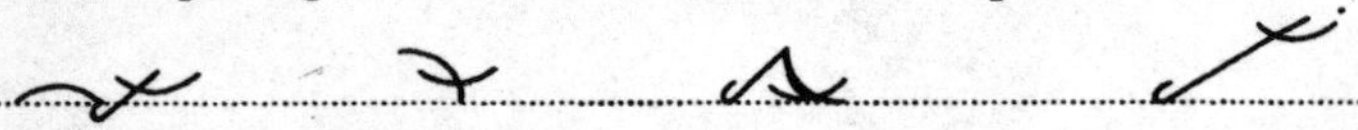

may we enquire your enquiry we have enquired we are enquiring

our enquiries enquiry bureau

2 An R upward may be intersected, when convenient, to represent *require*, *requirement*, *required*. A dot may be added to make *requiring*, or a circle S to make *requirements*:

we shall require your requirements we were required

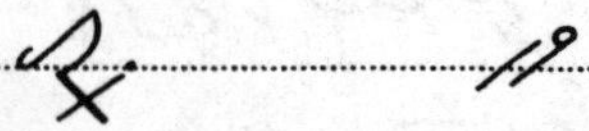

we shall be requiring our requirements

Phrasing

More phrases showing the omission of a word are:

1 *by*: 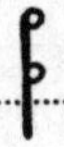 side by side  year by year

2 *have*:  would have been  must have been

3 *in*:  stock in trade  bear in mind

4 *of*:  point of view  first of all

EXERCISE 43

(*a*) 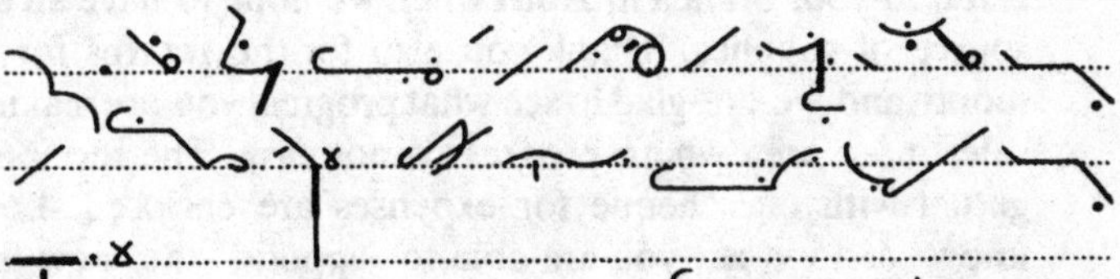

(*b*) 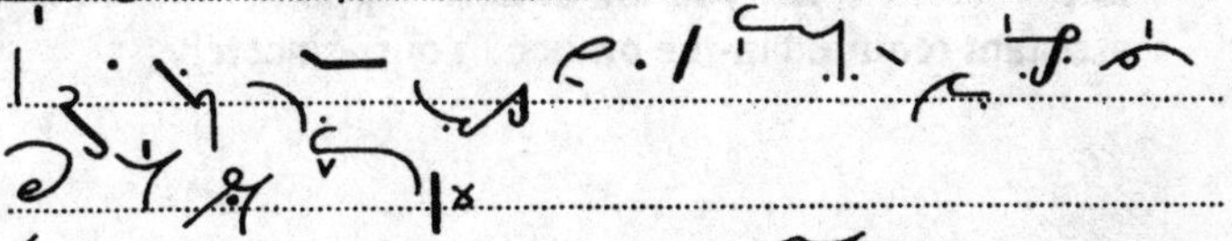

(*c*) 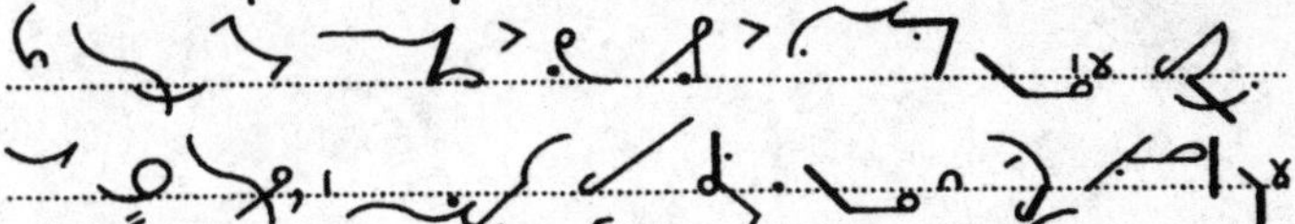

(*d*) 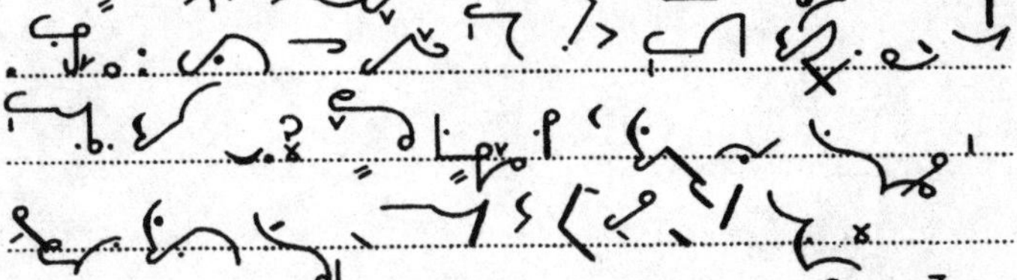

(*e*) 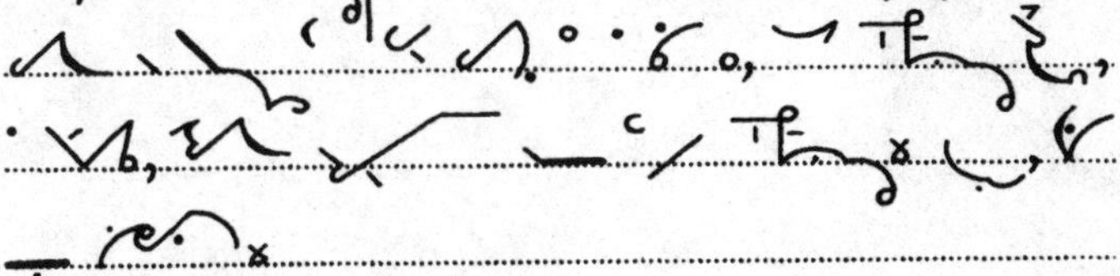

(*f*) 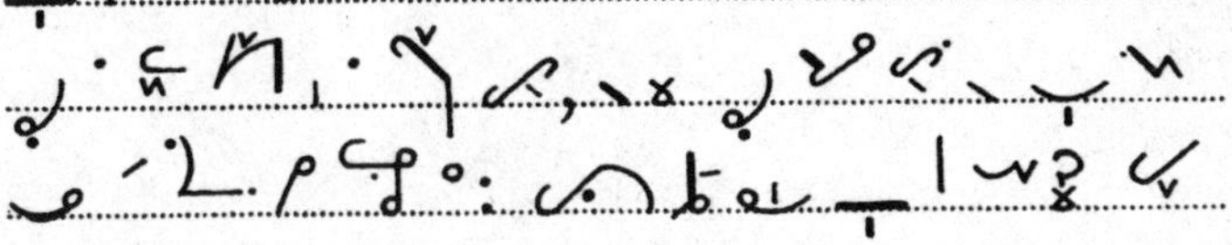

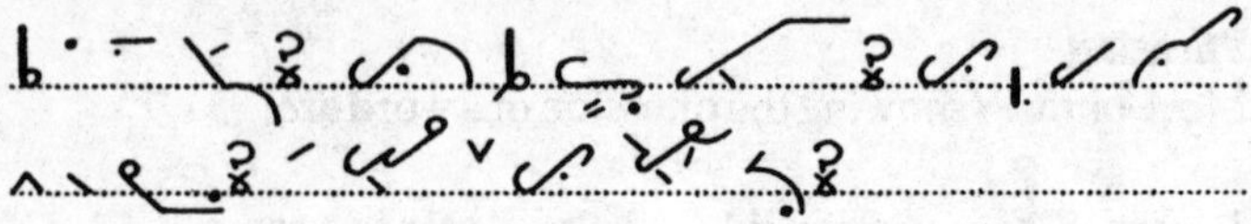

EXERCISE 44 Write in shorthand, afterwards checking with the key (phrasing is indicated by hyphens):

Dear-Miss Clark, Thank-you for-your-request for extra supplies of art paper for-your branch. We-are-able-to obtain only a few quires a month and-the demand is always much greater-than-the supply. We-will increase-the quantity allocated to-your branch in April when we-hope to-have an extra source of supplies. Thank-you also for-the returns for last-month and-we-are-glad to see what progress you-are making in sales in an area where progress is-not easy. The receipts together-with our cheque for expenses are enclosed. Let-us-know as-soon-as you-are-able-to appoint the new sales assistant required in-the branch. Yours-sincerely,

Section 16

Initial hooks to curved strokes

1 Just as the straight strokes have initial hooks L and R, so do the curved strokes. Hooks are always written *inside* curves, so to distinguish the two hooks the R hook is written small and the L hook is written large.

2 These are the initially hooked forms to curves:
R hooks:

FR VR ThR THR SHR ZHR MR NR

L hooks:

FL VL ThL SHL ML NL

Note that:
(*a*) Both the voiced and the unvoiced forms of TH have R hooks.
(*b*) Neither the voiced form of TH (TH-L) nor the voiced form of SH (i.e. ZHL) occur in normal English words, and there are no hooked forms for these sounds.

3 These hooks, just like those to the straight strokes may be used either consonantally or syllabically, as in  *frame* (consonantal) and  *differ* (syllabic), and in 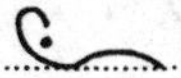 *flame* (consonantal) and  *shuffle* (syllabic).

Notice that

VR THR ZHR MR NR THL SHL ML NL

can be used syllabically.

Consonantal use examples:

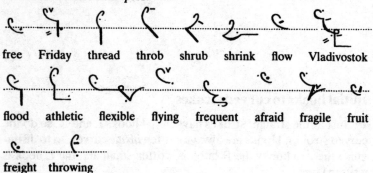

free Friday thread throb shrub shrink flow Vladivostok

flood athletic flexible flying frequent afraid fragile fruit

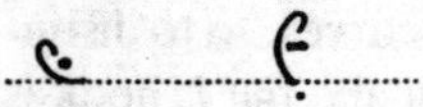

freight throwing

Syllabic use examples:

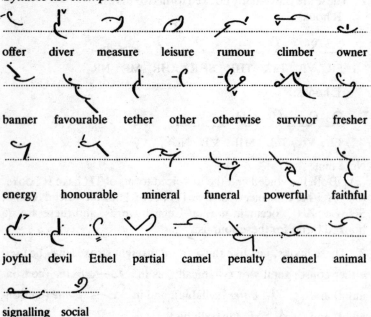

offer diver measure leisure rumour climber owner

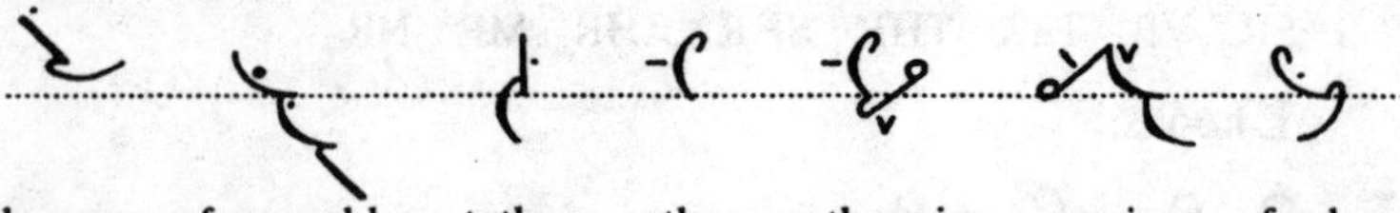

banner favourable tether other otherwise survivor fresher

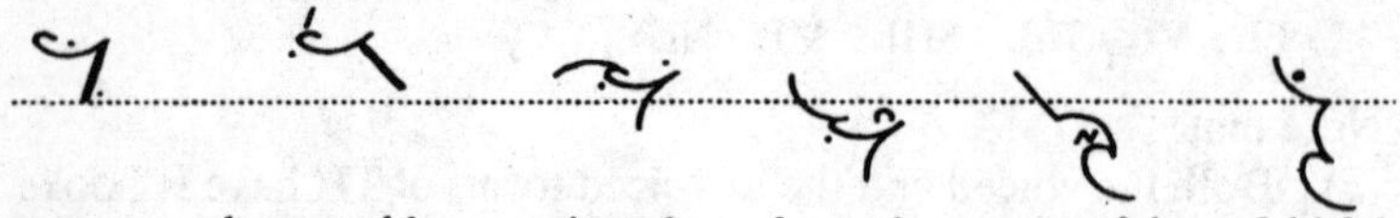

energy honourable mineral funeral powerful faithful

joyful devil Ethel partial camel penalty enamel animal

signalling social

4 Note the examples  *mineral* and  *funeral*. L is downward after N, N halved, -ING, and also N hooked for R, as above.

EXERCISE 45 From this point onwards many vowels will be omitted.

(*a*) 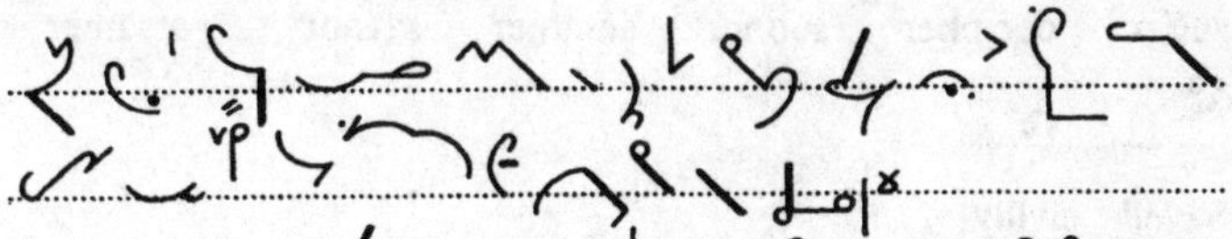

(*b*) 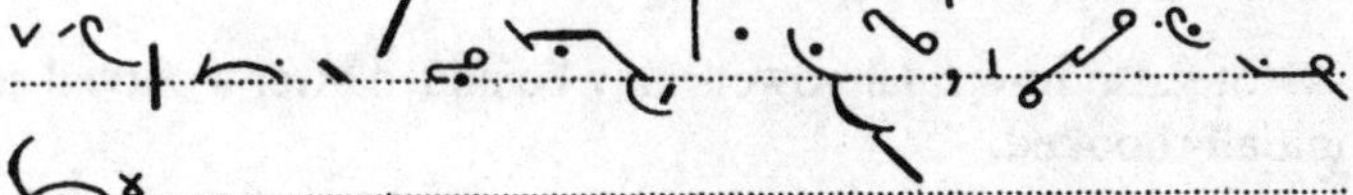

(*c*) 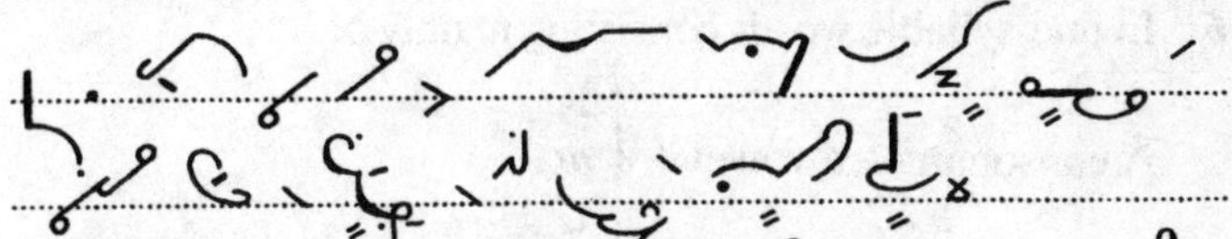

(*d*) 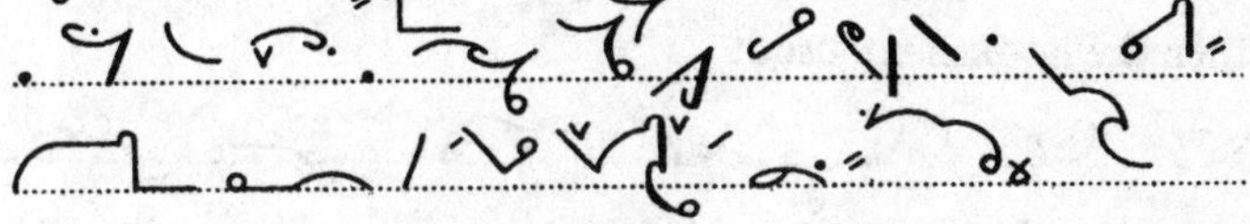

(*e*) 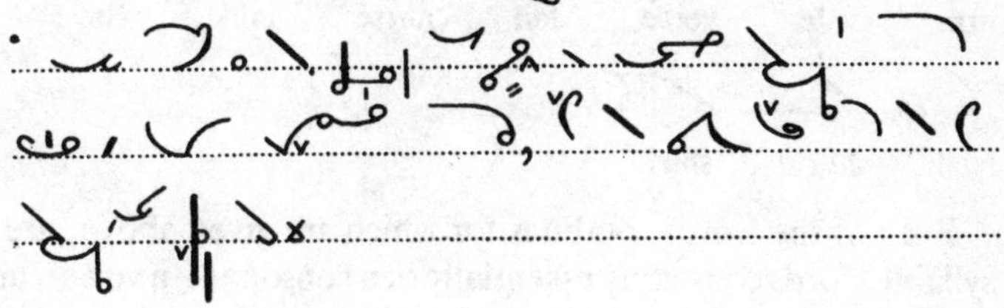

Writing note When writing the initial hooks to curved strokes:

(*a*) Keep the hooks round.
(*b*) Keep the R hook small.
(*c*) L hook must be large, even perhaps exaggerated a little, to make the distinction between R and L hooks plain.
(*d*) Do not let the size of the L hook induce you to increase the size of the stroke to which the hook is written.
(*e*) Keep the shape of the stroke correct.

Finally, remember that writing lightly is vital for writing quickly. There are no heavy strokes in shorthand – only light strokes and still lighter strokes.

5 Circles to initial hooks to curved strokes. The circle S may be tucked inside either an R hook or an L hook to a curved stroke and used medially too, as in:

suffer decipher sooner summer savoury gossamer civil

Savell civilly

Note also how final vowels may be added after a curved stroke initially hooked.

6 In one-syllable words consisting mainly of:

A consonant + a vowel + { R *or* L

then the hook is *not* used:

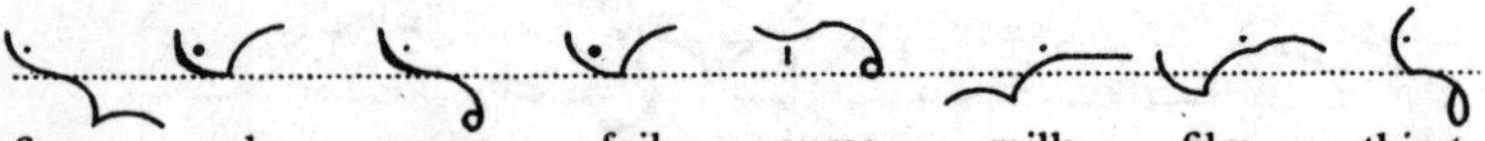

firm vale verse fail nurse milk film thirst

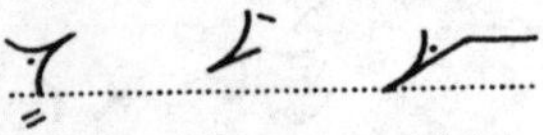

Nell short shirk

Each of the words, outlines for which are given above, are one-syllable words consisting essentially of a consonant, a vowel, and an R or an L. Therefore, the hooks R and L are *not* used.

7 Moreover, if the hooks are not used in the root word, then they are not used in the derivatives either. In this way families of words can have similar basic outlines and are thus easier to read and to write:

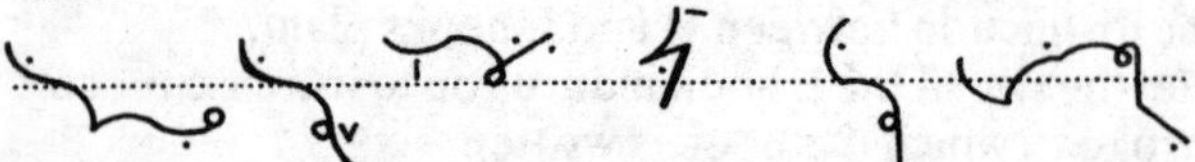

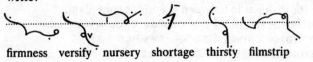

firmness versify nursery shortage thirsty filmstrip

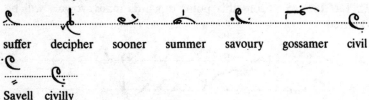

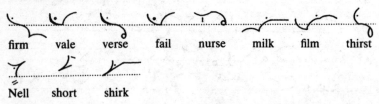

All the words in the preceding line are examples of derivatives from the words given in 6. They all retain the root form.

8 In words that have:

a consonant + a diphthong + { R *or* L }

or

a diphone

or

a triphone

the hooked form is *not* used. Examples of such words now follow:

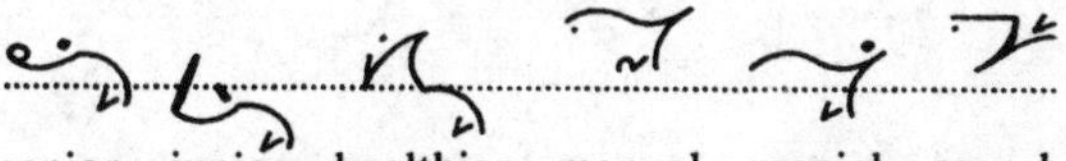

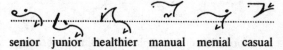

senior junior healthier manual menial casual

9 Stress.

(*a*) The rules about stress in relation to strokes initially hooked for R and L are the same for initially hooked curves as they are for initially hooked straight strokes.

As it is important to know when initially hooked curves may be used and when they may not, the rule is explained again here. This time initially hooked curves will serve as our examples.

All English words of more than one syllable have one syllable that is strongly stressed. For example in the three following words *car*amel, in*ven*tion and enter*tain* the stress falls on the first, the second, and the third syllable respectively.

Now, in any combination:

a consonant + a vowel + { R *or* L }

we have the chance of writing the initially hooked form or the separate strokes – consonant and R or consonant and L.

The rule is that if this combination occurs in an *unstressed* syllable, then we use the initially hooked form regardless of what the vowel between the consonant and R or L is (except, of course, that the rule in 8 above must be followed). For example, in *forestall* the

FORE- syllable is unstressed so we can use the hooked form and write  *forestall*. The intervening vowel is not written in.

Similarly, in *volcano* the VOL- syllable is unstressed so we can use the hooked form and write 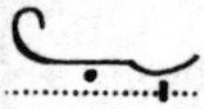 *volcano*. The vowel intervening between V and L is not written in, but it decides the place of the outline.

Here are some words where unstressed syllables with curve stroke consonant + vowel + R or L are written with the hooked form:

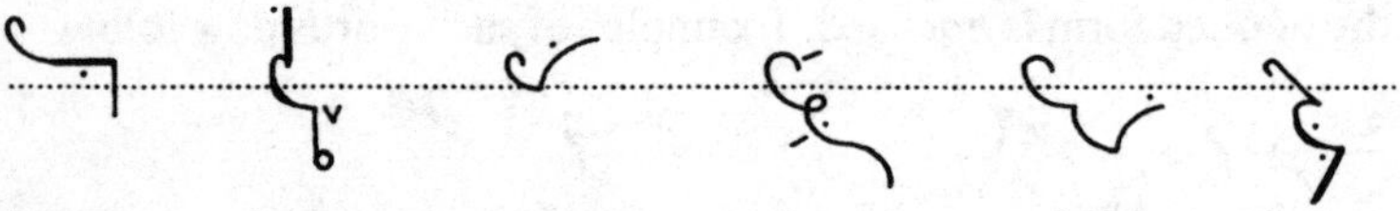

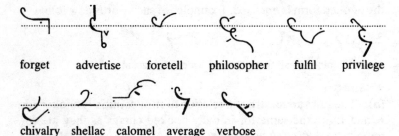

forget advertise foretell philosopher fulfil privilege

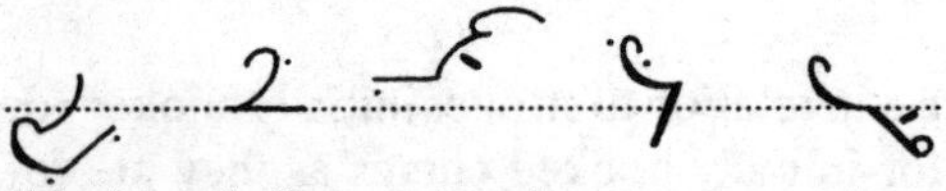

chivalry shellac calomel average verbose

(*b*) If the hooked form is used in a root word it is retained in derivatives even though, as sometimes happens, the stress shifts, as in:

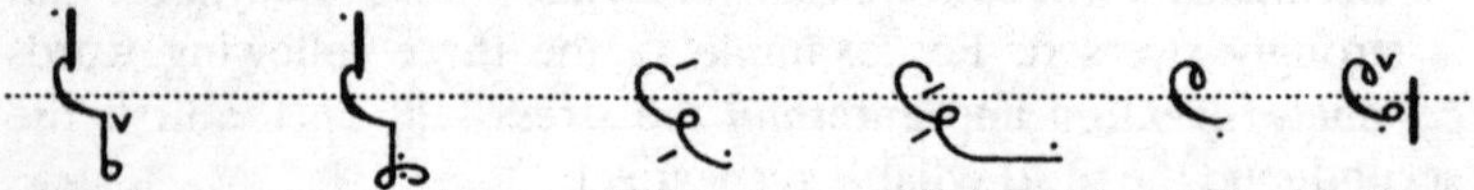

advertise advertisement philosophy philosophic civil civilised

civility

Conversely, if the hooked form is *not* used in a root word, then it is not used in derivatives either, even though the stress may shift, as in:

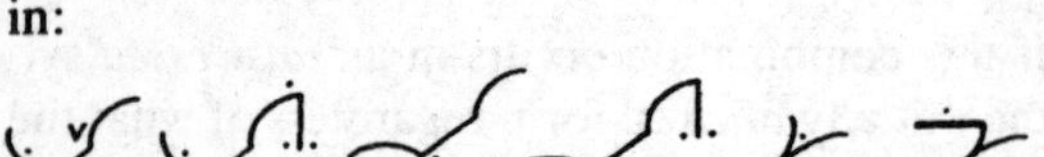

fertile fertility moral morality shell eggshell

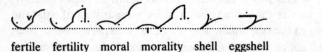

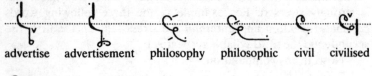

EXERCISE 46

(*a*) 

(*b*) 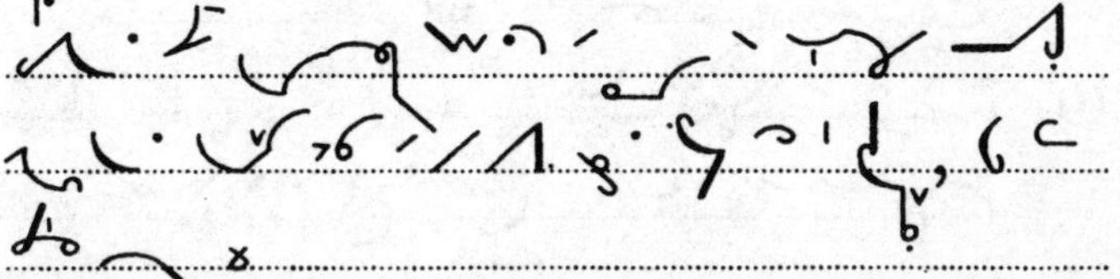

(*c*) 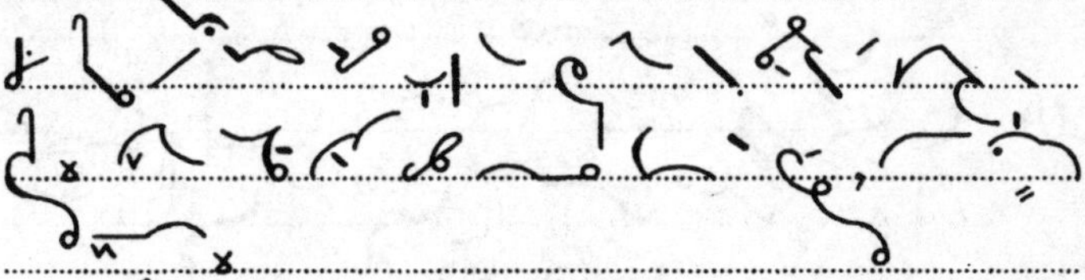

(*d*) 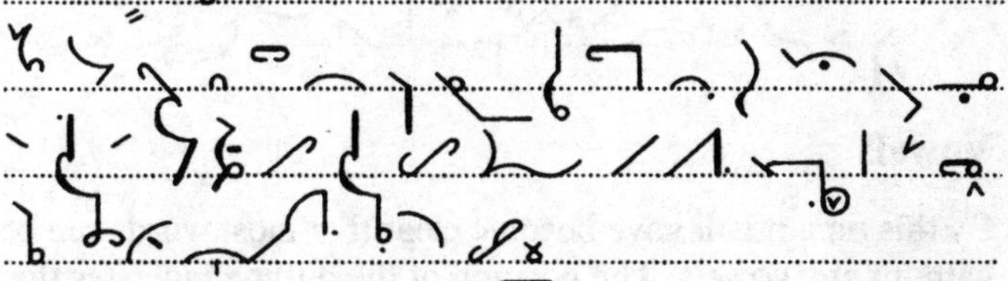

(*e*) 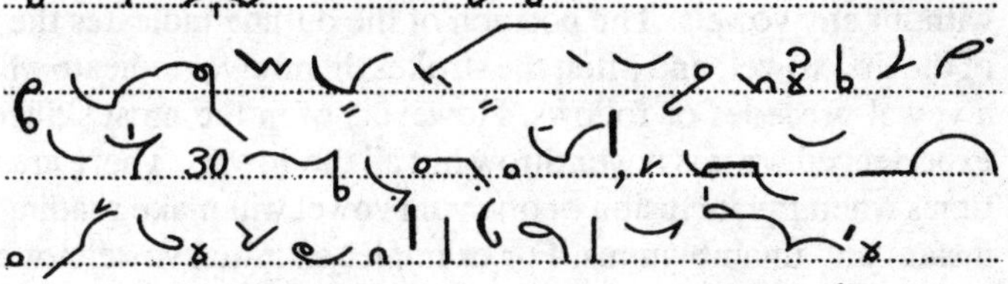

(*f*) 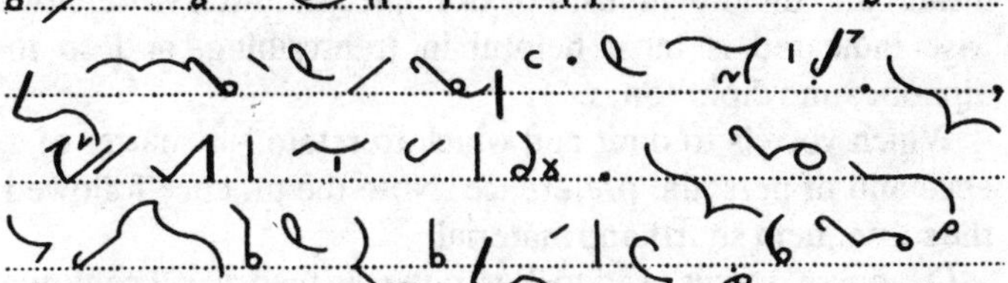

(*g*) 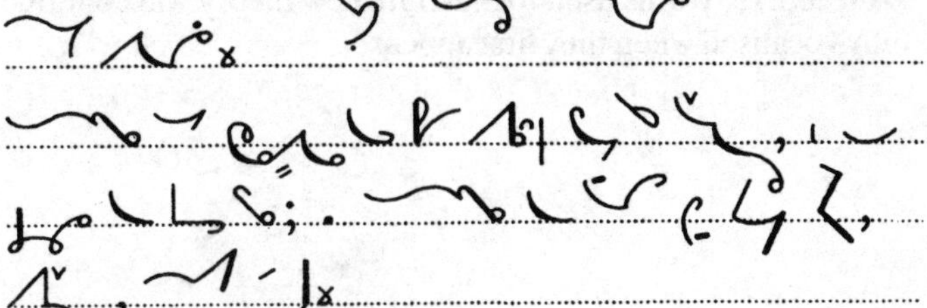

(*h*)

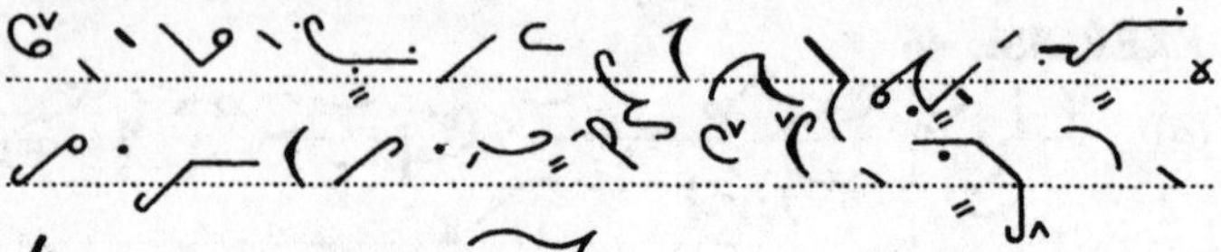

(*i*)

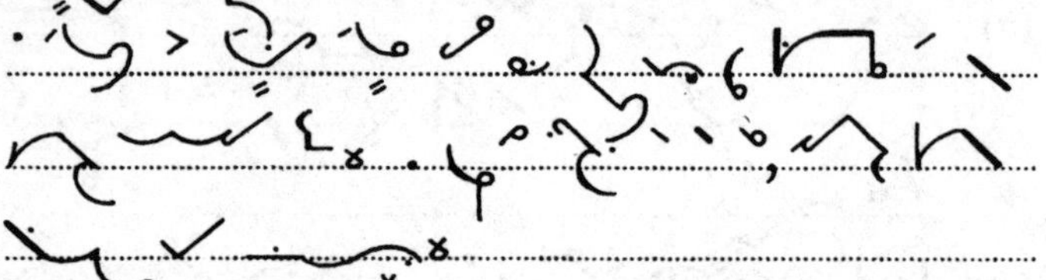

(*j*)

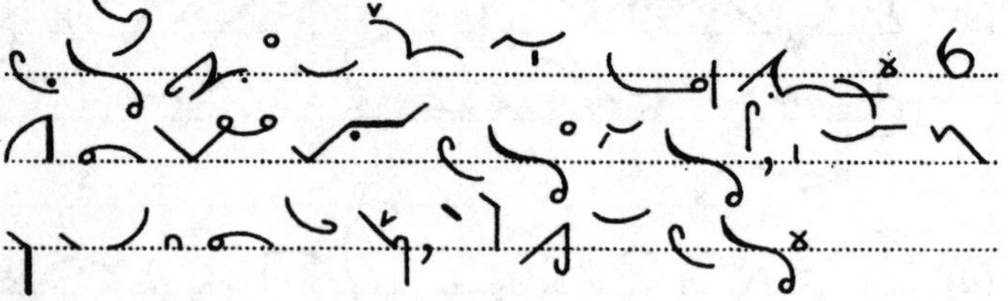

Vowels

By this time it will have become clear that most words can be read without any vowels. The position of the outline indicates the place of the first vowel, and often the strokes themselves indicate whether a vowel precedes or follows. However, even the most skilled and experienced writers never throw out all the vowels. There are many times when the inclusion of one vital vowel will make reading back instant and unambiguous. For example, an initial vowel not otherwise indicated is most helpful in transcribing, and so too are diphones and diphthongs.

Which vowels to omit and which to retain is a matter of experience and of personal preference. Note the practice followed in all the subsequent shorthand material.

Of course, words used to illustrate new theory will continue to be fully vocalised when they first appear.

Section 17

Reverse forms of initially hooked curves

1 The initially hooked curves

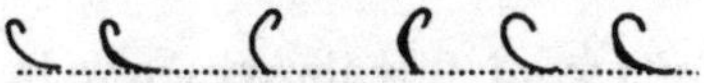

FR VR ThR THR FL VL

have reverse forms. These are written with the clockwise right motion ⟶ and appear as:

FR VR ThR THR FL VL

2 These reverse forms are always used after all horizontals and all upstrokes, whether straight strokes or curved strokes. The reason for the rule is, of course, that it is not possible to write the ordinary forms of the initially hooked curves after horizontals or upstrokes:

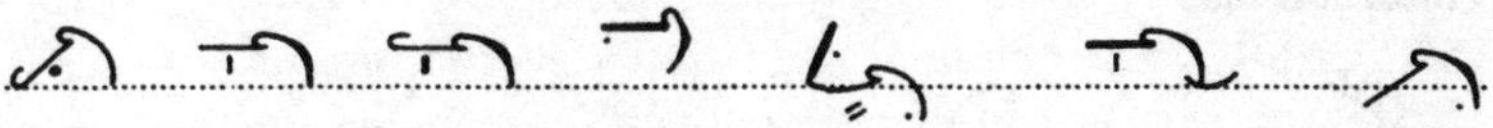

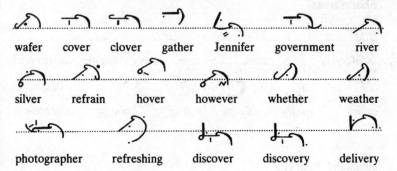

wafer cover clover gather Jennifer government river

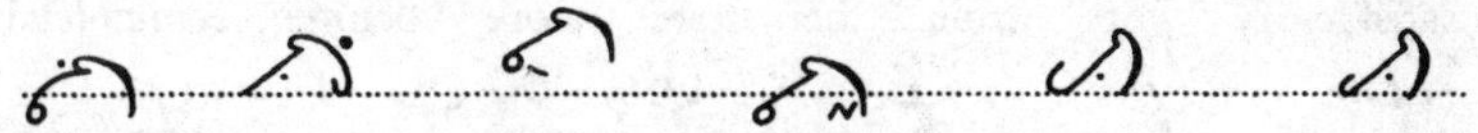

silver refrain hover however whether weather

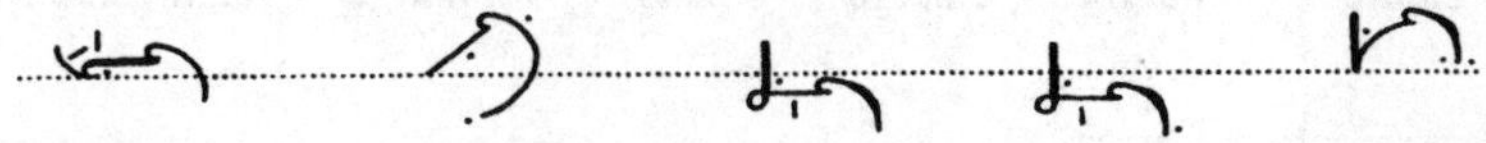

photographer refreshing discover discovery delivery

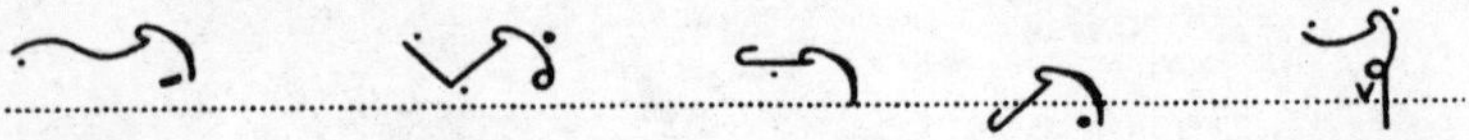

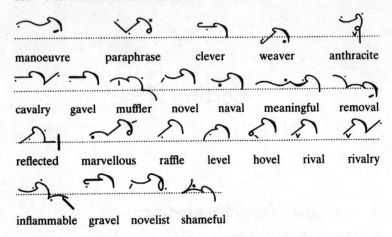

manoeuvre paraphrase clever weaver anthracite

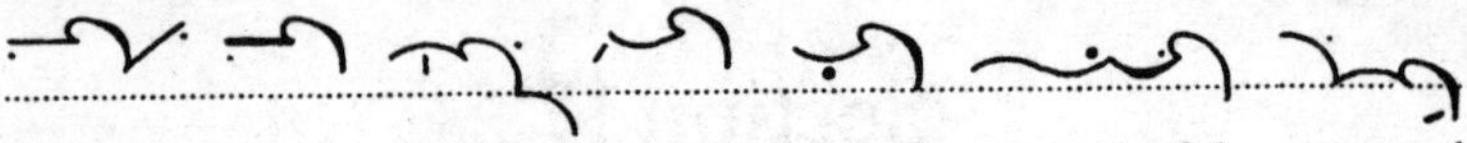

cavalry gavel muffler novel naval meaningful removal

reflected marvellous raffle level hovel rival rivalry

inflammable gravel novelist shameful

3 If an R appears in the spelling of a word, it is always shown in shorthand even though it may not seem to be pronounced. Compare .... *fought* and .... *fort*.

The reasons for this are:

(*a*) The inclusion of the R always makes reading easier and helps to distinguish words that might otherwise have identical outlines.

(*b*) The presence of an R often has a modifying effect on the vowel or diphthong that precedes it.

(*c*) In some forms of spoken English (as, for example, in Scotland) the R has a much more noticeable consonantal significance than in other forms.

Short forms

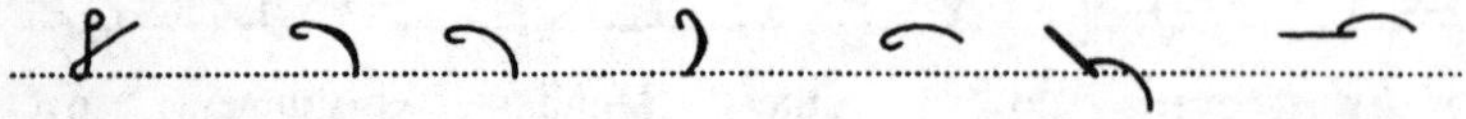

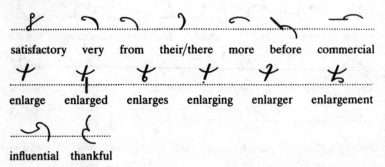

satisfactory very from their/there more before commercial

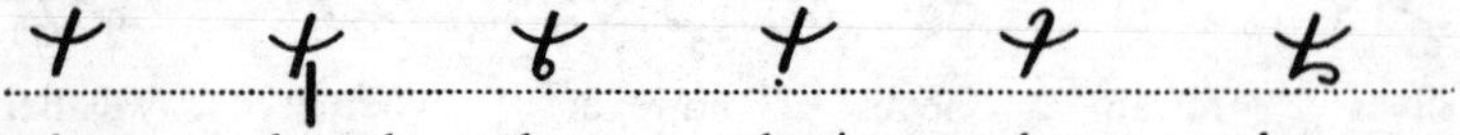

enlarge enlarged enlarges enlarging enlarger enlargement

influential thankful

Notes on short forms

(*a*) Note the important short forms *very*, *from*, *their*/*there* formed from simple reverse forms.

(*b*) *Before* is a short form because a reverse FR is used contrary to the rule given in 2 above.

(*c*) Once you learn *enlarge* as , all the rest of this group of six follow on naturally.

(*d*) In writing *influential*, ensure that the reverse form FL comes through the line.

EXERCISE 47

(*a*) (*b*) (*c*) (*d*) (*e*)

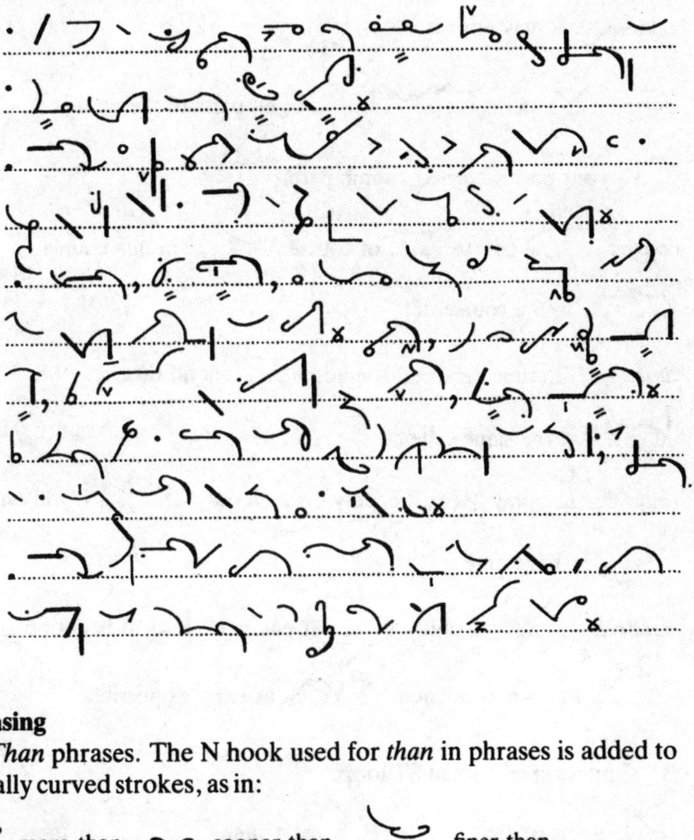

Phrasing

1 *Than* phrases. The N hook used for *than* in phrases is added to initially curved strokes, as in:

 more than sooner than finer than

2 Initially hooked strokes are used in phrasing as follows:

our: .... in .... in our .... in our own

.... in our interests

far: .... far .... so far .... very far .... too far

.... how far

appear: .... appear .... it appears .... which appear

.... it may appear

part: .... part .... in all parts of the world

.... your part .... some parts

course: .... course .... of course .... in due course

.... in the course of

time: .... time .... sometime .... at all times

.... at the same time

only: .... only .... it is only .... if only .... it will only

.... I have only

possible: .... possible .... if possible .... it is not possible

.... as soon as possible .... as early as possible

3 Omission of T from ST loop:

.... we trust that .... next time .... in most cases

Below, the intersection TH for *month* is shown. This gives us phrases like:

 this month  six months 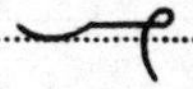 next month

4 *There* phrases:

 there is  there is no doubt  there are

 there will be

Intersection

A TH may be intersected, or where convenient joined, to represent *month*:

 several months  in the month  every month

 some months  for a month

EXERCISE 48

(a) (b) (c) (d)

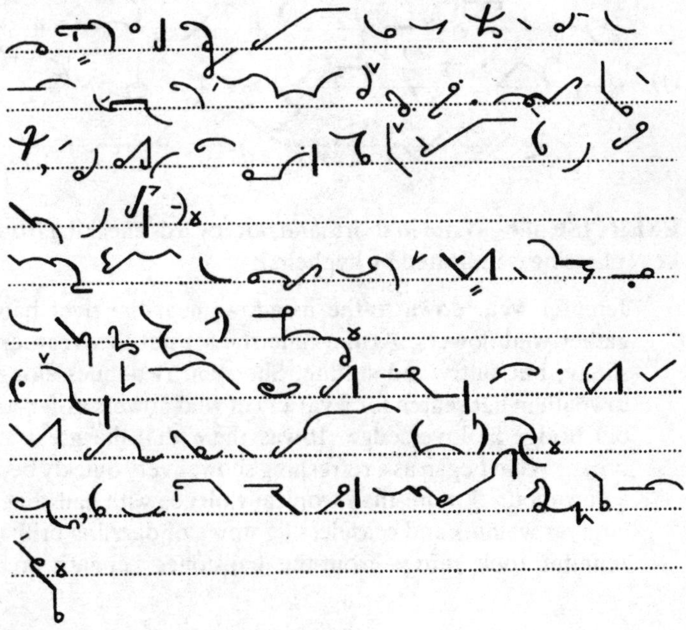

(*e*) 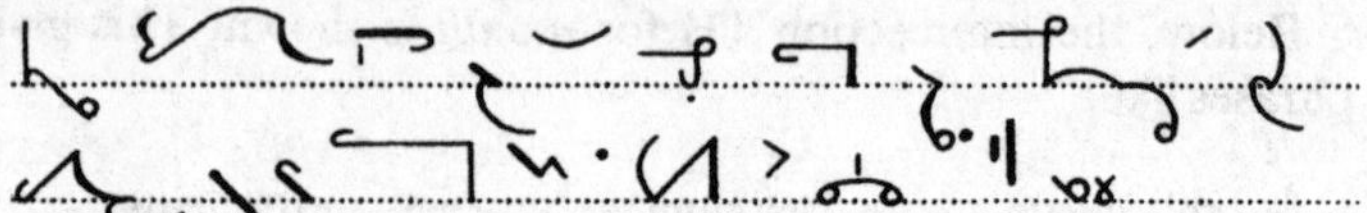

(*f*) 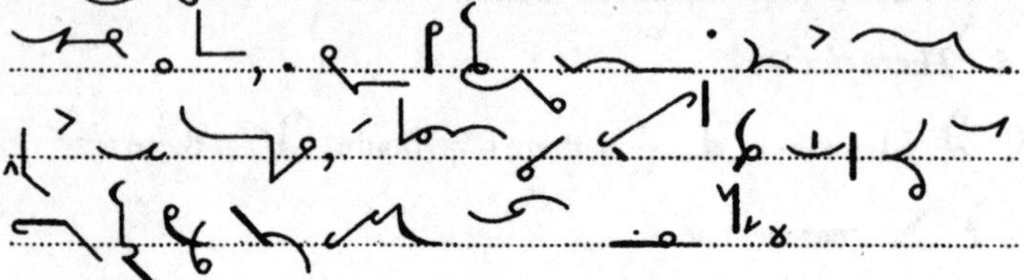

(*g*) 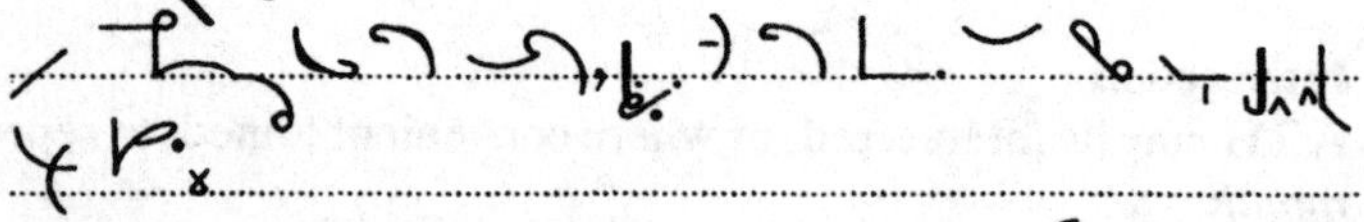

(*h*) 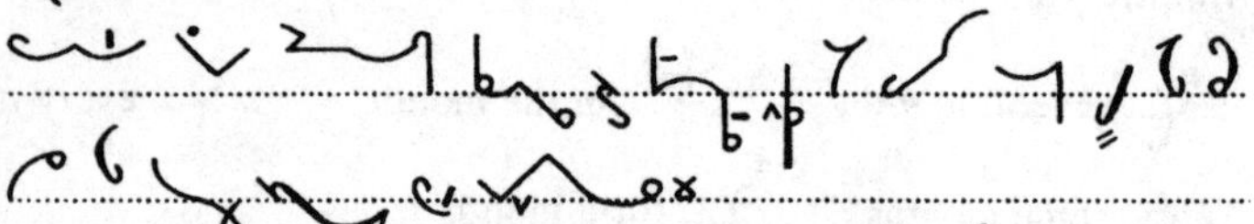

(*i*) 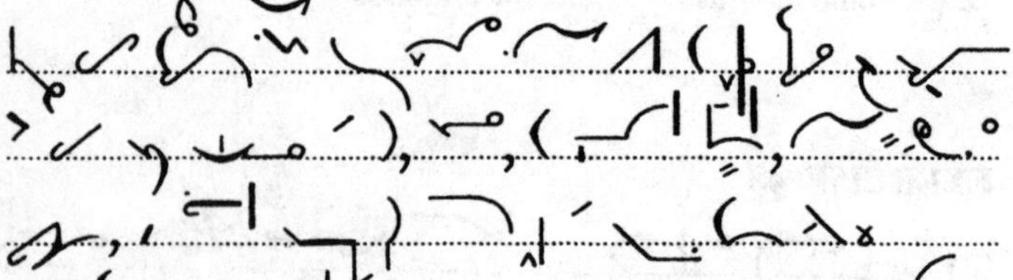

(*j*) 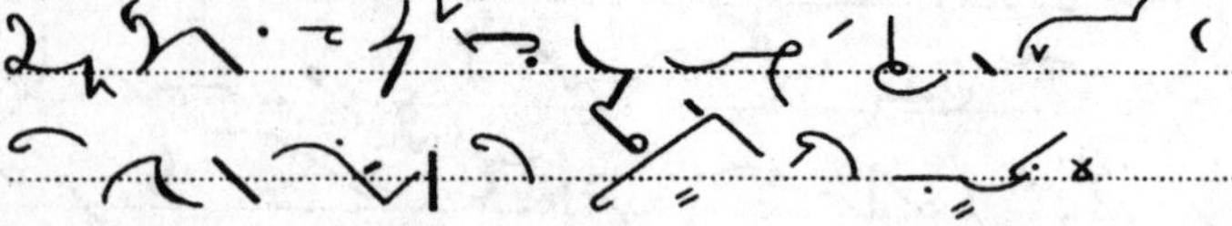

EXERCISE 49 Write in shorthand, afterwards checking from the key (phrasing is indicated by hyphens):

Jennifer went down to-the meadows near-the river bank to gather wild flowers. At-the-time she set out the weather was sunny, but sultry and stifling. She went two-miles along-the towpath in her search for a variety of wild flowers as-far-as-the old bridge at Liversedge. It-was there that-the great storm broke. What began as a refreshing shower very quickly became a downpour of more-than tropical violence with hailstones as-large-as walnuts and ceaseless lightning of dazzling brilliance. Jennifer took refuge from-the hailstones beneath an arch of-the bridge. But such was-the quantity of-water that fell, that-the river soon became a torrent, and she was obliged to-seek help from-the Glover family. They lived in a large grange close by-the bridge at Liversedge. It-was this chance meeting that began-the famous romance which this novel tells.

Section 18

Review

Read, copy, and then re-read from your own copy each of the four passages that follow. Then re-transcribe them back into shorthand from the key without reference to your original shorthand. Check the result.

1

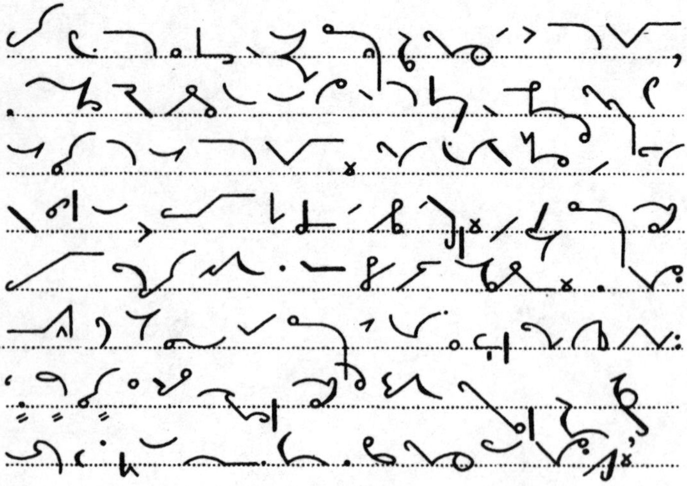

2

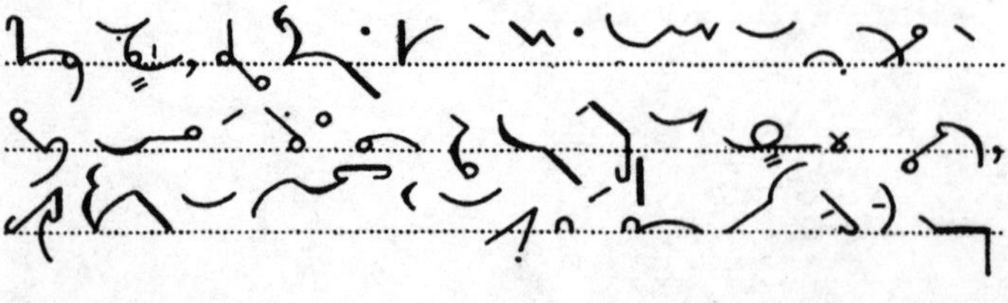

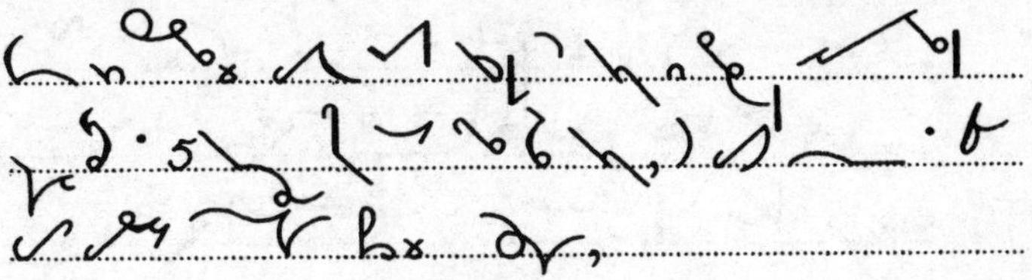

3

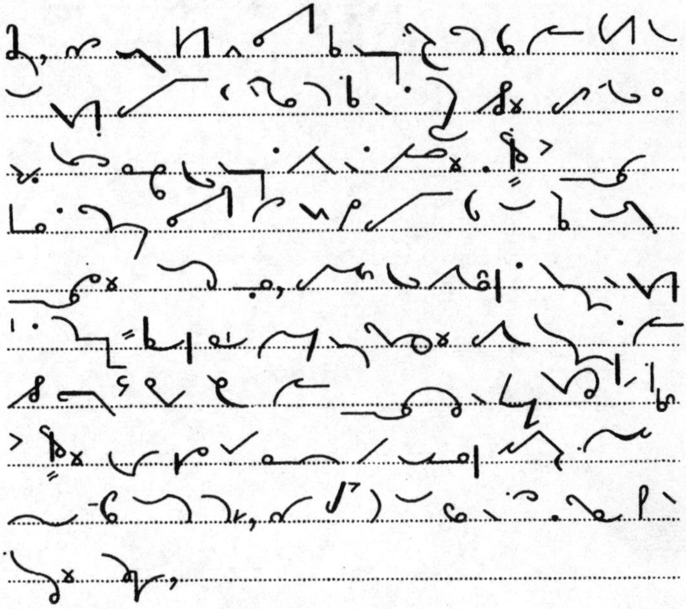

4

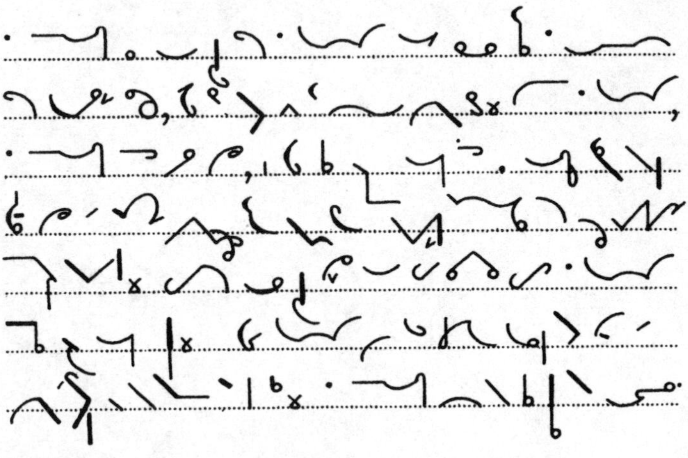

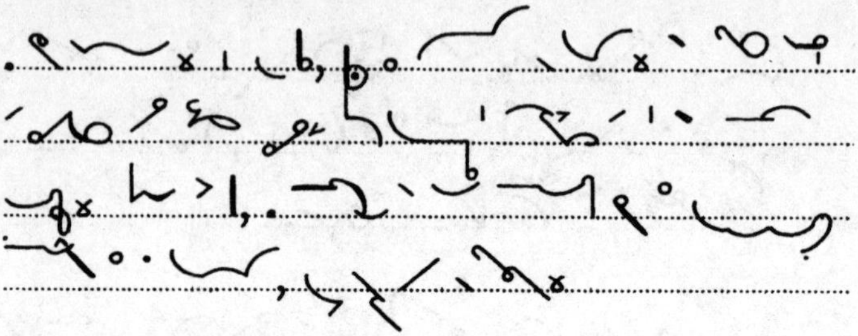

Section 19

-SHUN hook

1 The suffix -SHUN, pronounced sometimes with unvoiced SH and sometimes with voiced ZH, is very common in English. It is variously spelled, as in the following examples: *fashion*, *relation*, *Persian*, *invasion*, but of course it is the sound that is represented in shorthand and not the spelling.

Note that the pronunciation of the -SHUN in the first two examples, *fashion* and *relation*, is with the unvoiced SH and of the last two examples, *Persian* and *invasion*, is with voiced ZH.

2 -SHUN hook to curves. -SHUN is written as a large hook inside a curved stroke, and at the end of the stroke. Circle S may be added:

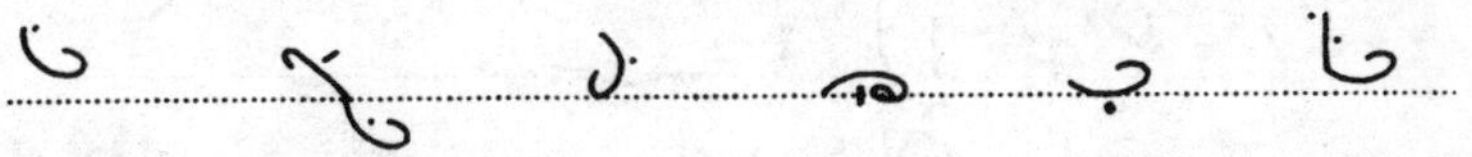

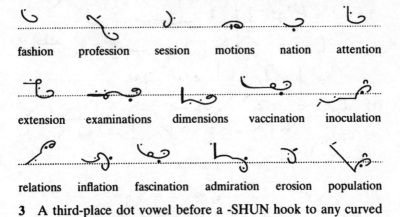

fashion profession session motions nation attention

extension examinations dimensions vaccination inoculation

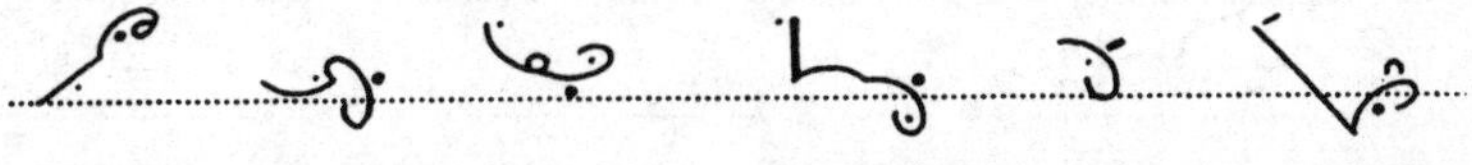

relations inflation fascination admiration erosion population

3 A third-place dot vowel before a -SHUN hook to any curved stroke is written inside the hook. All other third-place vowels, diphthongs, triphones or diphones are written outside the hook in the third place:

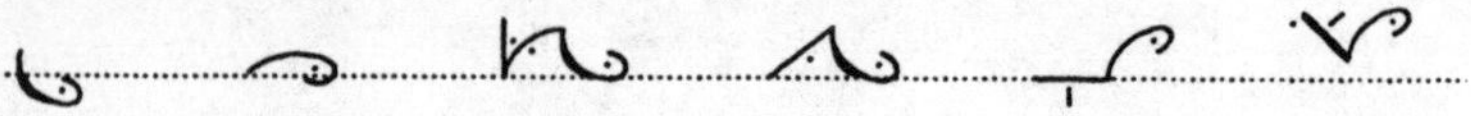

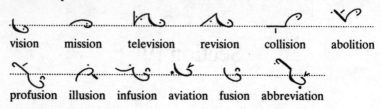

vision mission television revision collision abolition

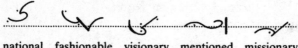

profusion illusion infusion aviation fusion abbreviation

4 Although -SHUN is always written at the end of a stroke, it is often found medially, as in:

national fashionable visionary mentioned missionary

5 The ending -ABLE, when following a -SHUN hook, is written with  or 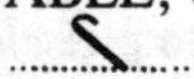 disjoined and written close to the -SHUN hook, as:

unfashionable tensionable mentionable

EXERCISE 50

(*a*)

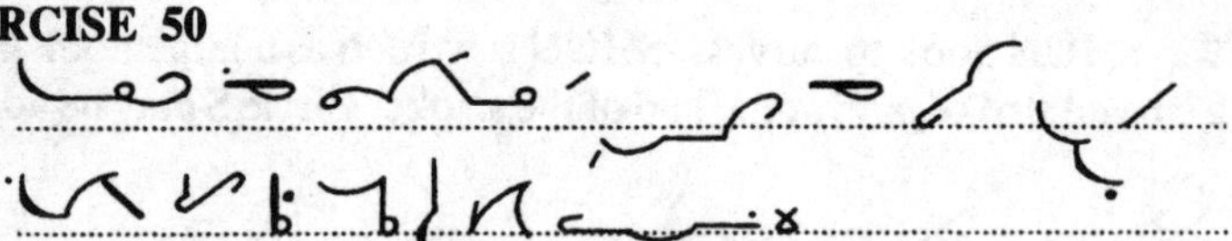

(*b*)

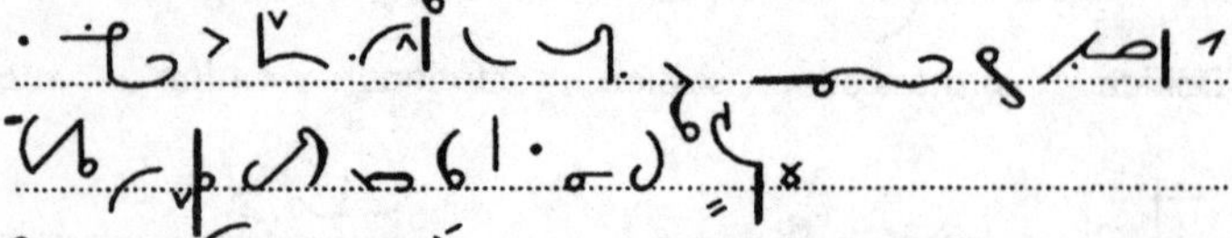

(*c*)

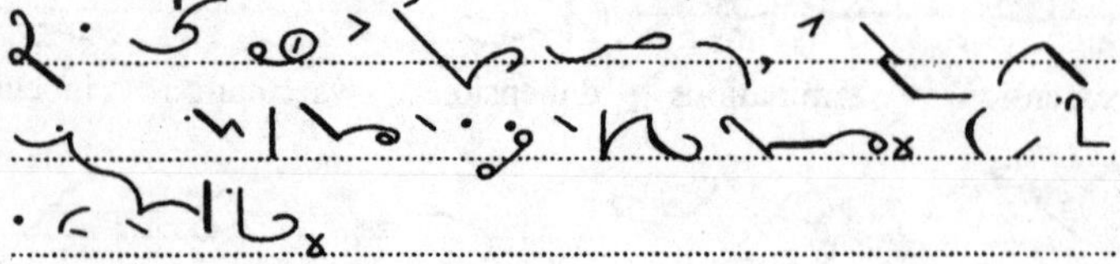

(*d*)

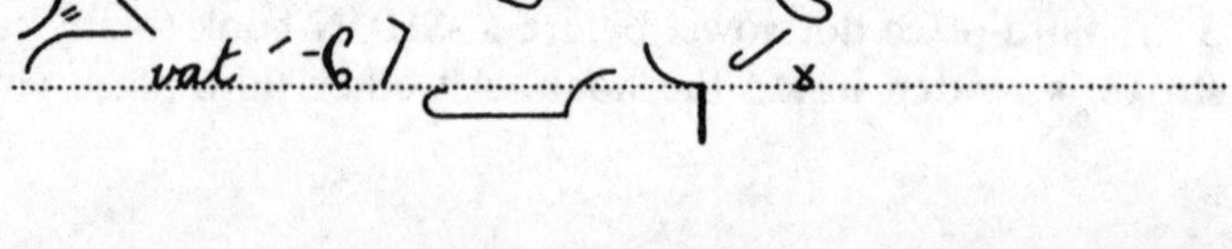

(*e*) 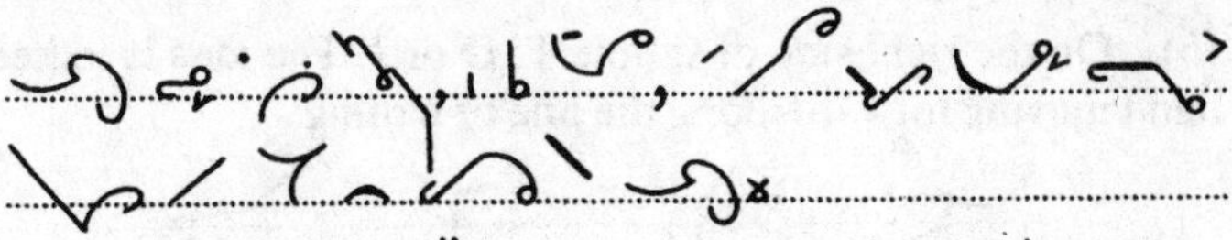

(*f*) 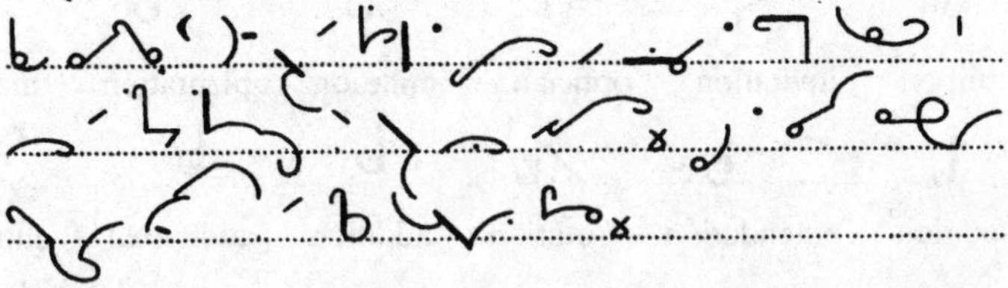

6 -SHUN to straight strokes. When -SHUN follows a straight stroke, it is obvious that it may be written either on one side of the stroke or on the other, as in  or . The rules that now
K-SHUN K-SHUN
follow show how the decision is made about which side of a straight stroke to write the -SHUN. These rules are given in priority order. Reasons for the rules are given too.

(*a*) If the straight stroke has an initial hook or an initial circle, then the -SHUN is always written on the side opposite to that initial attachment. The reason for the rule is to make writing easier by keeping the straight stroke straight:

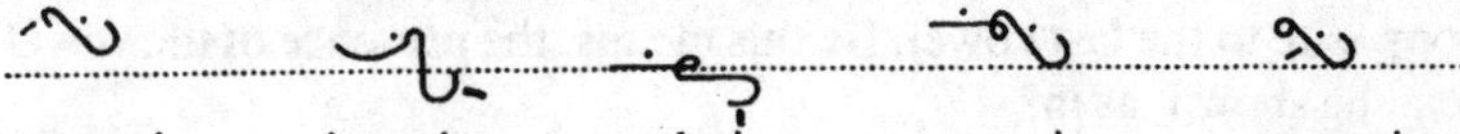

oppression intrusion exclusion expression suppression

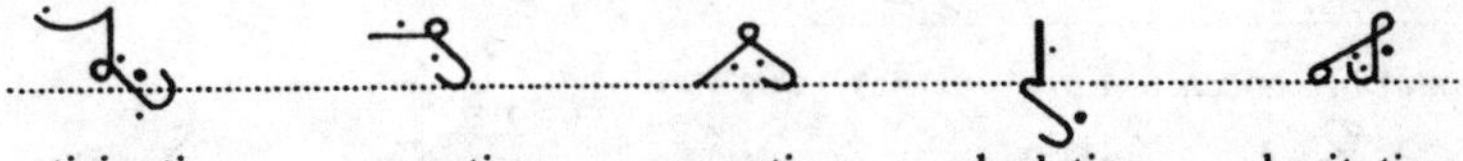

anticipation exception reception depletion hesitation

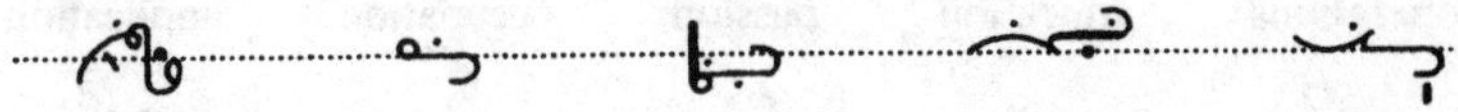

illustrations section discretion emigration inclusion

persuasion separation station

(Note  *stationary/stationery* in which the -SHUN hook is written on the same side as the initial attachment in order to enable the derivative word to be written from the root word. The same is true of  *exception* and  *exceptional*.)

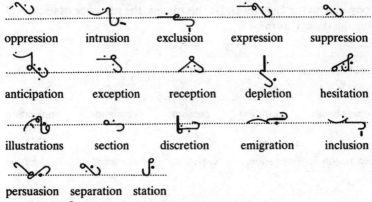

(*b*) On the right side of simple T, D or J. The idea is to keep the hand moving forward along the line of writing:

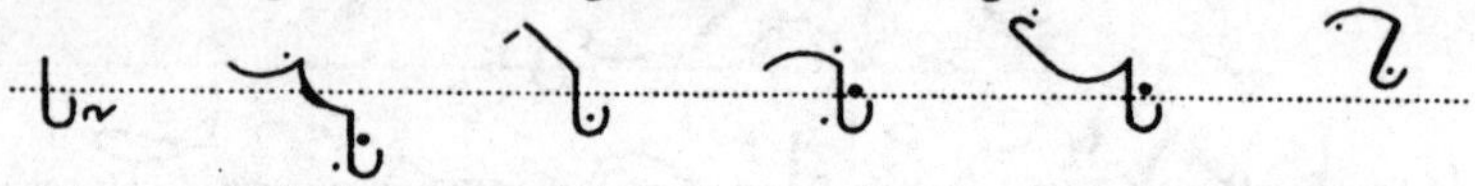

tuition invitation optician imitation plantation magician

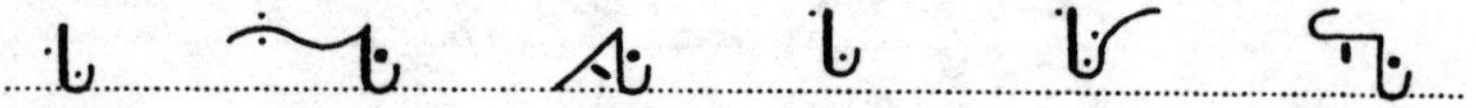

edition emendation rotation addition additional quotation

(*c*) After the consonant combinations .... F-K, ... V-K, ... V-G, ... L-K, ... L-G then -SHUN is written on the side opposite to the curve in order to balance the outline and enable the straight stroke to be clearly shown:

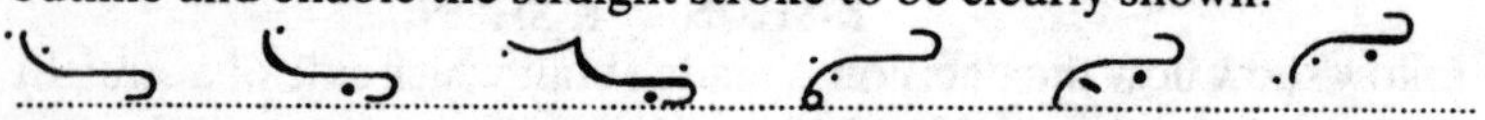

affection vacation navigation selection location allegation

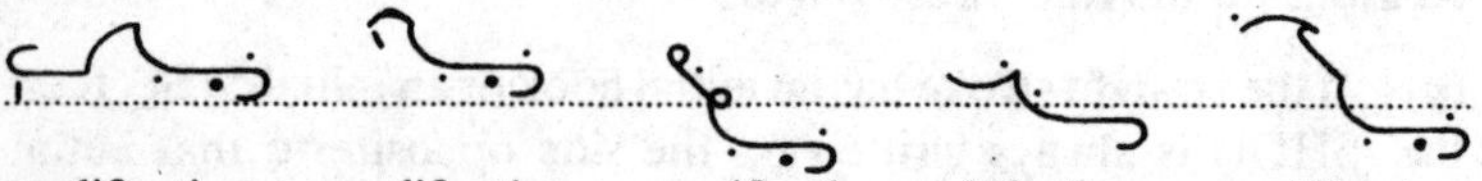

qualification modification specification infection amplification

(*d*) The -SHUN hook is written to a straight stroke on the side opposite to the last vowel. By this means, the presence of the vowel can be shown, as in:

caution occasion *but* action auction.

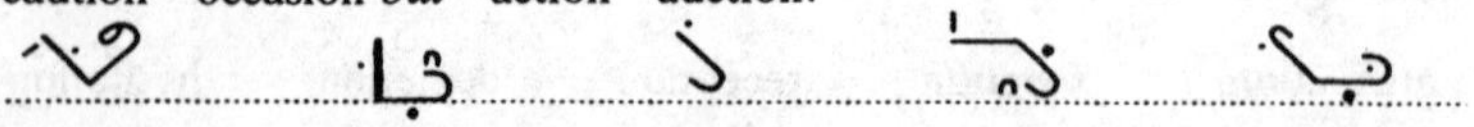

operations education passion occupation application

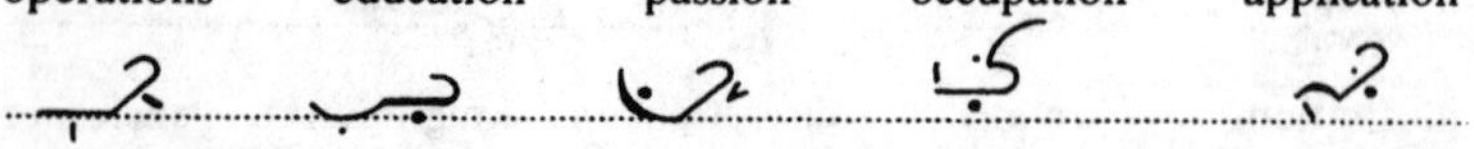

corrosion negation variation occasional moderation

co-operation rations

(*e*) When the form of the word is consonant + no vowel + -SHUN, then the rule is to write the -SHUN on the side of the straight stroke that will not imply a vowel. For example, in 

operation the fact that the -SHUN is written anticlockwise implies a vowel after the R, but in .... *portion* the -SHUN written clockwise implies no vowel after the R:

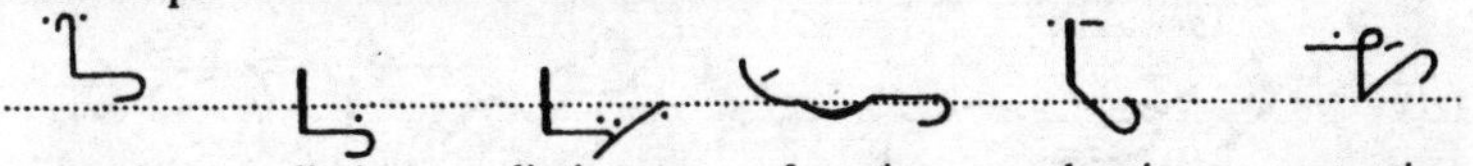

attraction diction dictionary function adoption extortion

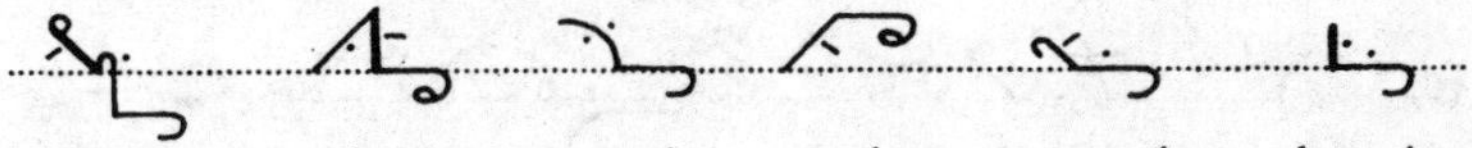

subtraction reductions erection ructions protection detection

(*f*) When -SHUN is followed by a vowel and then ST, the -SHUN hook is not possible, so SH or ZH + stroke N + ST is used, as in:

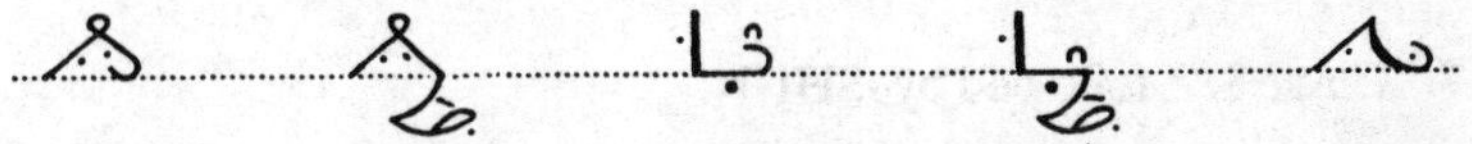

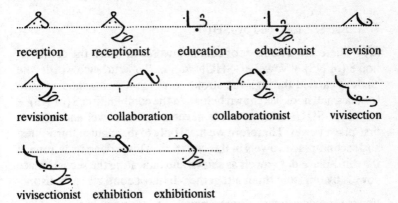

reception receptionist education educationist revision

revisionist collaboration collaborationist vivisection

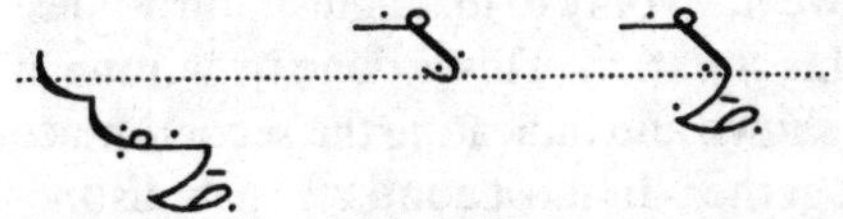

vivisectionist exhibition exhibitionist

EXERCISE 51

(*a*)

(*b*)

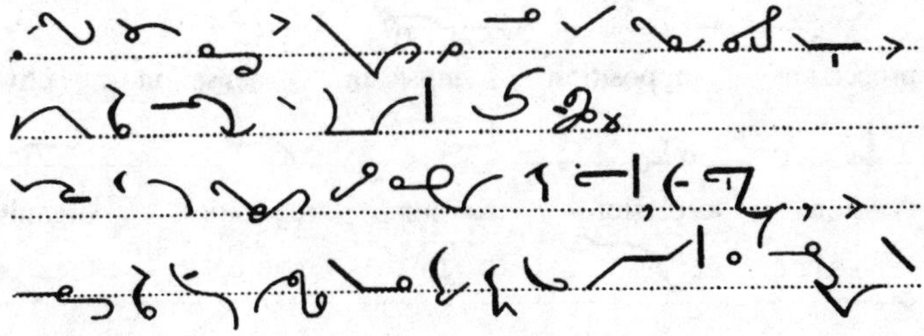

(*c*) 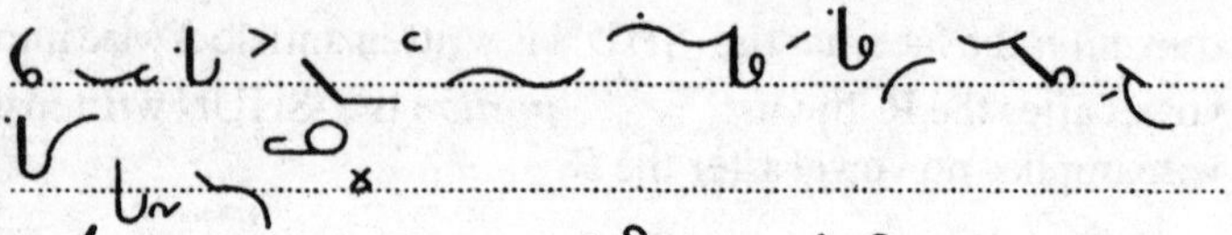

(*d*) 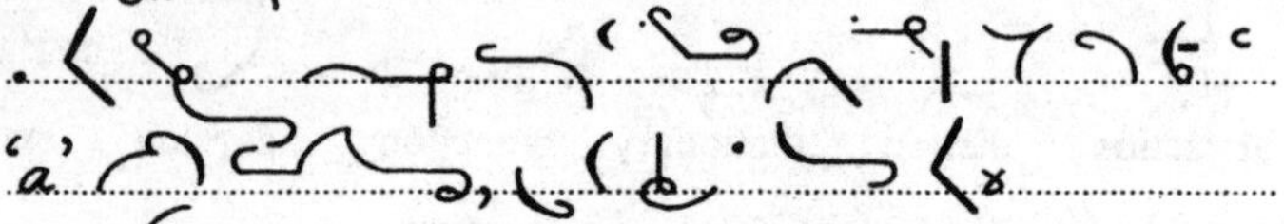

(*e*) 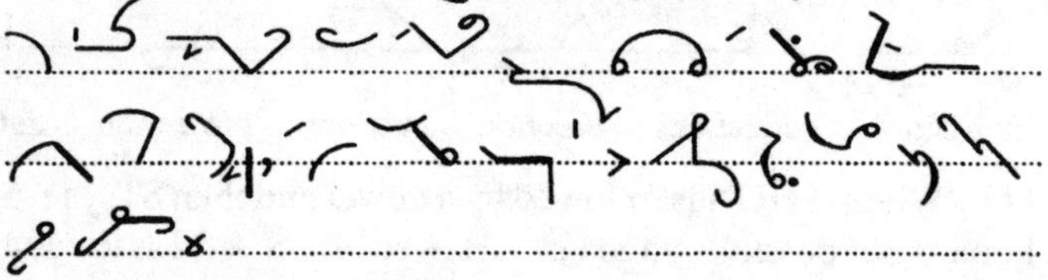

7 Circle S/Z followed by -SHUN.

(*a*) There are a number of common words in which the combination S (or NS) + vowel + -SHUN occurs. To write such words, the circle is carried through the stroke to which it is attached so as to form a small hook, as shown below. In the combination S (or NS) + vowel + -SHUN, the vowel is never a stroke vowel and never a first-place vowel. Therefore we have only to distinguish third-place and second-place vowels in this situation. This is done by writing in the third-place dot vowels as shown and indicating the second-place vowels by omitting them altogether. In most contexts such distinction is rarely necessary, for example:  *position* but  *possession*, or  *recision* but 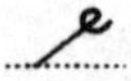 *recession*.

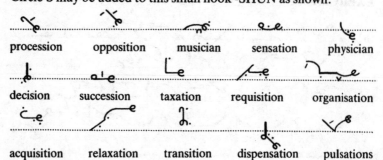

Circle S may be added to this small hook -SHUN as shown:

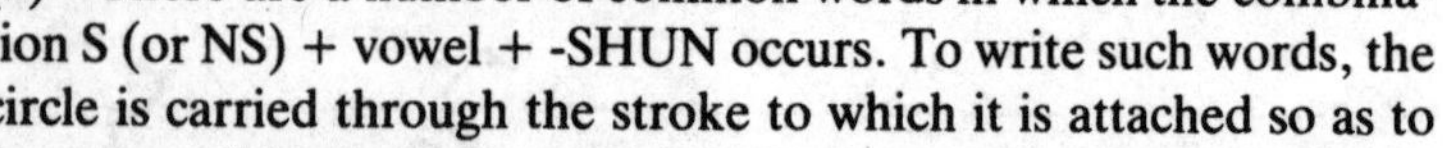

procession   opposition   musician   sensation   physician

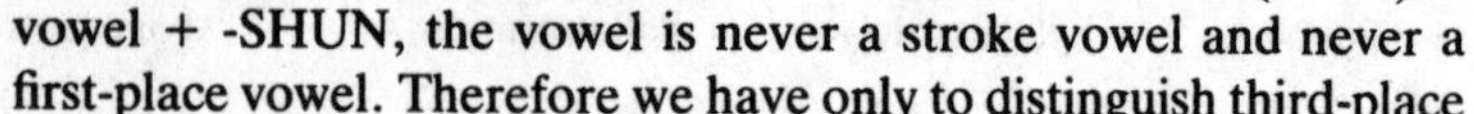

decision   succession   taxation   requisition   organisation

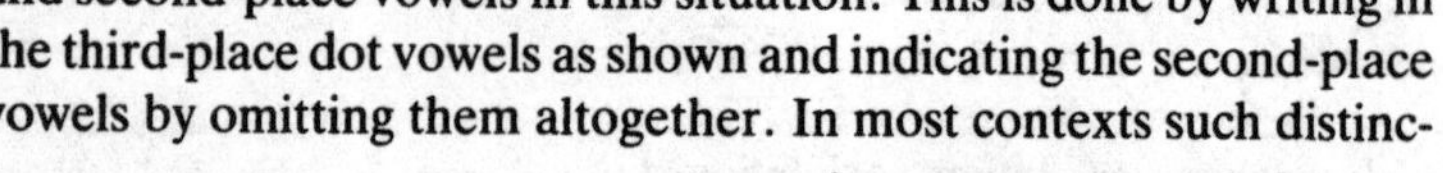

acquisition   relaxation   transition   dispensation   pulsations

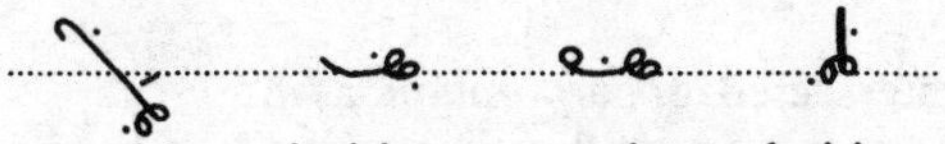

prepositions incisions sensations decisions

(*b*) S (or NS) + vowel + SHUN followed by L has to be written with a disjoined L close up to the root outline. Some other derivatives from roots having final -SHUN can be written joined. Others have to be written differently or disjoined:

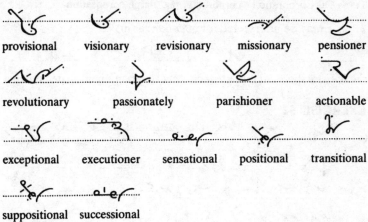

provisional visionary revisionary missionary pensioner

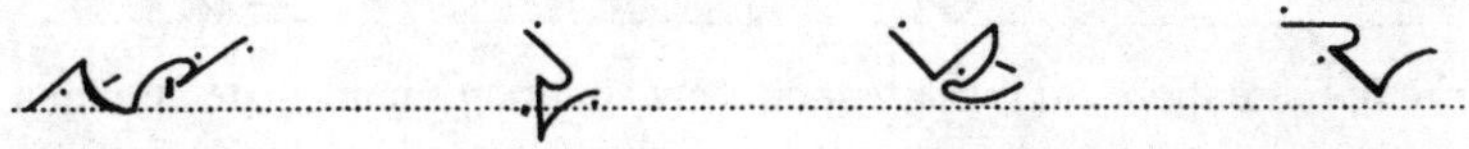

revolutionary passionately parishioner actionable

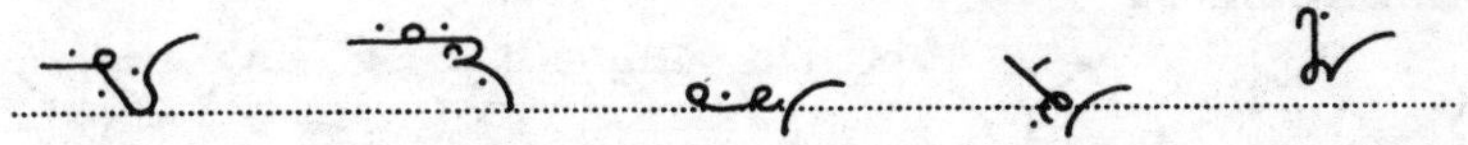

exceptional executioner sensational positional transitional

suppositional successional

Writing notes

(*a*) Write the -SHUN hook large and round.

(*b*) Do not allow its size to increase the size of standard length strokes.

(*c*) Keep the hook open.

(*d*) Write the S/SHUN or NS/SHUN by carrying the circle through the stroke no farther than is necessary to make a small, neat, open hook.

Short forms

information satisfaction unsatisfactory

Note how each of these short forms is made by omitting a whole syllable, yet leaving a readable and suggestive framework.

Intersections

1 A KR hook may be intersected for *corporation*, as in:

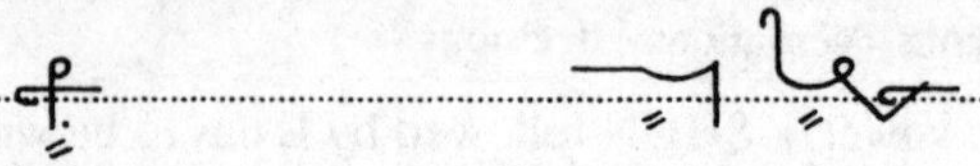

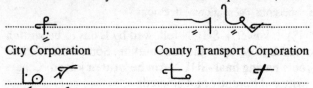

City Corporation County Transport Corporation

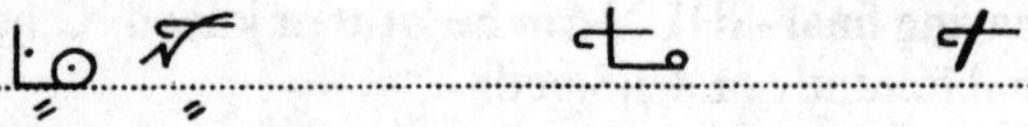

Texas Oil Corporation corporation tax large corporation

2 A T may be intersected for *attention*, as in:

prompt attention to our attention my attention immediate attention

EXERCISE 52

(a) (b) (c) (d) (e) (f)

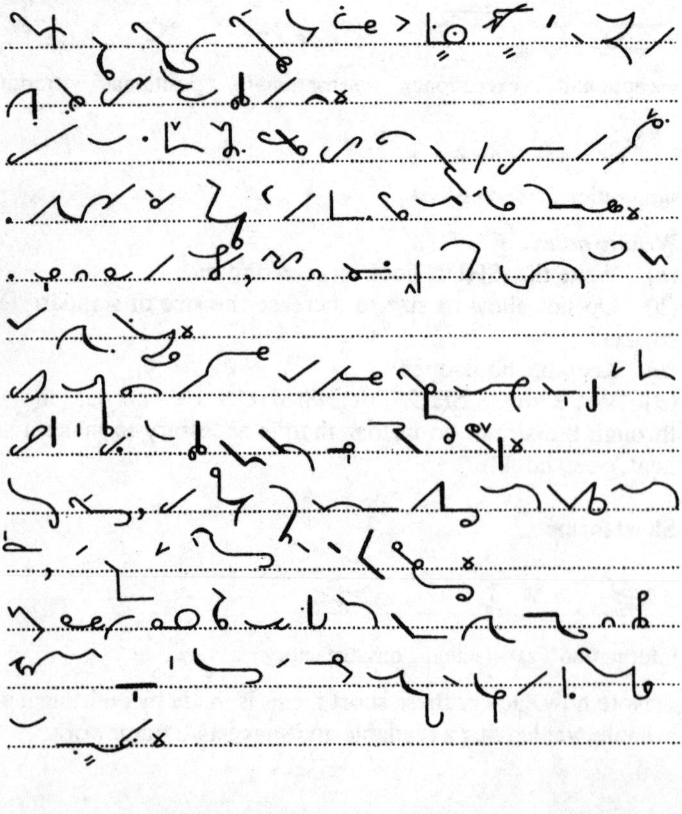

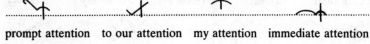

(*g*)

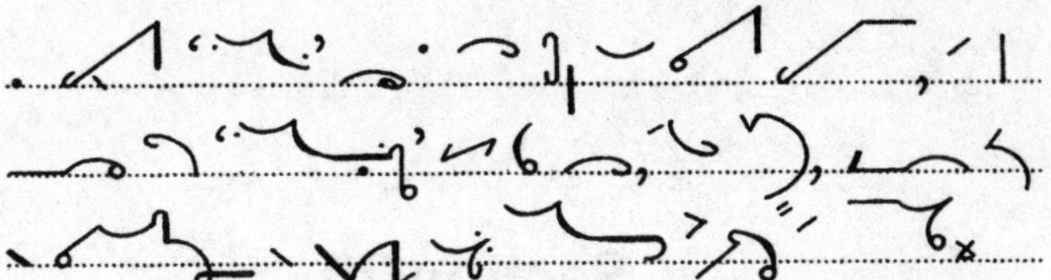

(*h*)

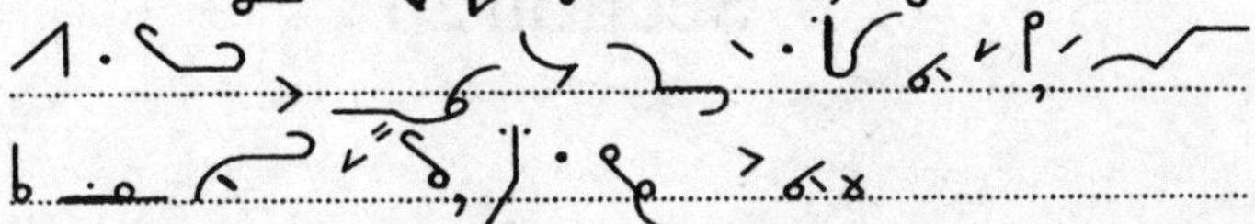

(*i*)

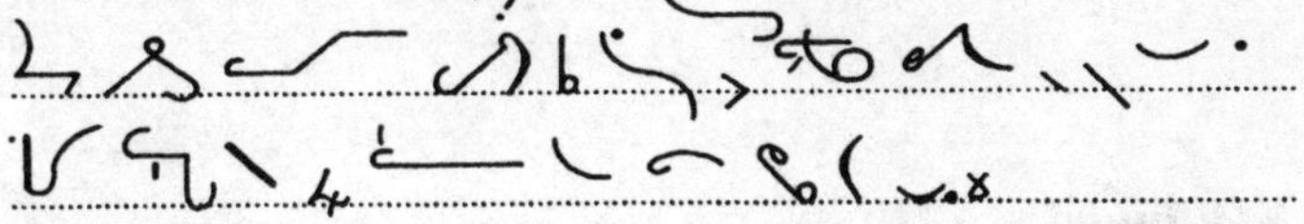

(*j*)

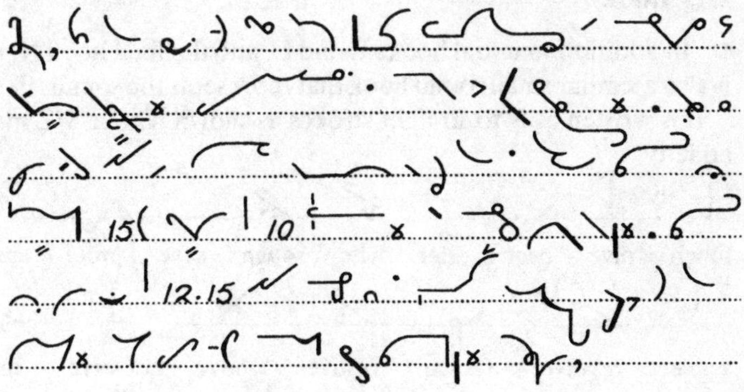

Section 20

F/V hook

1 In addition to initial hooks R and L, and the final hook N, there is also a similar small round hook that represents the sounds F or V.

It is written only to straight strokes as shown. Circle S/Z may be added:

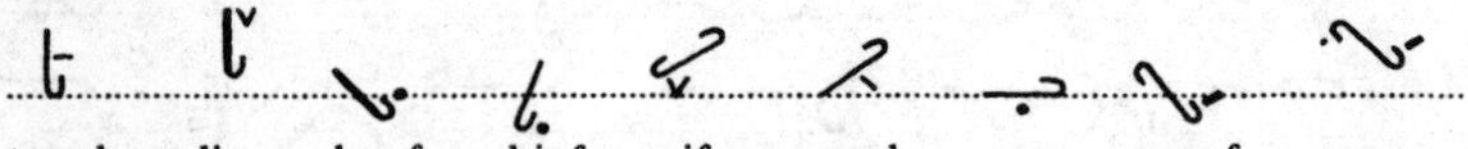

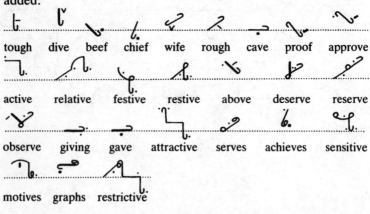

tough dive beef chief wife rough cave proof approve

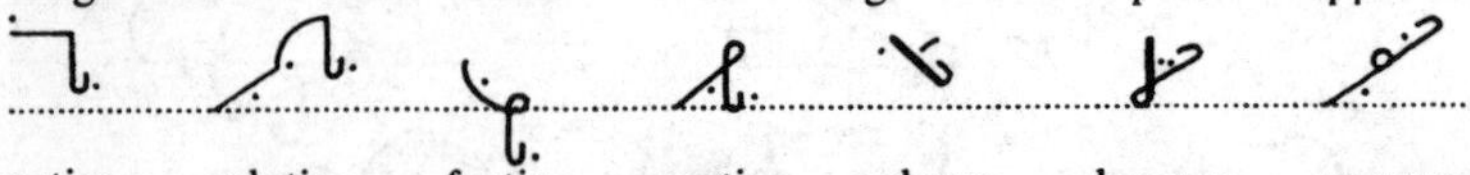

active relative festive restive above deserve reserve

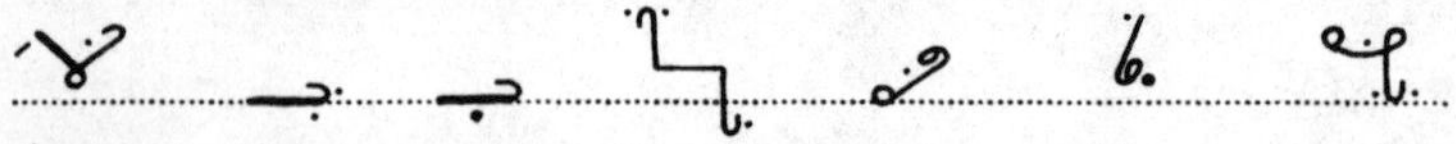

observe giving gave attractive serves achieves sensitive

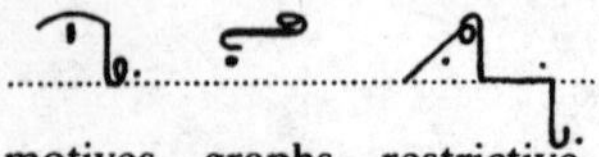

motives graphs restrictive

2 In a word ending with F or V plus vowel, then the stroke must be used. This is a further instance of the fact that the way in which an outline is written often indicates the presence or absence of vowels:

cough café serve survey puff puffy deaf defy rave

review wave wavy

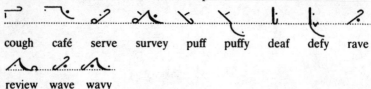

The same is true of words that end in F or V plus any vowel(s) plus S/Z. They, too, must be written with stroke and circle:

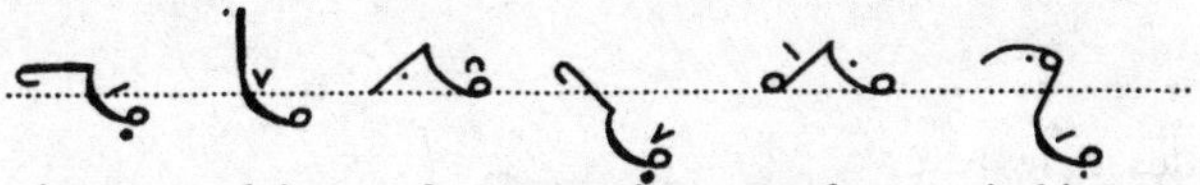

grievous advise refuse previous surface mischievous

These two rules illustrate a more general rule of Pitman 2000 Shorthand: in the shorthand writing of any word, the outline must be written in such a way that there is a place for every vowel, should it be necessary to insert all the vowels.

Writing note Notice that the hook F/V, written to straight strokes only, is (*i*) small, (*ii*) round and (*iii*) anticlockwise. When the circle S/Z is tucked inside the hook, it takes an oval rather than a circular form, and this is acceptable.

3 A straight stroke hooked for F/V is halved for the addition of T or D and this applies whether the word is a monosyllable or not:

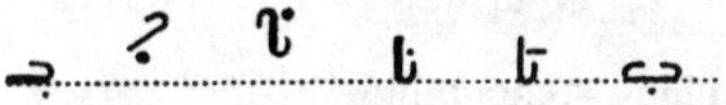

gift raft draft deft tuft cleft

EXERCISE 53

(*a*) 

(*b*) 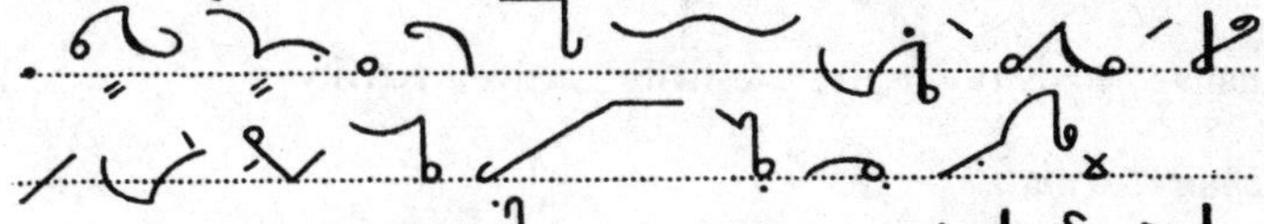

(*c*) 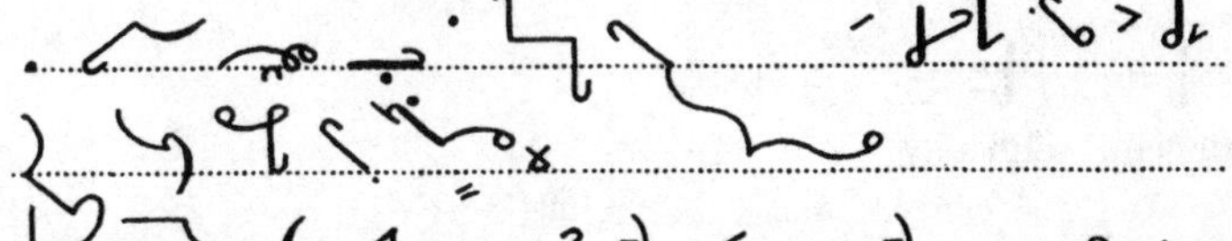

(*d*) 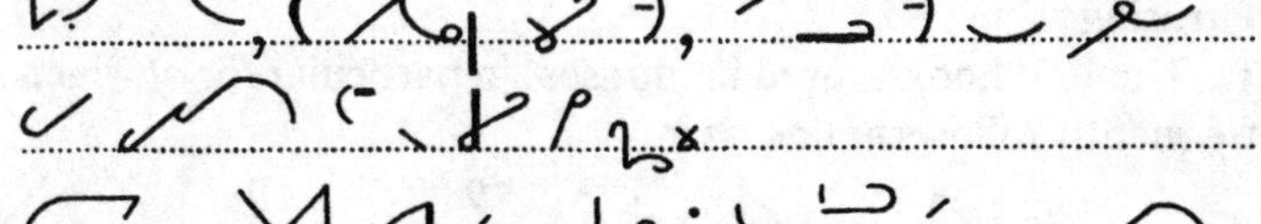

(*e*) 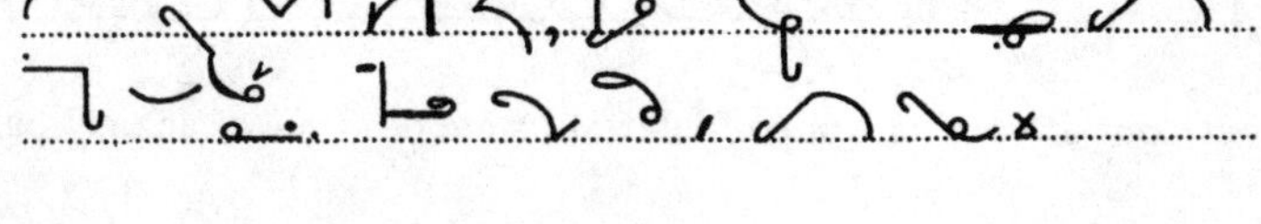

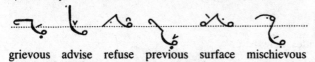

4 The final F/V may also be used medially.

(*a*) between two straight downstrokes, as in:

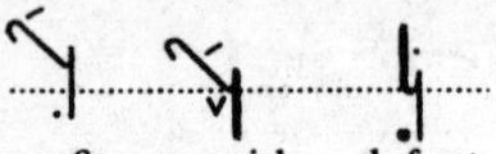

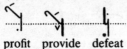

profit provide defeat

(*b*) between a straight downstroke and strokes Th, S, Z, K, G, N, as in:

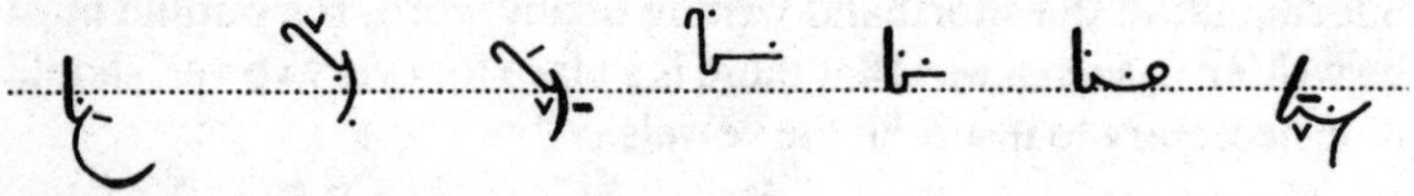

diphthong privacy proviso traffic defect defence juvenile

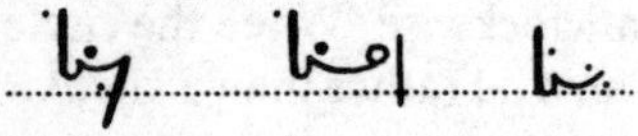

advantage advanced definite

(*c*) between two straight horizontal strokes, as in:

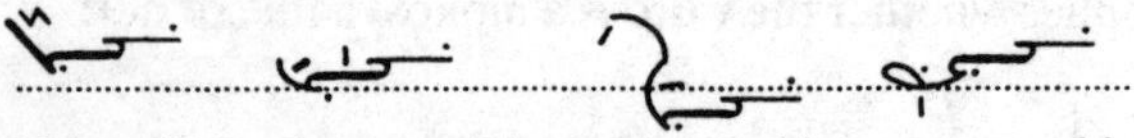

biographic photographic orthographic stenographic

5 If a root word is written with an F/V hook finally, derived or compound words retain this hook, as in:

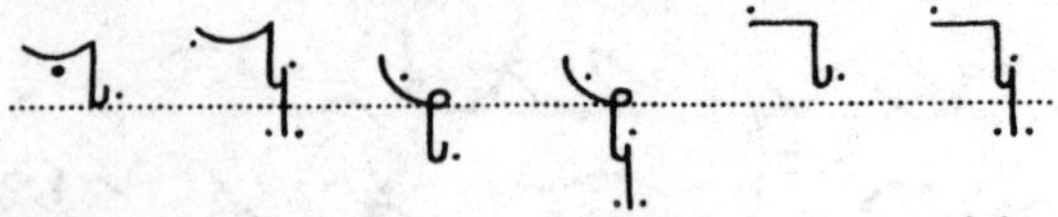

native nativity festive festivity active activity

Short forms

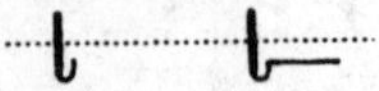

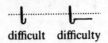

difficult difficulty

Phrasing

1 The F/V hook is used in phrases, in particular for *of* which very frequently follows nouns, as in:

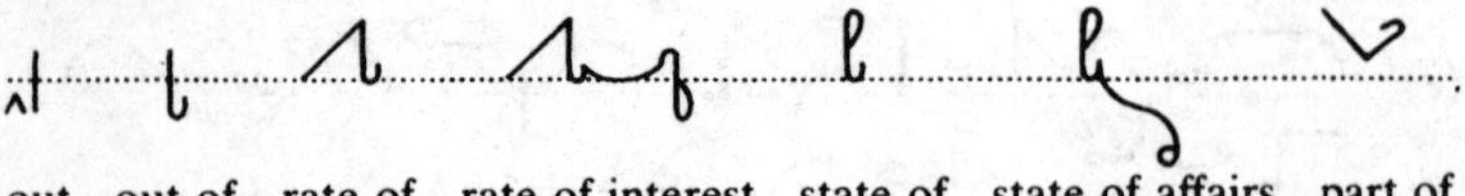

out out of rate of rate of interest state of state of affairs part of

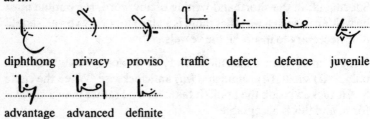

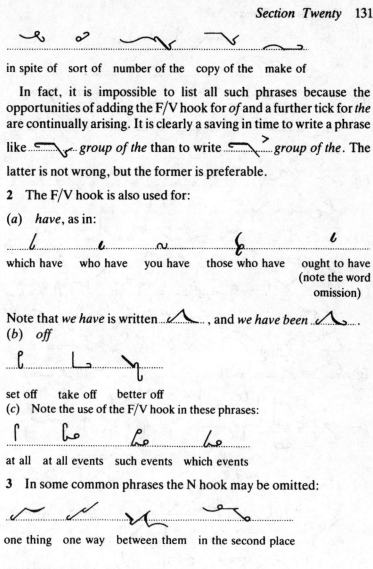

in spite of sort of number of the copy of the make of

In fact, it is impossible to list all such phrases because the opportunities of adding the F/V hook for *of* and a further tick for *the* are continually arising. It is clearly a saving in time to write a phrase like 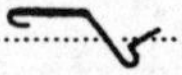 *group of the* than to write 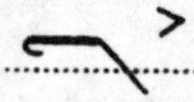 *group of the*. The latter is not wrong, but the former is preferable.

2 The F/V hook is also used for:

(*a*) *have*, as in:

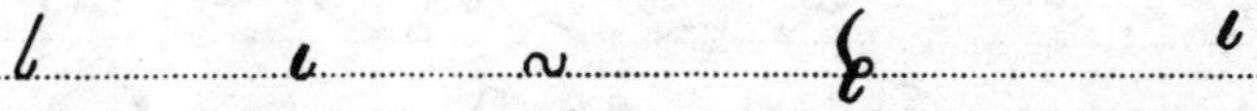

which have who have you have those who have ought to have (note the word omission)

Note that *we have* is written 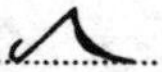, and *we have been* .

(*b*) *off*

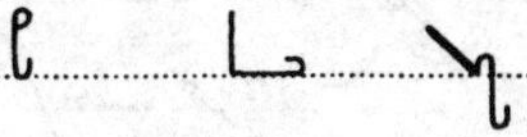

set off take off better off

(*c*) Note the use of the F/V hook in these phrases:

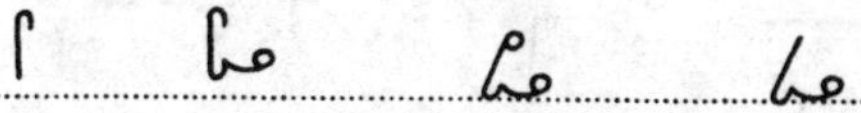

at all at all events such events which events

3 In some common phrases the N hook may be omitted:

one thing one way between them in the second place

EXERCISE 54

(*a*)

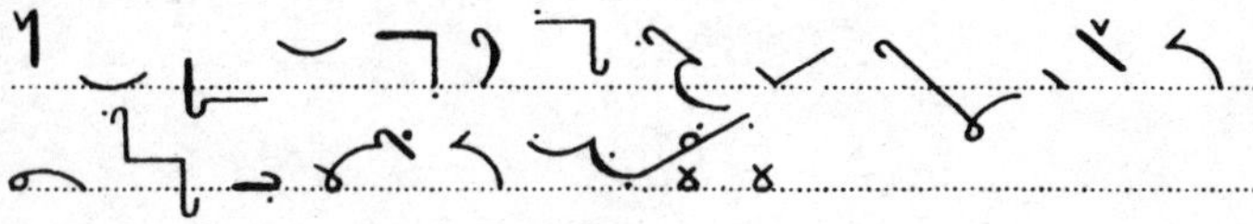

(*b*)

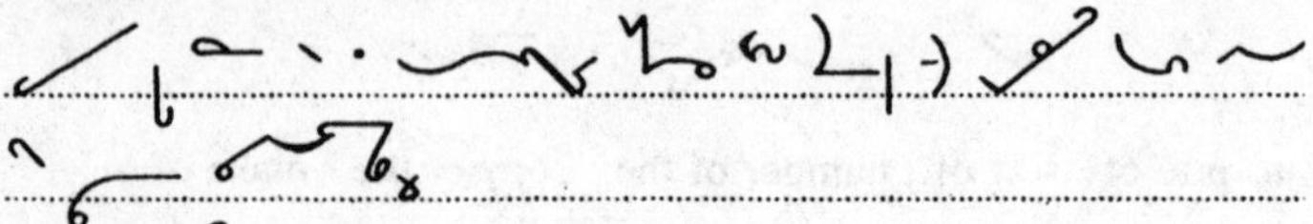

(*c*)

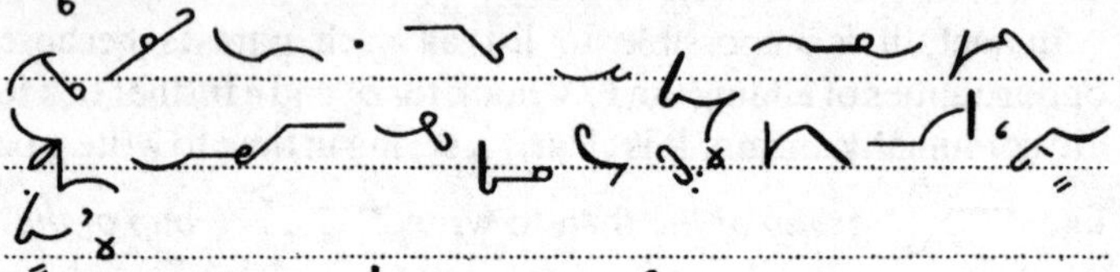

(*d*)

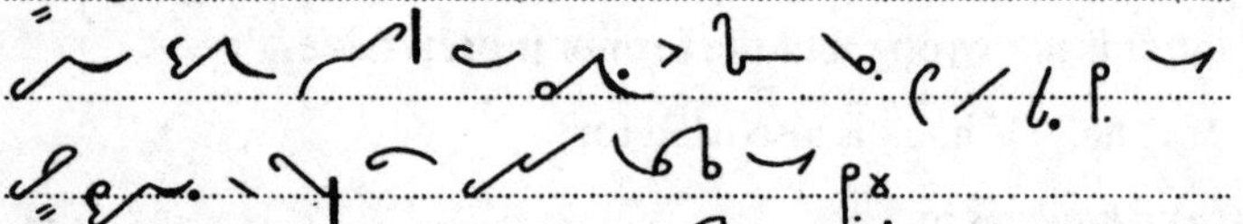

(*e*)

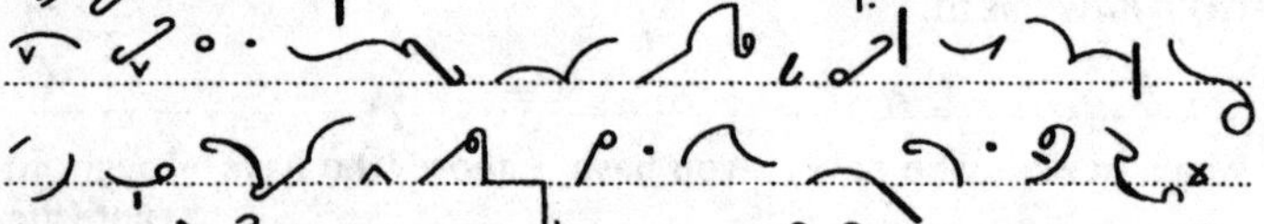

(*f*)

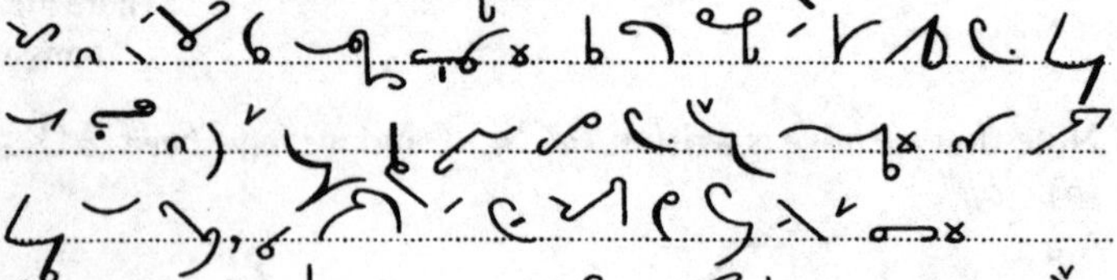

(*g*)

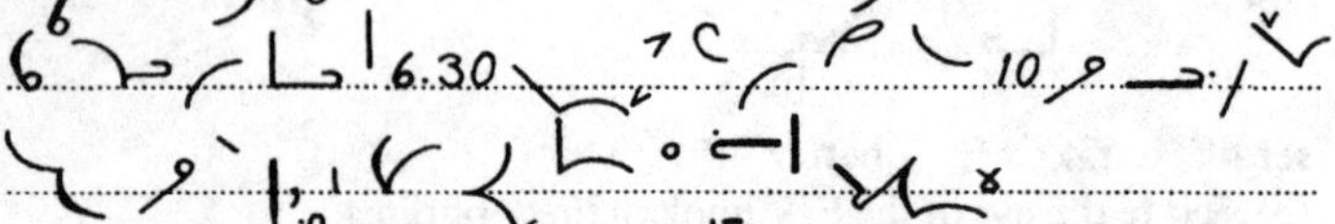

(*h*)

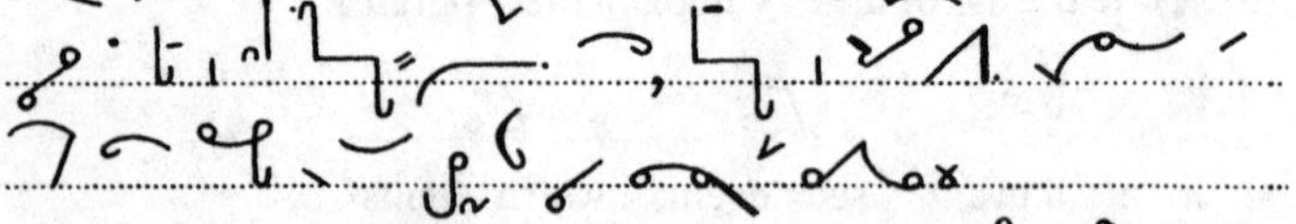

(*i*)

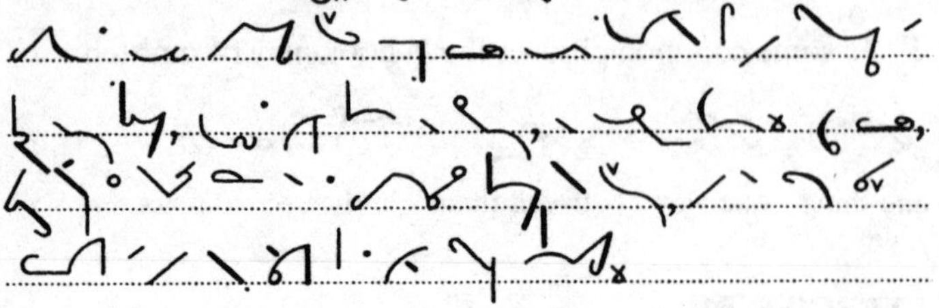

EXERCISE 55 Write in shorthand, afterwards checking from the key (phrasing is indicated by hyphens):

> The cafe at-the top-of-the hill called Kate's Cook-In is well worth a visit as-those-who-have-been will tell-you. They serve you with very-good meals at low-prices and in-your-present state-of lack-of money, you-have good reasons for spending as little as-possible. At-all-events, you-will-be better-off taking one hot meal a day there than eating the poor fare that-they serve up in-your guest house. This-is a copy-of-the menu at-the cafe for Tuesday of-last week.

Section 21

Doubling

Writing a stroke twice its normal length adds the syllable -TER or -DER or -THER or (in common words) -TURE to it.

1 Any curved stroke may be doubled in length to add the final syllables -TER or -DER or -THER or -TURE, as in:

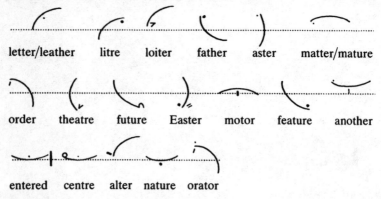

letter/leather litre loiter father aster matter/mature

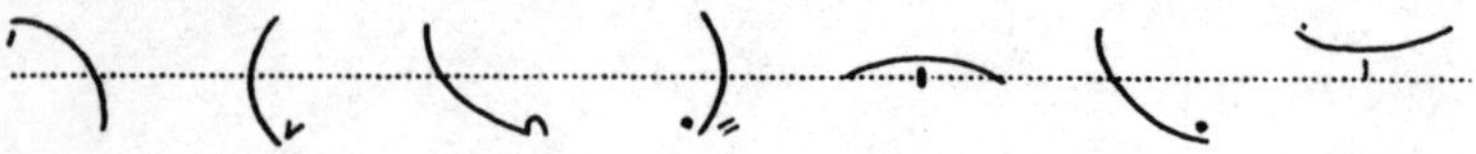

order theatre future Easter motor feature another

entered centre alter nature orator

Writing note

(*a*) Write a double-length stroke with a free cursive movement. As long as the stroke is at least twice as long as normal, its exact length does not matter.

In fact, this, like all the other shorthand principles that require something large – like SES, STER, SHUN, KW, GW, WH, L hook to curves – may be written in a slightly exaggerated form, but *only* if that does not affect the size of the connected or adjacent strokes.

(*b*) Note that all the downward curves are bound to come through the line. Strokes L (up), M, and N may take their correct positions according to the first vowel in the words.

2 This doubling of curved strokes may be used in the middle of an outline, as shown in some of the following outlines:

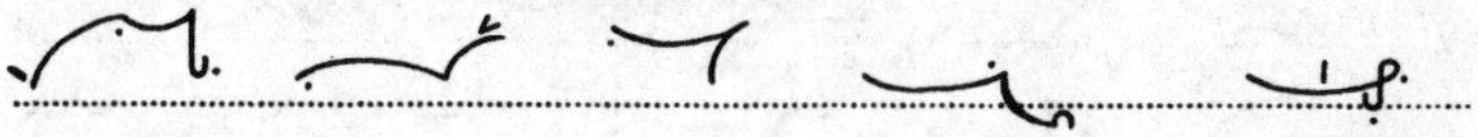

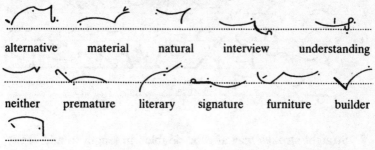

alternative material natural interview understanding

neither premature literary signature furniture builder

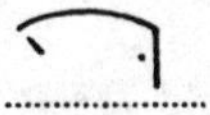

moderate

3 Curved strokes with an initial hook R or L or a final N hook may be doubled, as in:

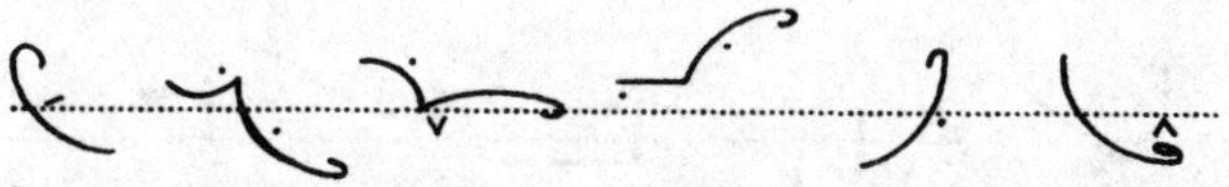

flutter inventor reminder calendar shredder founders

4 In a small group of words curved strokes may be doubled for the addition of the sound -TEER, however spelled, as in:

austere frontier volunteer muleteer arterial

EXERCISE 56

(*a*)

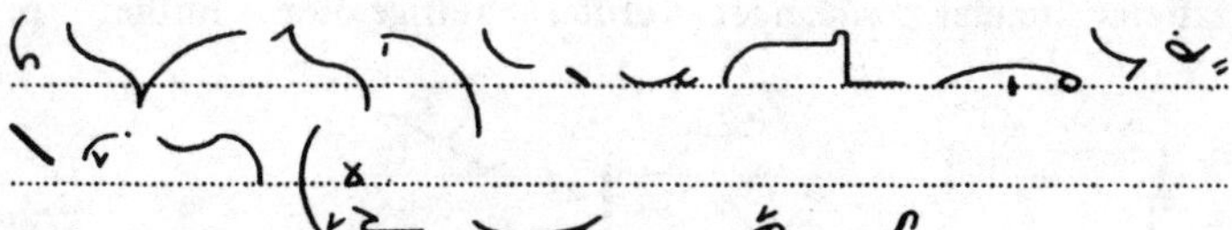

(*b*)

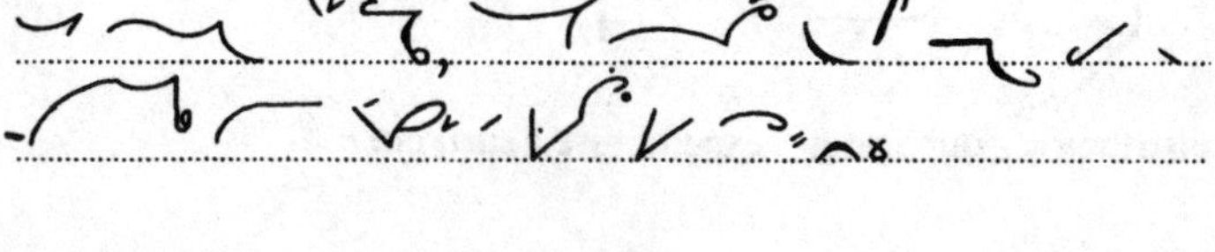

(*c*)

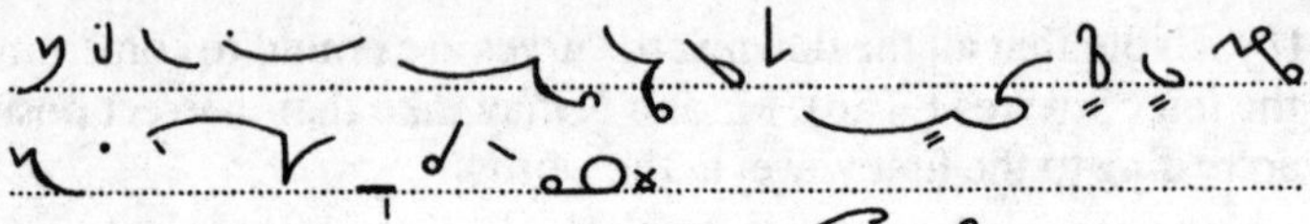

(*d*)

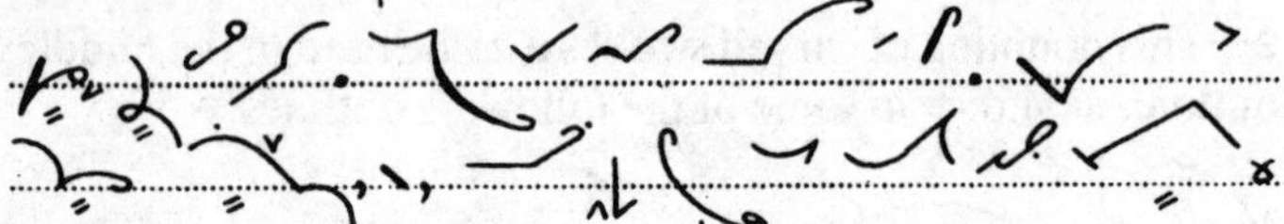

(*e*)

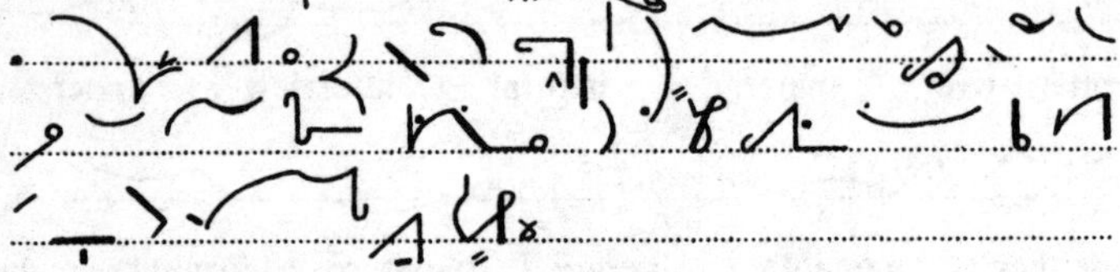

5 Straight strokes may also be doubled in length to add -TER, -DER, -THER or -TURE, but only:

(*a*) when they follow another stroke, or
(*b*) are finally hooked for N or F/V, as in:

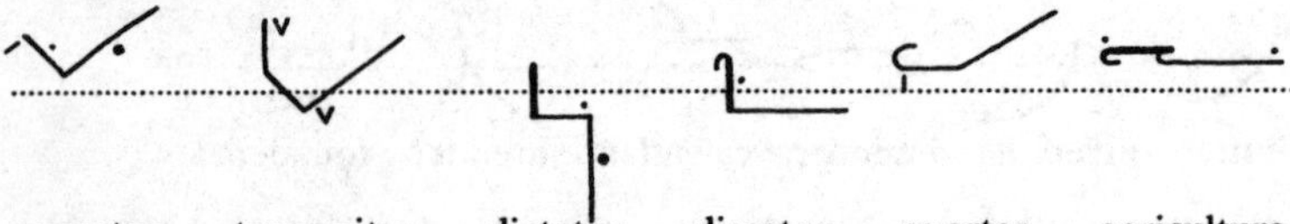

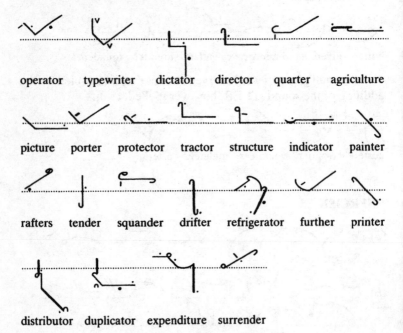

operator typewriter dictator director quarter agriculture

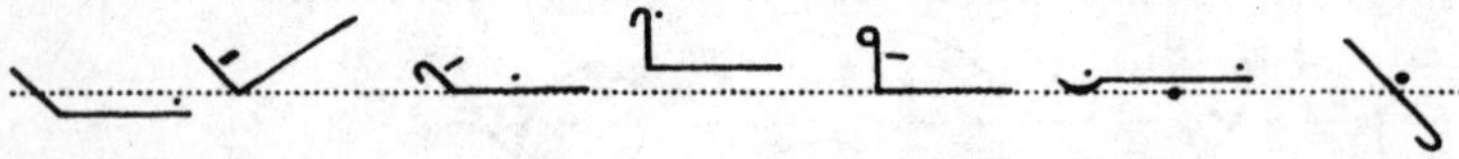

picture porter protector tractor structure indicator painter

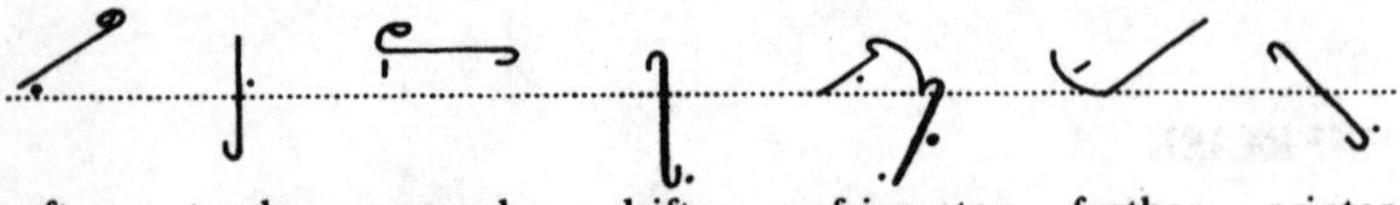

rafters tender squander drifter refrigerator further printer

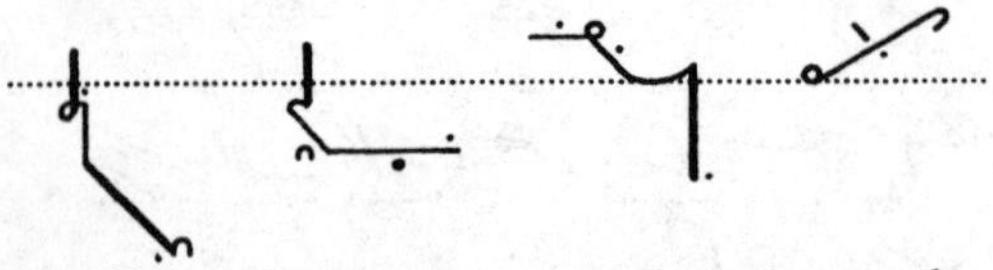

distributor duplicator expenditure surrender

6 In outlines with two strokes of unequal length and no angle between them that makes them easily readable, the doubling principle is not used, as in:

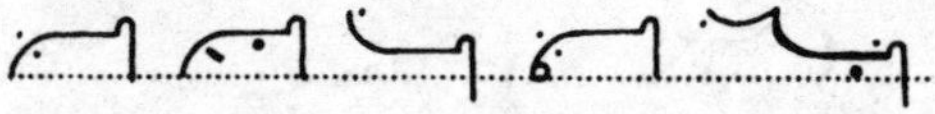

elector locater factor selector navigator

7 Straight stroke doubling is *not* used in the middle of an outline. This is because it would not be obvious whether two identical strokes followed one another (as in *cook* or *cake*) or whether doubling was being used. So we write:

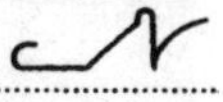 not , 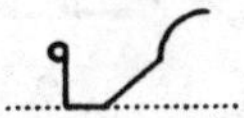 not 

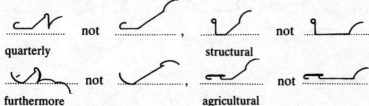

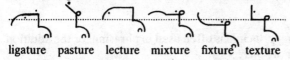

quarterly structural

 not 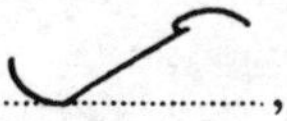, 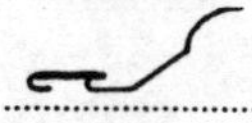 not 

furthermore agricultural

8 Sometimes, if the final syllable -TURE cannot be represented by doubling, then it is written with T and R down, as in:

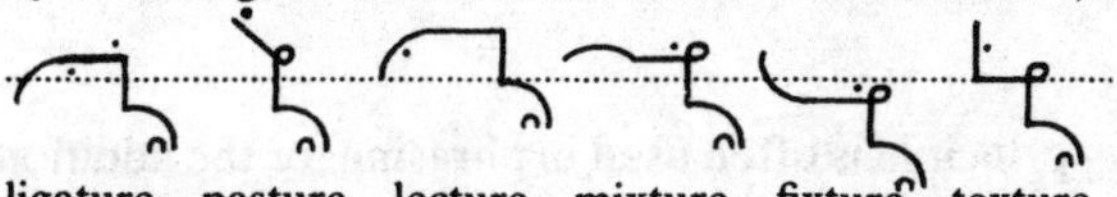

ligature pasture lecture mixture fixture texture

9 If a final vowel follows the syllables -TER, etc., then doubling is not used, as in:

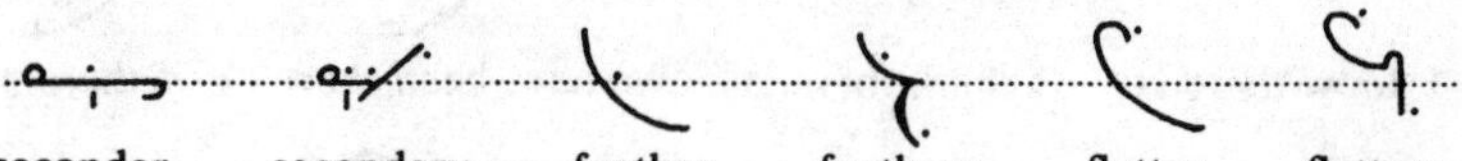

seconder secondary feather feathery flatter flattery

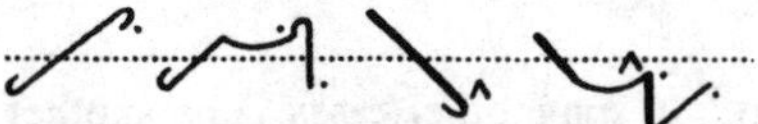

winter wintry bounder boundary

EXERCISE 57

(*a*) 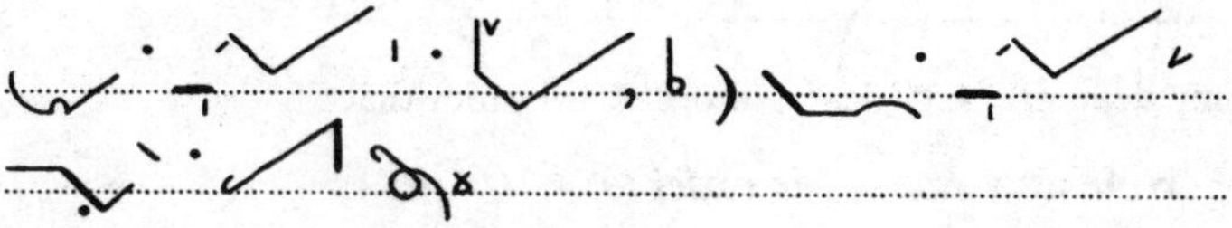

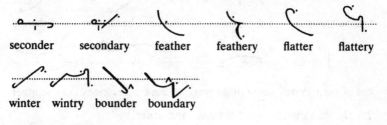

(b) (c) (d) (e)

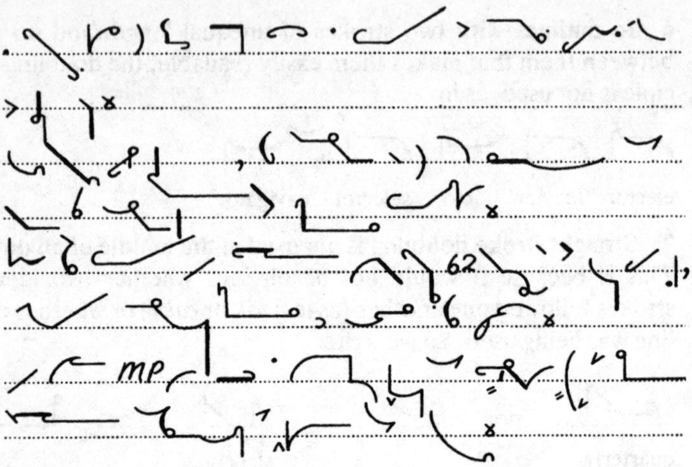

Short forms

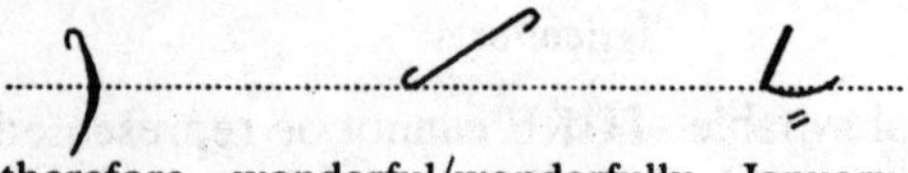

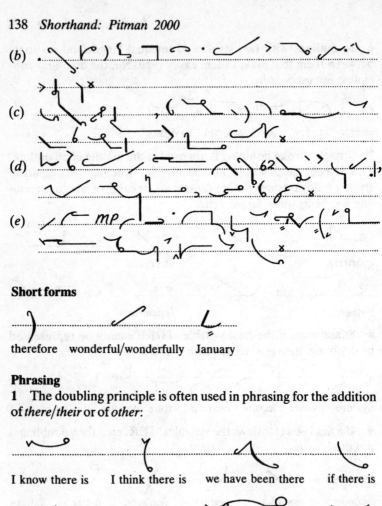

therefore wonderful/wonderfully January

Phrasing

1 The doubling principle is often used in phrasing for the addition of *there/their* or of *other*:

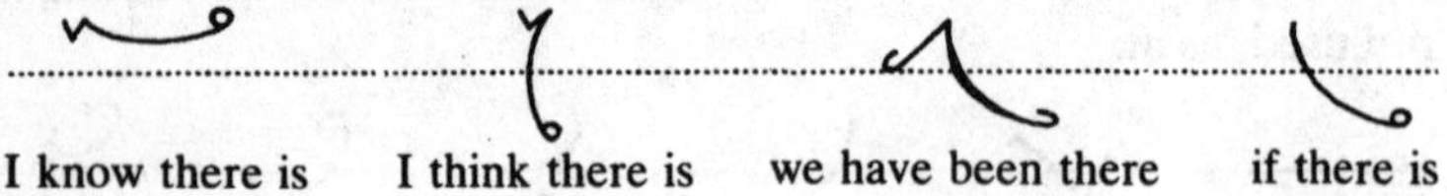

I know there is I think there is we have been there if there is

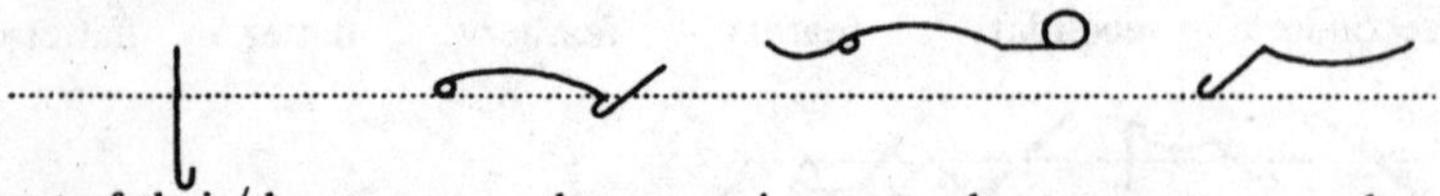

out of their/there some other way in some other cases one another

2 Doubling is also used for *dear* and *order*:

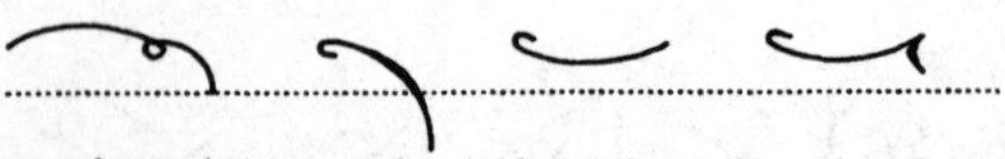

my dear sir very dear in order in order that

Note also  *in order to*.

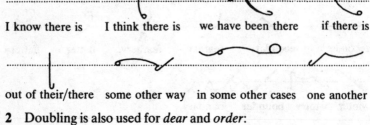

3 Omission of *of the*:

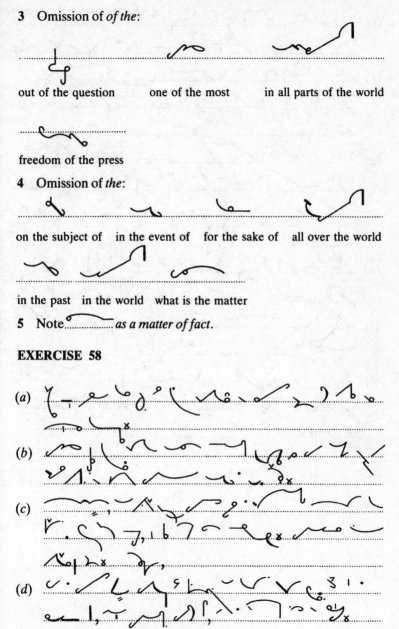

out of the question | one of the most | in all parts of the world

freedom of the press

4 Omission of *the*:

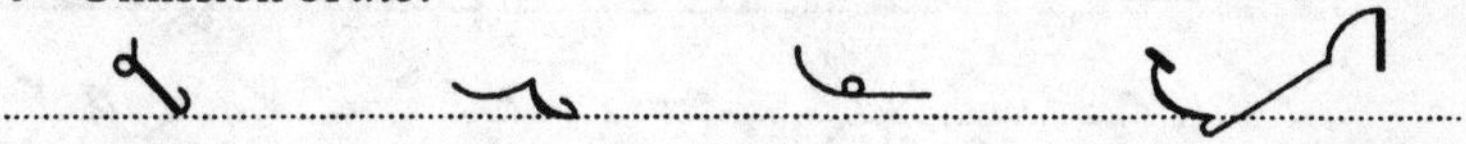

on the subject of | in the event of | for the sake of | all over the world

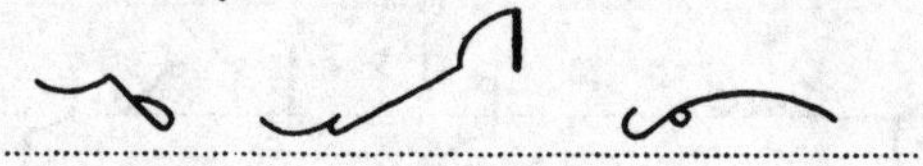

in the past | in the world | what is the matter

5 Note  *as a matter of fact*.

EXERCISE 58

(*a*)

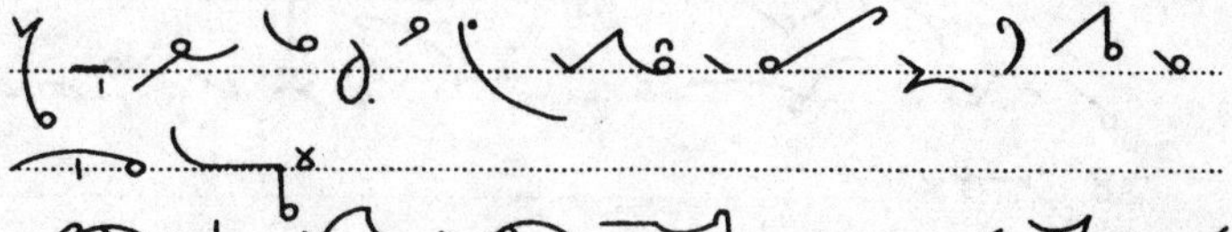

(*b*)

(*c*)

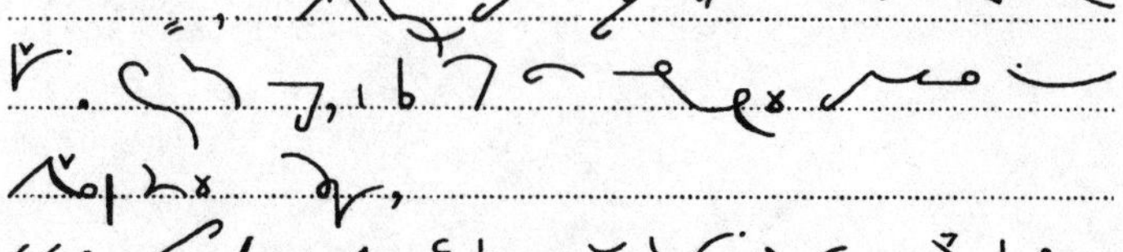

(*d*)

(*e*) 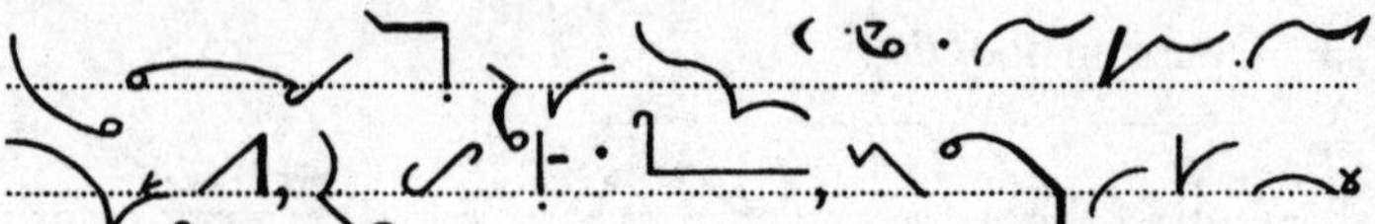

(*f*) 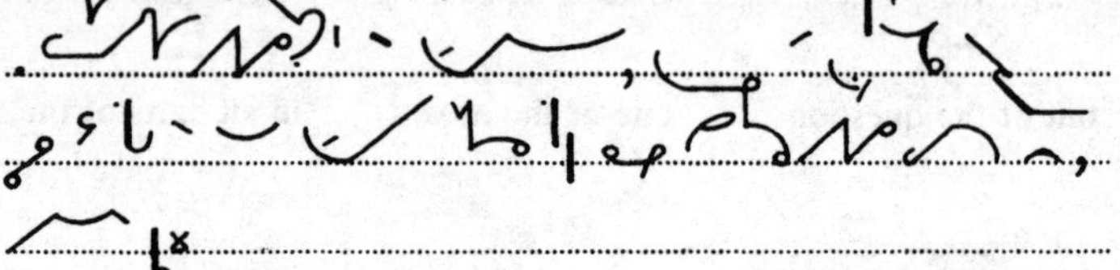

(*g*) 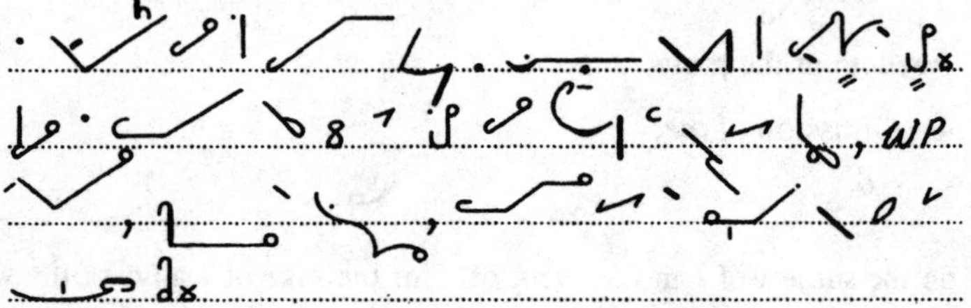

(*h*) 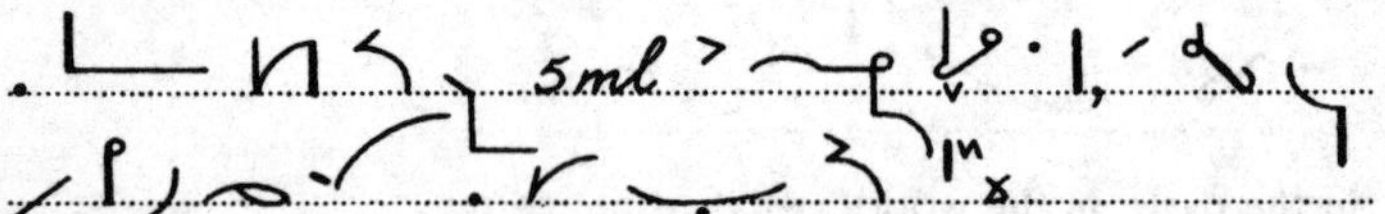

(*i*) 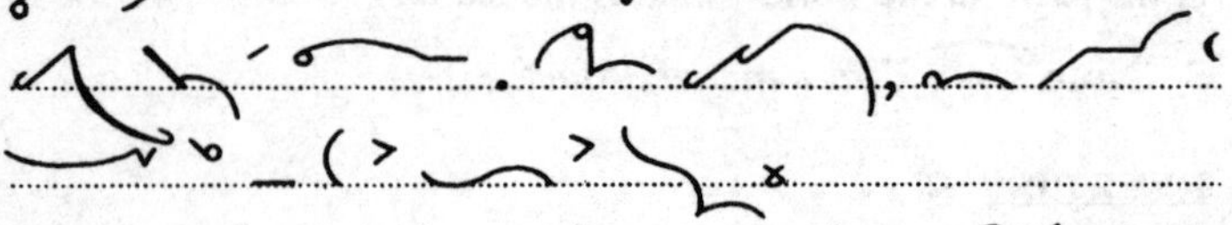

(*j*) 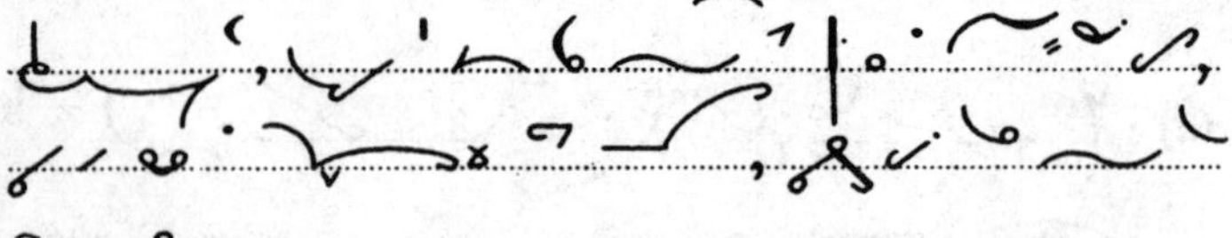

Section 22

Prefix CON- or COM-; Medial -CON-, -COM-, -COG-, -CUM-

1 In the *Concise Oxford Dictionary* (1982) there are twenty-two pages of words listed that begin with CON- or COM-, totalling nearly five hundred words, most of them common ones.

Shorthand represents this initial prefix with a dot placed just before the first stroke in the outline begins. The position of the outline is fixed by the vowel place of the first vowel after the CON- or COM-:

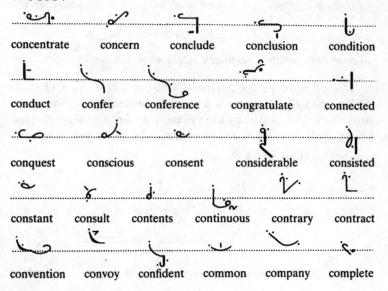

concentrate concern conclude conclusion condition

conduct confer conference congratulate connected

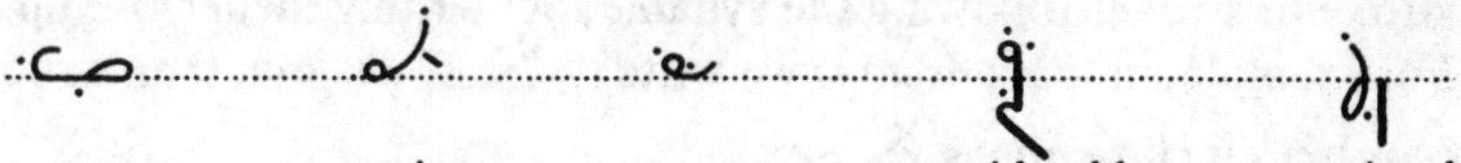

conquest conscious consent considerable consisted

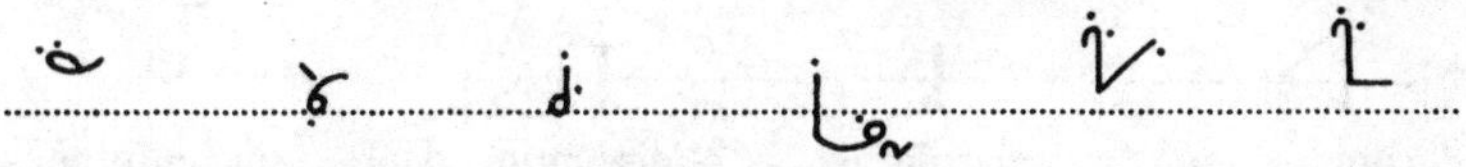

constant consult contents continuous contrary contract

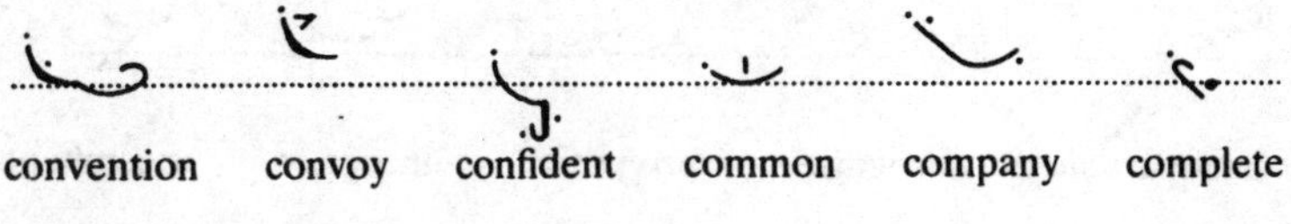

convention convoy confident common company complete

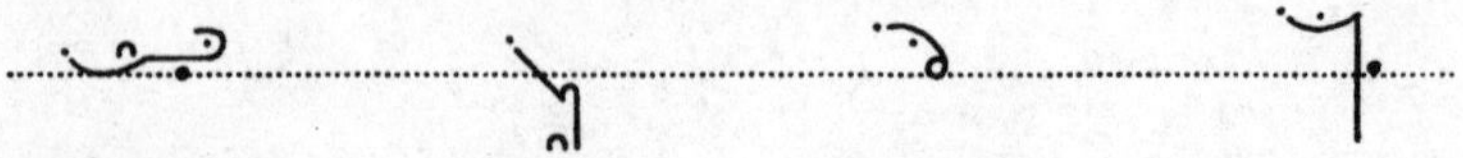

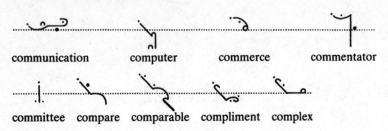

communication computer commerce commentator

committee compare comparable compliment complex

2 A second way of writing initial CON- or COM- is to write the outline for the word that begins with CON- or COM- close up to the one that precedes it:

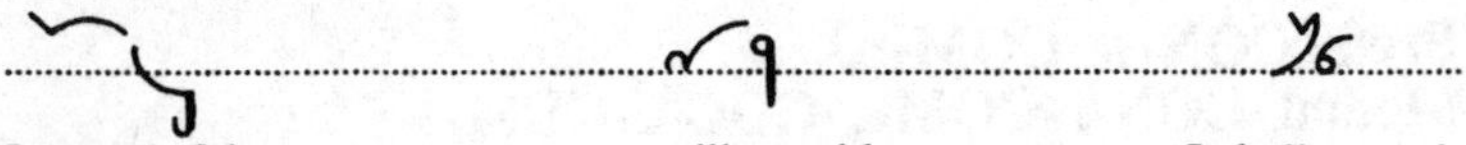

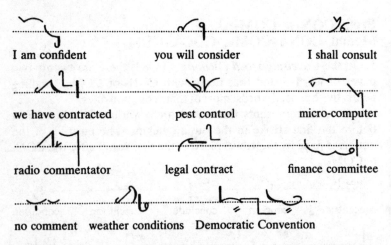

I am confident you will consider I shall consult

we have contracted pest control micro-computer

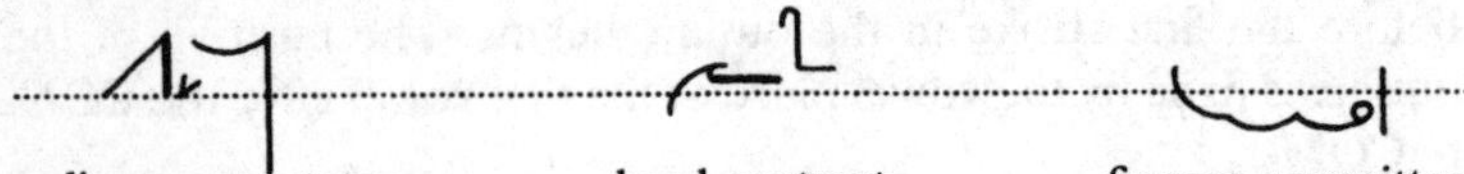

radio commentator legal contract finance committee

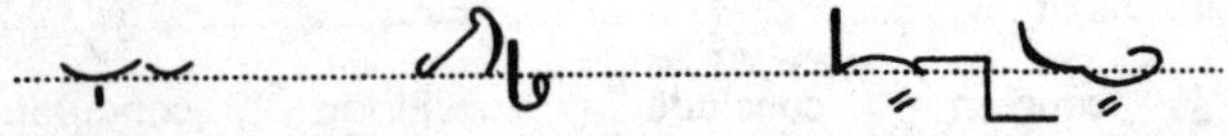

no comment weather conditions Democratic Convention

3 When a word has the syllable -CON-, or -COM-, or -COG-, or -CUM- medially, then such a word is written by disjoining the stroke or strokes following the syllable, but writing them close up. For example, in *subconscious* we write 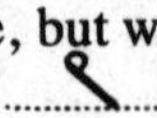, disjoin, then write (*con*)*scious* close up, as :

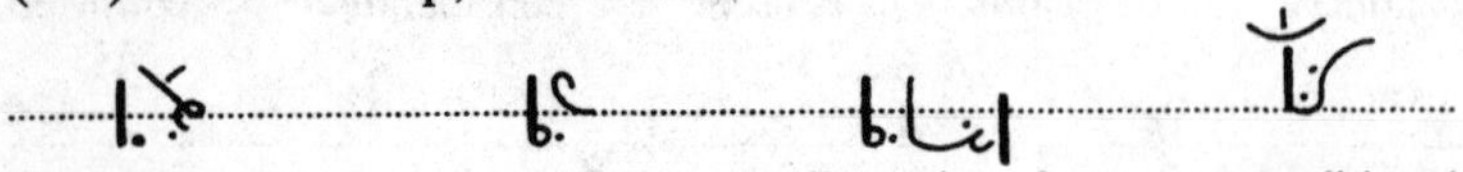

decomposition discomfort discontinued unconditional

incomparable recognise recognition incognito incumbent

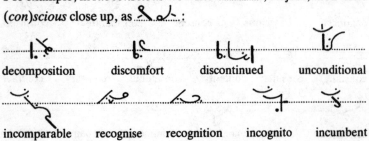

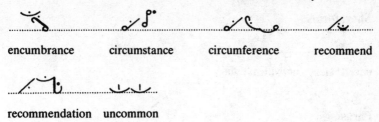

encumbrance circumstance circumference recommend

recommendation uncommon

EXERCISE 59

(*a*) 

(*b*) 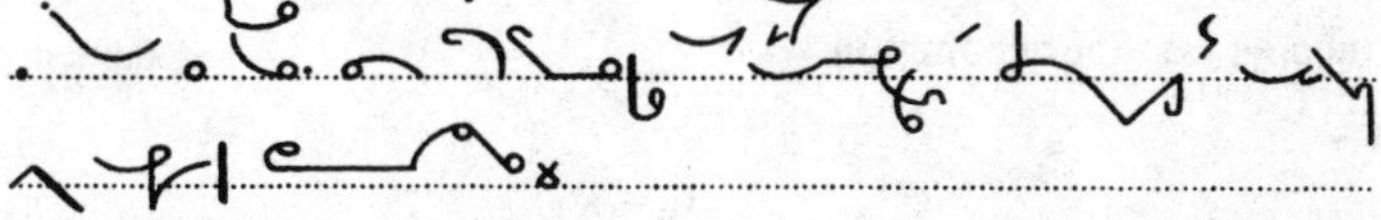

(*c*) 

(*d*) 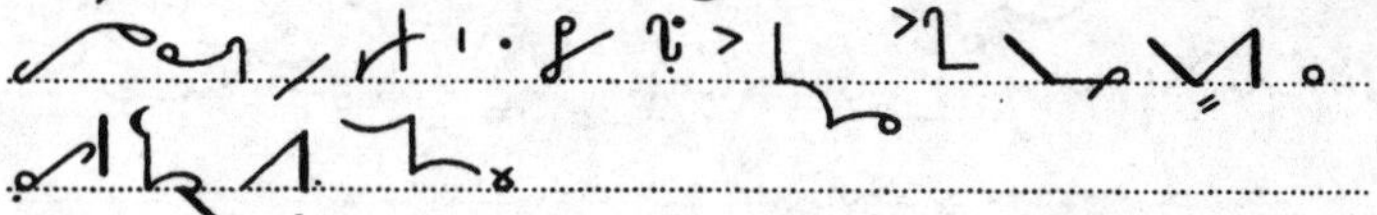

(*e*) 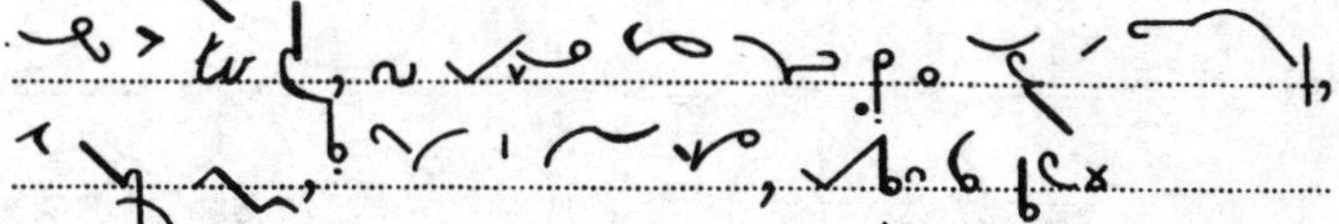

(*f*) 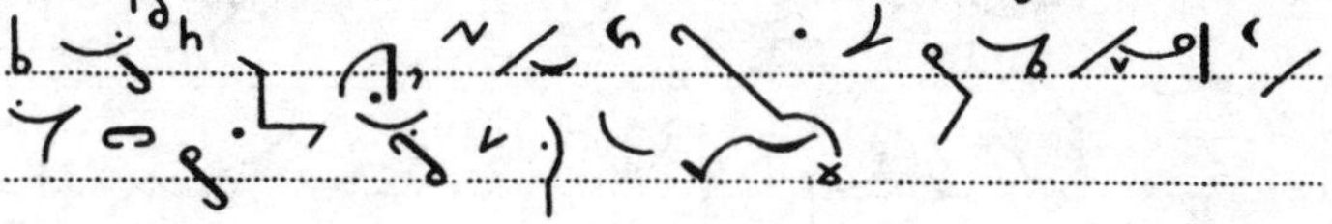

4 Omitting the CON- dot is permissible when writing a word close up to an upward dash short form, but not single downward or dot short forms:

and contact the on the computer all committees of the committee

Short forms

nevertheless   notwithstanding

Phrasing

I shall continue   I will consider   in connection   in connection with the

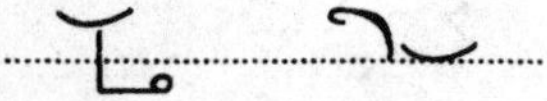

income tax   very common

EXERCISE 60

(*a*) 

(*b*) 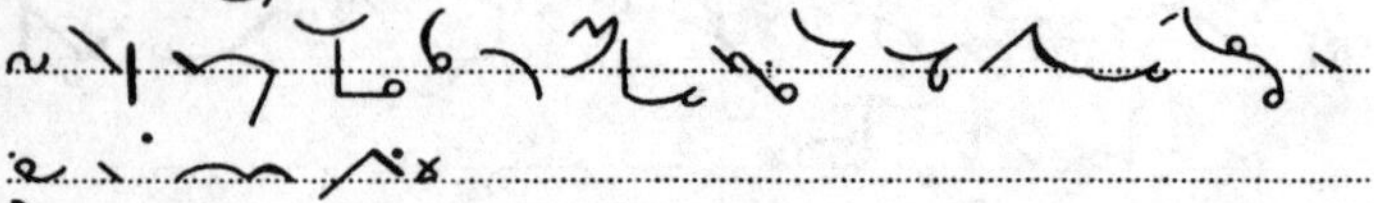

(*c*) 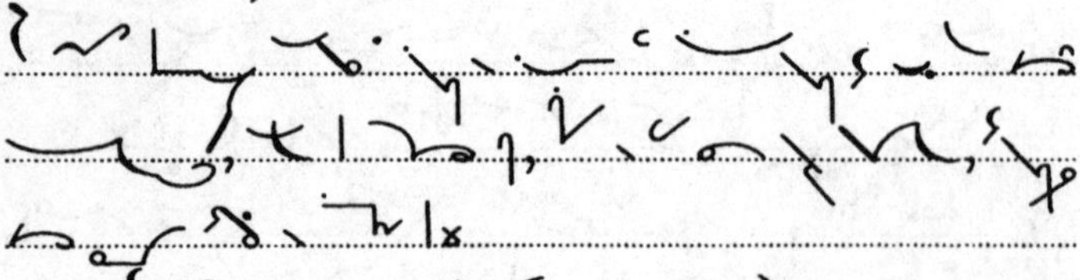

(*d*) 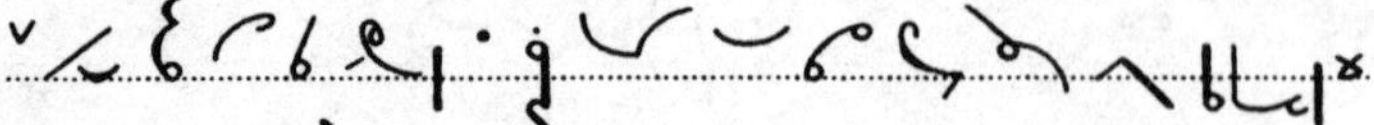

(*e*) 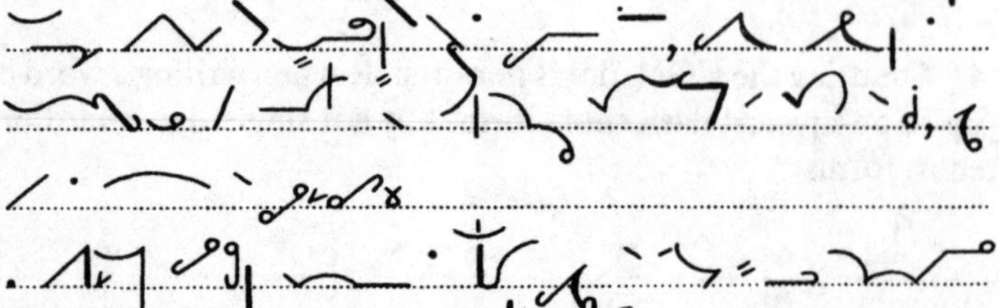

(*f*) 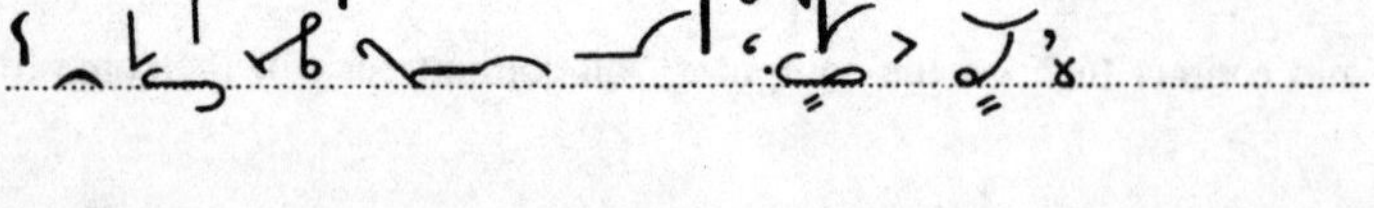

(g)

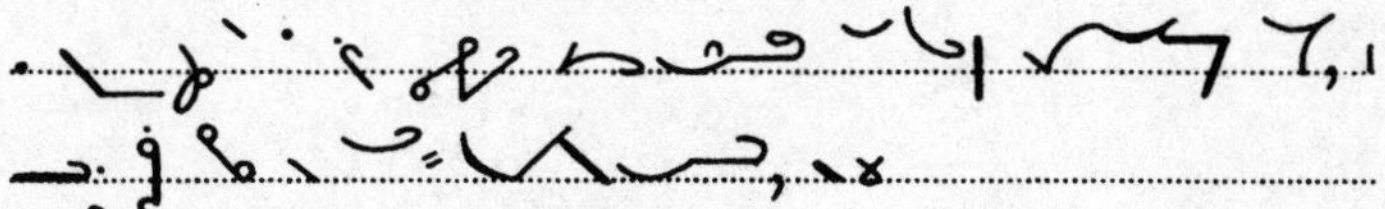

(h)

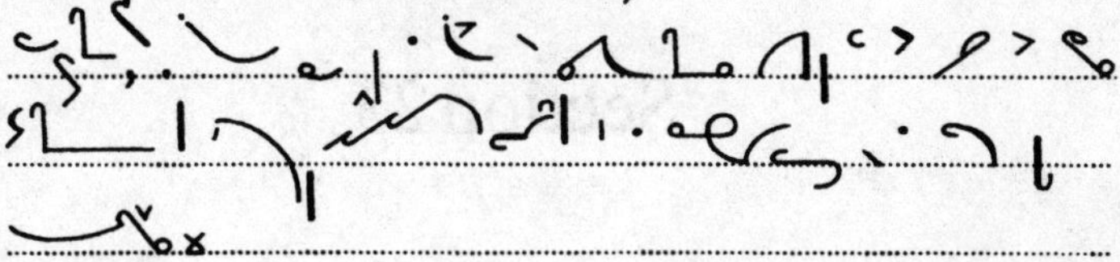

Section 23

Figures

1 Omitting 0 and 8, it is usual in a continuous English context to write the figures up to ten in shorthand, and so too for round numbers like .... (*30*) or .... (*90*). However, this is not a hard and fast rule. For example, in dates it is quite common to write 4.......... (*4th August*), or 2.......... (*2nd January*).

2 N may be used for *hundred*, Th for *thousand*, M for *million* and B for *billion* in the manner shown:

7...... = seven hundred, 5...... = five thousand,

23...... = twenty-three million, 7...... = seven hundred thousand,

2, 4...... (or 2 4......) = two million, four hundred thousand,

3 4...... = three billion, four hundred million.

3 Adapted to sums of money, these devices appear as:

3...... = £3,000, 242...... = £242,000,000 (or £242 million)

7 22 = £7.22.

Irregular numbers are shown normally by Arabic numbers:

17,222 = £17,222, 437, 260...... = 437,260 tons of coal.

4 The 24-hour clock may be written as shown:

 = 1800 hours, 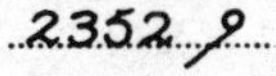 = 2352 hours.

5 Normal time references to *am* and *pm* are as shown:

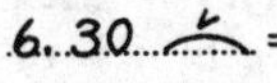 = 6.30 am,  = 4 pm.

EXERCISE 61

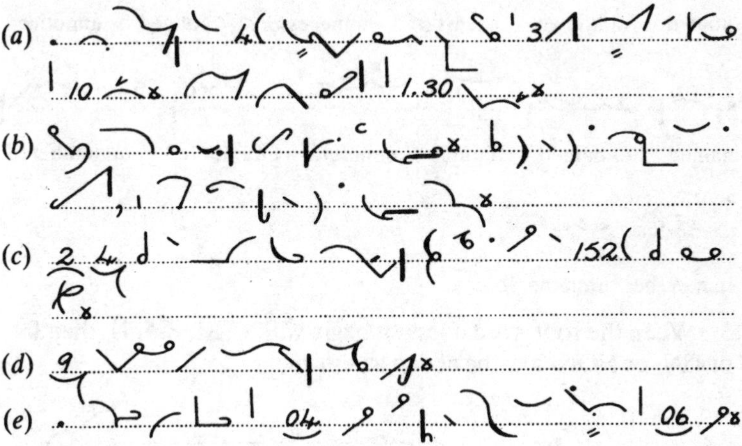

Negative words

English uses several prefixes to mean *no*, *not* or *opposite*. The chief of these are IN-, UN-, and NON-.

1 When IN- is affixed to words beginning with the 'liquid' consonants L, M, R, it is coalesced into IL-, IM-, IR-, and so, to show the negative, the first consonants are repeated as shown:

logical illogical legal illegal literate illiterate material

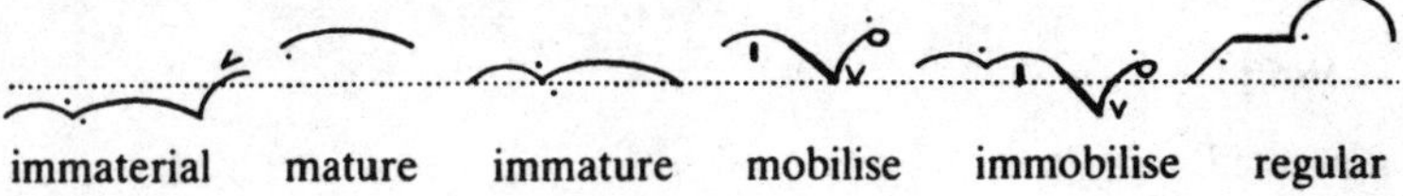

immaterial mature immature mobilise immobilise regular

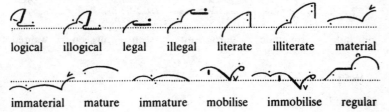

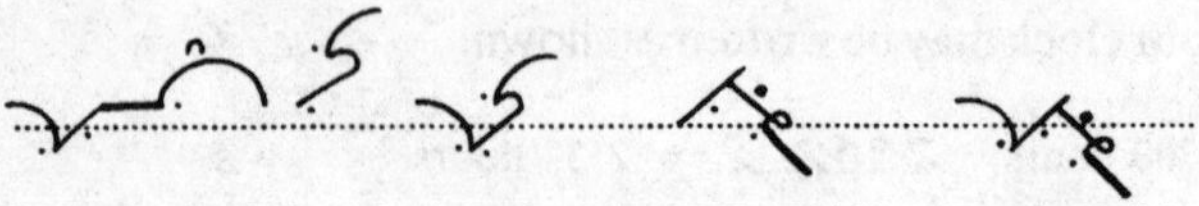

irregular rational irrational replaceable irreplaceable

2 The same principle of repeating the initial consonant N is used when root words beginning with N are made negative by IN- or UN-:

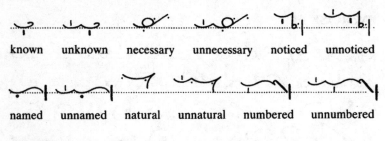

known unknown necessary unnecessary noticed unnoticed

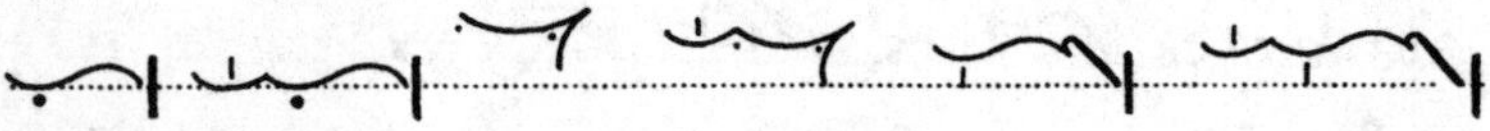

named unnamed natural unnatural numbered unnumbered

numerable innumerable

3 When the root word does not begin with L, M, R or N, then IN- or UN- or NON- may be added as shown:

decent indecent clement inclement comparable

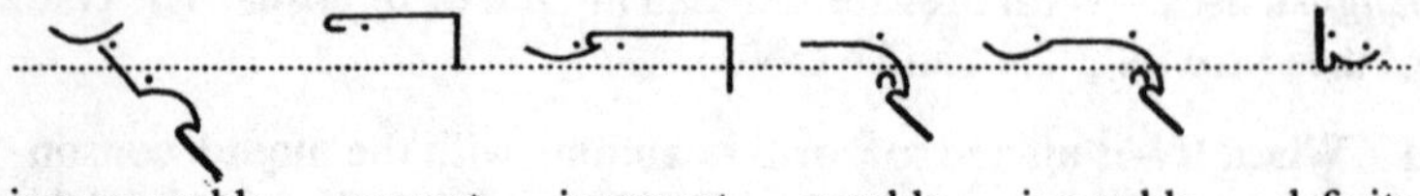

incomparable correct incorrect curable incurable definite

indefinite romantic unromantic seen unseen wanted

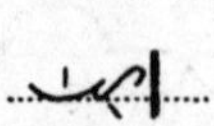

unwanted

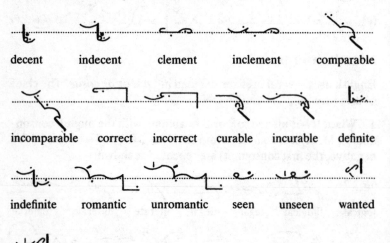

4 The prefix NON- can sometimes be joined, but it may have to be disjoined in some words:

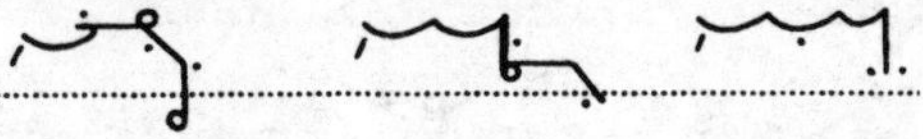

but

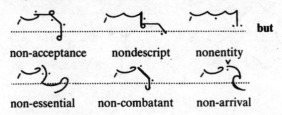

non-acceptance nondescript nonentity

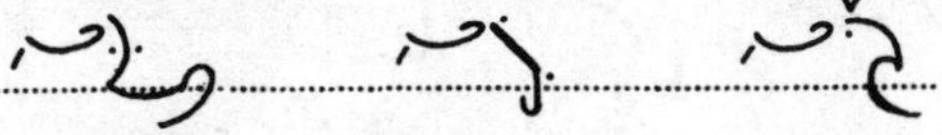

non-essential non-combatant non-arrival

Suffix -SHIP

A stroke SH represents the ending -SHIP. It is joined when it can be joined easily, but otherwise it is disjoined.

hardship authorship fellowship citizenship lectureship

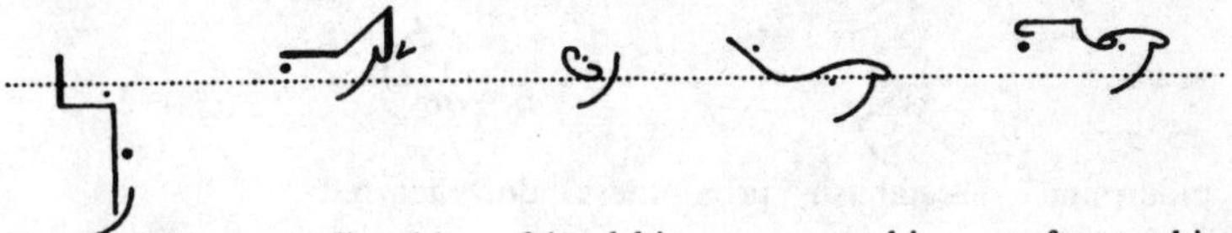

dictatorship guardianship friendship penmanship craftsmanship

chairmanship

EXERCISE 62

(*a*)

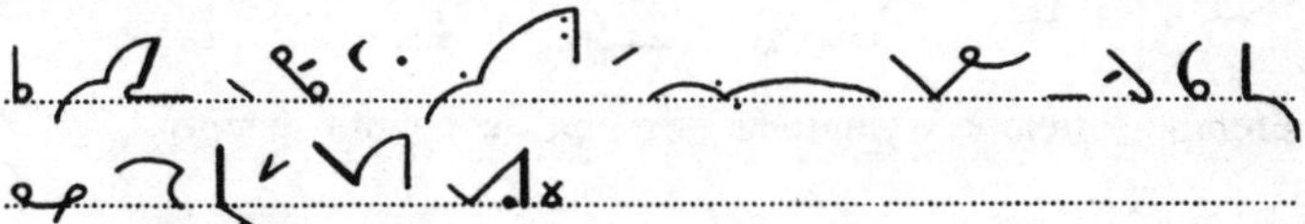

(*b*)

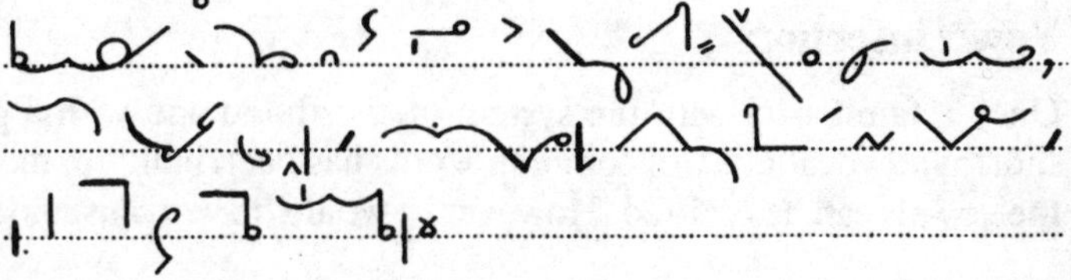

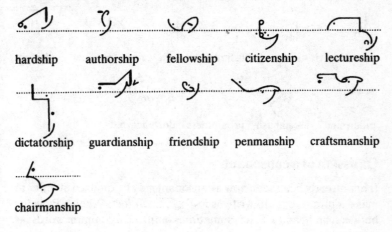

(c) 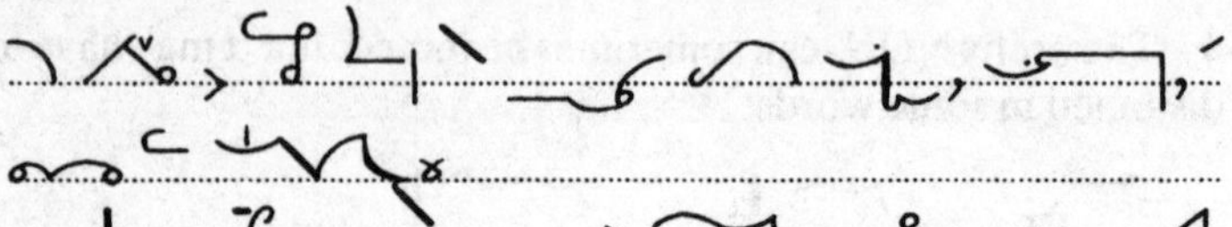

(d) 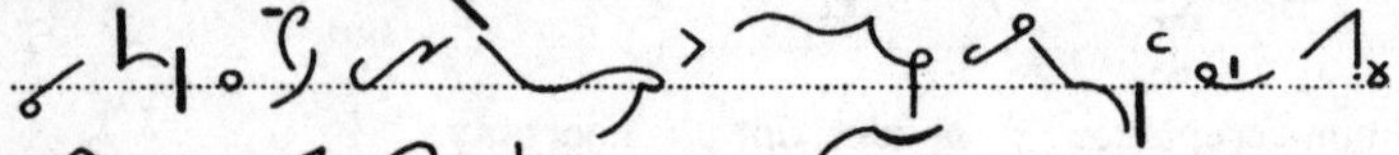

(e) 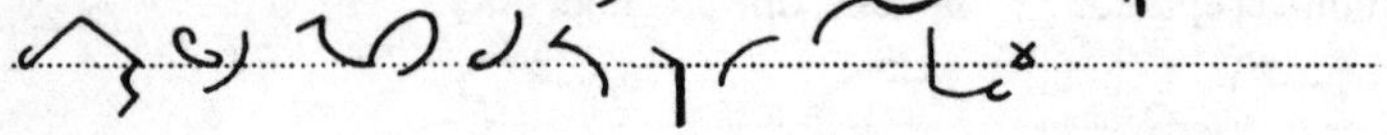

Disjoining

Most words in the language can be written in shorthand without a lift of the pen, but sometimes it is necessary to disjoin a part of a word. This is particularly so when there is no angle to show the joining of strokes of unequal length, as in:

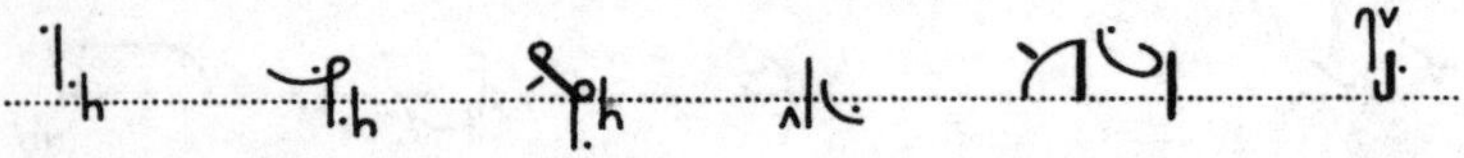

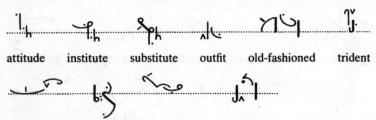

attitude institute substitute outfit old-fashioned trident

undermine disestablish promptness downhearted

Omission of a consonant

It has already been seen how a consonant may be omitted in order to make a phrase easy to write as in 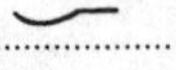 *in fact*. When a P occurs between an M and a T, it is sometimes omitted in common words, as in:

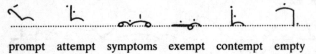

prompt attempt symptoms exempt contempt empty

Vowel insertion

Once a familiarity with the system of shorthand and with a good shorthand vocabulary of common words has been built up, most of the vowels can be omitted. However, it would be very misguided to try to do without vowels altogether. It is a matter of experience to know when it is the right time and place to insert a vowel, but it is certainly true that the more vowels you can insert, the easier the task of reading and transcribing becomes.

There are occasions when it is very desirable that a vowel should be inserted:

1 To distinguish common word collocations like  *at last* from  *at least*, or  *in another case* from  *in neither case*.

2 To show initial vowels or final vowels where these are not indicated by a rule. For example, it is needless to insert an initial vowel in  *ask* or  *art*, or a final vowel in  *penny* or  *coffee* or  *borrow* because the rules indicate the vowels.

However, an initial or final vowel is very useful in words like  *appeal*, 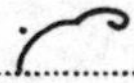 *element*,  *physically*, 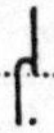 *totally*, 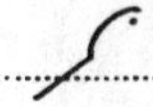 *really*.

3 Diphthongs, triphones, and diphones are most helpful in quick reading and transcribing, and should be inserted as often as possible especially in short words, for example:  *road*, 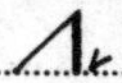 *radio*,  *doll*,  *dial*, 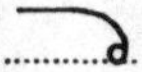 *cares*,  *coerce*.

4 In uncommon words it is helpful to include the vital vowel. To many, the word *egregious* will appear uncommon, even unknown, and in such instances the key vowels help in ensuring that the word can be read:  .

5 Single strokes, and particularly single strokes without initial or final hooks or circles, and half-length single strokes, may often need a vowel if their reading is to be made easy.

Words like *cut*, *lot*, *out*, *up*, *oppose*, *guide* and so on are better written with a vowel, and most experienced verbatim writers would do so, as in: .... *cut*, ... *lot*, ... *out*, ... *up*, ... *oppose*, ... *guide*.

EXERCISE 63

(a) (b) (c) (d) (e) (f)

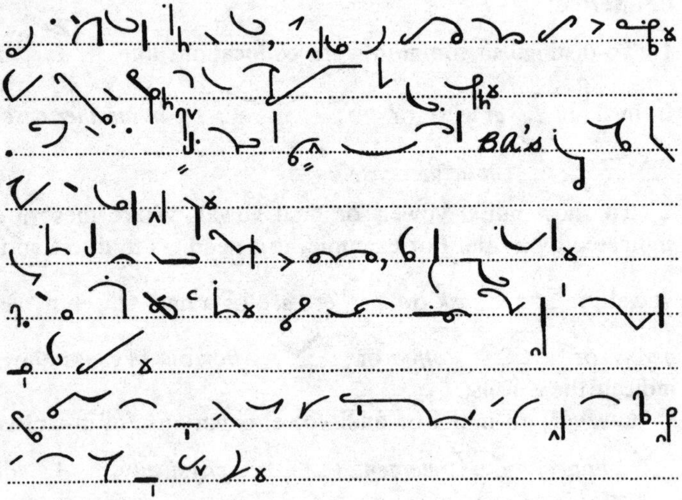

Section 24

Review

Read, copy, and then re-read from your own copy each of the three passages that follow. Then re-transcribe them back into shorthand from the key without reference to your original shorthand. Check the result.

1

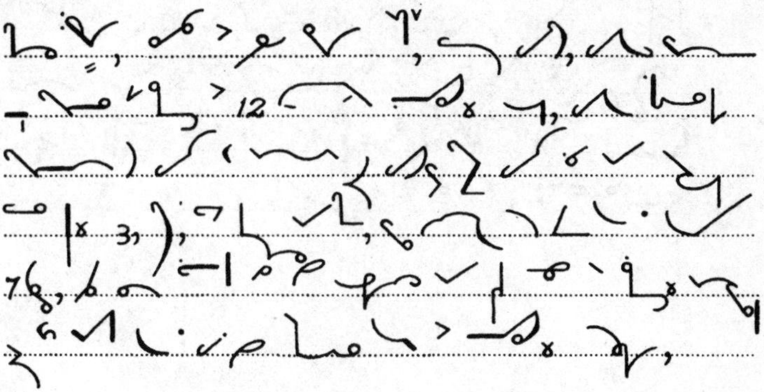

2

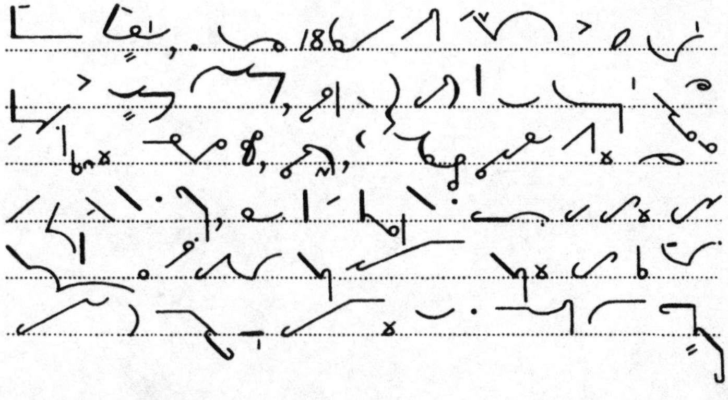

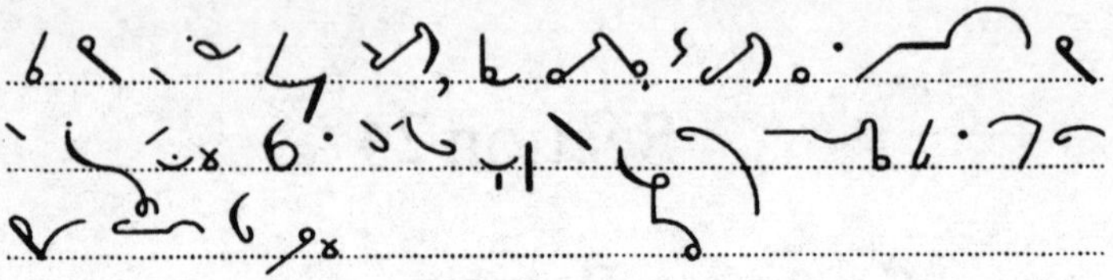

3

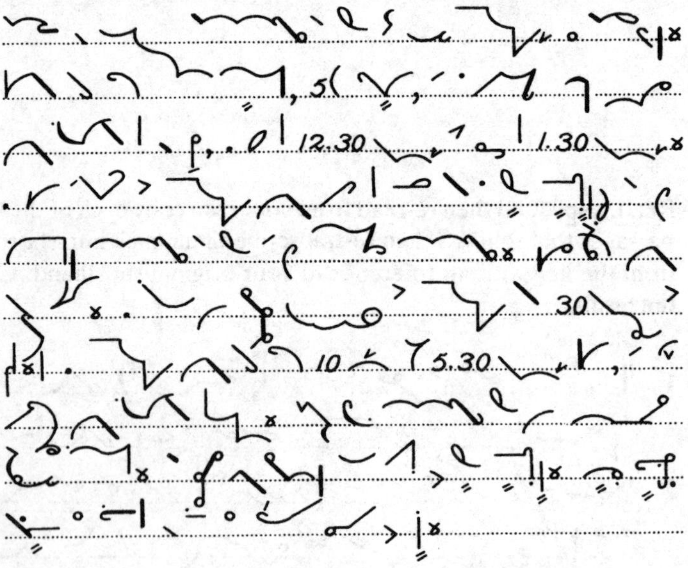

Keys to the Exercises

Section 1

Exercise 3

(*a*) 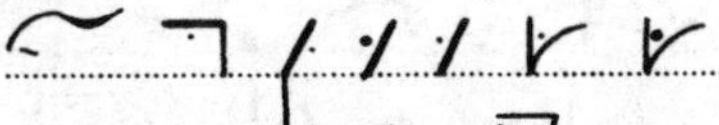

(*b*) 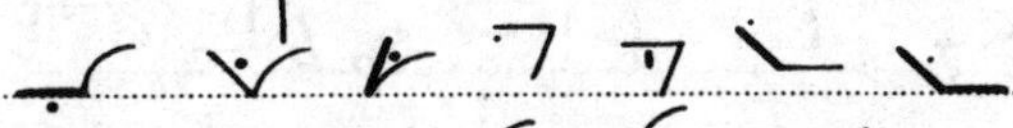

(*c*) 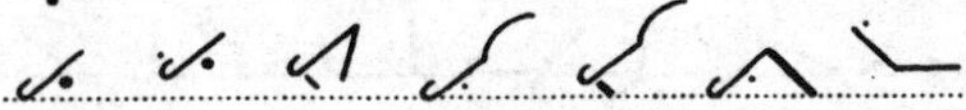

Exercise 4

(*a*) We may make some losses on the day's sales at the Boat Dock.
(*b*) You ought to do the job of checking the boxes.
(*c*) You may go to the docks today to fetch the cases of soap.
(*d*) I ought to take the watches to the lads today as we said.
(*e*) I bought some of the locks and catches, but the lass at the depot said the boxes in which the things came had to go back.
(*f*) You may go in today and pay in the cheque to the bank.
(*g*) Nothing may change, but we ought to do something to aid the lads dwelling along the edge of the lake, in case it does.
(*h*) Some of us ought to fetch the spades and pails and take back the boxes in which the things came.
(*i*) It is too much to walk all the way and we ought to take the coach to the top; maybe we may pass you on the way.
(*j*) We may be at the game on Monday, and we ought to tell Jack and Anne because the two always come to the games at the Dell.

Exercise 5

(*a*) We may go to the bank today as it is on the way to the lodge and the coach passes it.

(*b*) I had some cases of soap and two bags of cabbages on the boat, but I suppose Tom had to take all the things in the boat to the docks.
(*c*) Some tell us we ought to locate the luggage at the coach depot and Tom knows the way to get to it.
(*d*) We aim to catch the coach at two which goes along the edge of the lake and passes the old gates of the lodge on the way.
(*e*) Tom has a tape of the jet coming in and all the things the lads said at the check-in.

Exercise 6

(*a*)
(*b*)
(*c*)
(*d*)
(*e*)

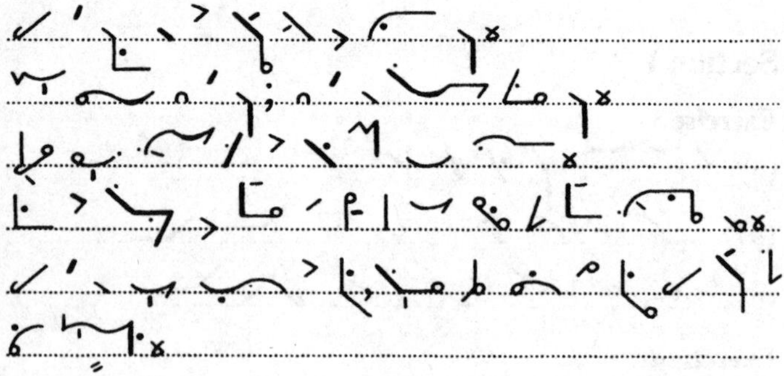

Section 2

Exercise 7

(*a*) We ought to ask them to take the photos to the shop and thus save some cash.
(*b*) Follow the path along the vale to the lake and fetch them back on the boat.
(*c*) We may make a cassette of the songs they sang on the way to the cafe.
(*d*) You know the facts of the case and they show us the way to vote today.
(*e*) In the Gazette, Tom has an essay on the customs of the folk in the vale.

Exercise 8

(*a*) Thank you for the desks and chairs which came yesterday and which we despatched to our customers on the same day.

(*b*) Your message came as we were packing the rugs for carriage to the vessel Red Rose which will be in dock tomorrow, so we packed the dozen wraps you asked for in with them.

(*c*) We shall go to the bank tomorrow to pay in a cheque for the rail charges and for the repair work on the two cars.

(*d*) Have you mailed the customs form for the manufactures we are despatching to our customer in Rhodes? We referred to this in the message we passed on to you yesterday.

(*e*) I think we ought to share the repair charges for this work on the doorway and gates as we were both careless in parking the firm's cars.

(*f*) Will you be coming with us to the cafe tomorrow? I know that it is a long way for you, but as Jack and Carol will be with us and we are having eggs, sausages, and tomatoes, we think you ought to come.

(*g*) We are going to Rome for a month and taking with us some of our range of manufactures. Our customers in Rome have asked for them as they think they may sell well in the shops.

(*h*) We borrowed the firm's car and followed the path along the edge of the vale as far as the copse to take some colour snaps of the lake.

(*i*) We shall have to make repairs to the shed and in fact we have chosen Rob Wade for that job. We have asked Paul Shore to do the thatching for us.

(*j*) We think you are wrong in paying in so much cash to the bank today, as we shall have to have change for our customers at the sale of charms and badges in the shop.

Exercise 9

(*a*) 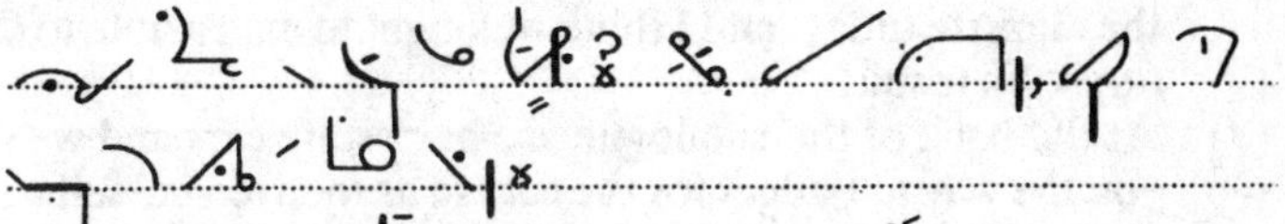

(*b*) 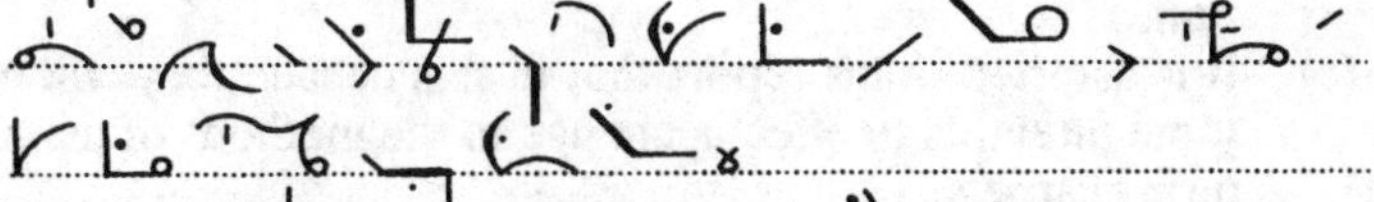

(*c*) 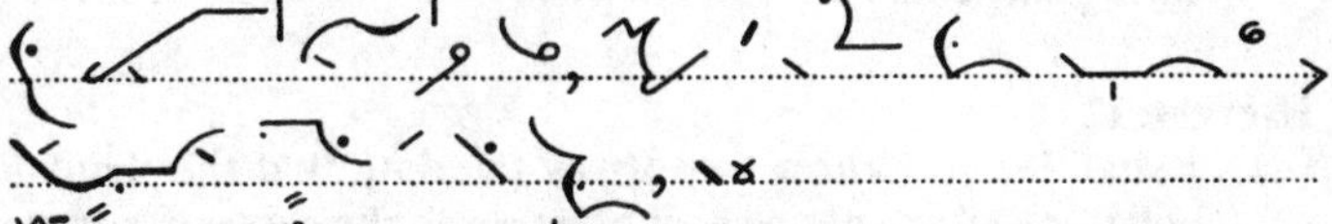

(*d*) 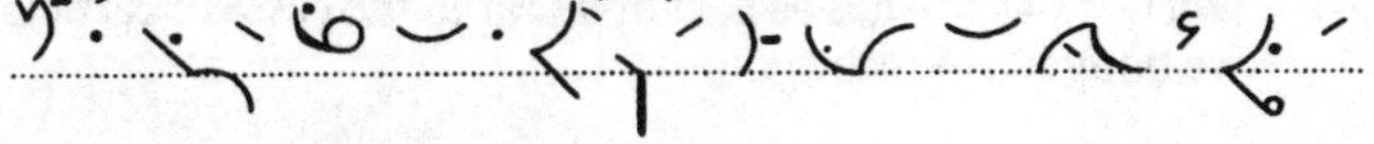

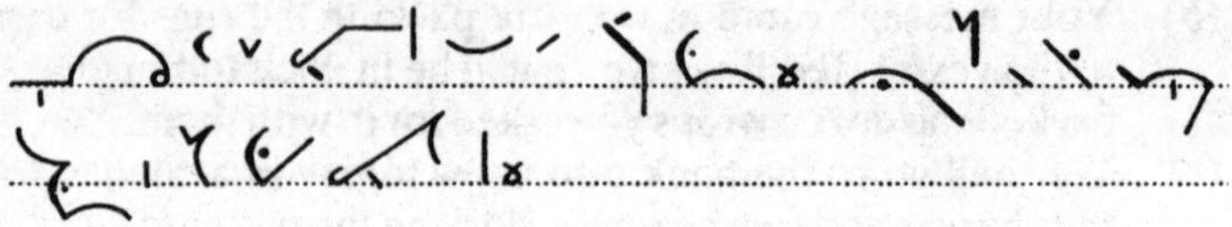

Section 3

Exercise 10

(*a*) I shall go to the college sports day and make some notes for the Sports Gazette, as they asked us to let them have something late in the day for the sports page.
(*b*) As I left our depot having worked all day I met our boss, a Scot named MacCabe, with spare parts for our car.
(*c*) In court, the judge said that the theft of some pots of jam was not such a small affair as was thought.
(*d*) We are manufacturers of coats and today we have sent two cases to the port for loading on the vessel 'Arab Rose' which will sail tomorrow. We were paid spot cash for the coats.
(*e*) I had a chat with the girls in the workshop, and they said they were waiting for soft soap to wash the walls of the workshop which have the dirt of long months on them.

Exercise 11

(*a*) We have to pay our rates tomorrow and that will affect our balance at the bank.
(*b*) We expect the results of our methods of manufacturing bolts and padlocks to show a rise though it may be slow.
(*c*) Carol wrote a ballad which Tom reports will be on page 17 of the Gazette today, and I think we ought to mail a note to Carol on such a result.
(*d*) At the back of the catalogue are our estate cars and we show you the way to budget for the cars so as to save yourself a large sum.
(*e*) It is asserted in his report that in this decade they will make some attempts to effect a change in the methods of manufacturing carpets.

Exercise 12

(*a*) I shall let you know tomorrow the date that the 'Gulf Rose' will dock which has as part of its cargo the cases of carpets that we bought a month ago.

(*b*) I have, in fact, sent a note with a customs form to the dock, and I would think that the cargo could be off the vessel tomorrow.

(*c*) You owe us two small sums for the manufactures that we let you have in March and May, but we expect you to deduct anything owing to you for the repair work on the estate car.

(*d*) Could you let us have tomorrow all the sports wear you have in the shop for us? Thank you for having kept them for us for so long. We are despatching a cheque for the sports wear today and you ought to get it tomorrow.

(*e*) I slept late, yet on awaking I felt doped. A cold bath had some effect and as I walked to work, thoughts came back and I recalled the tale that the tall Scot had told and resolved to take on the job of checking on all the facts.

Exercise 13

(*a*) 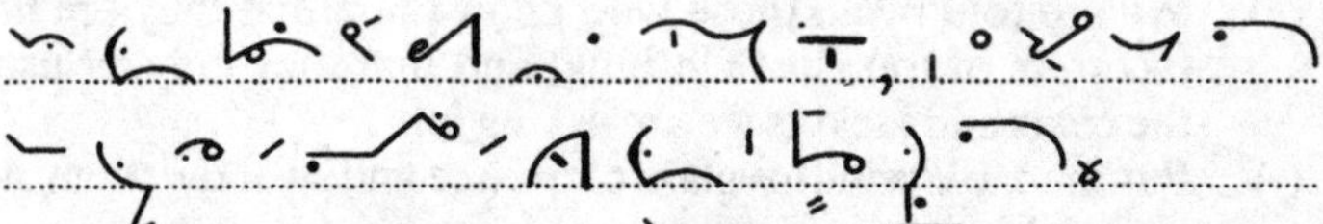

(*b*) 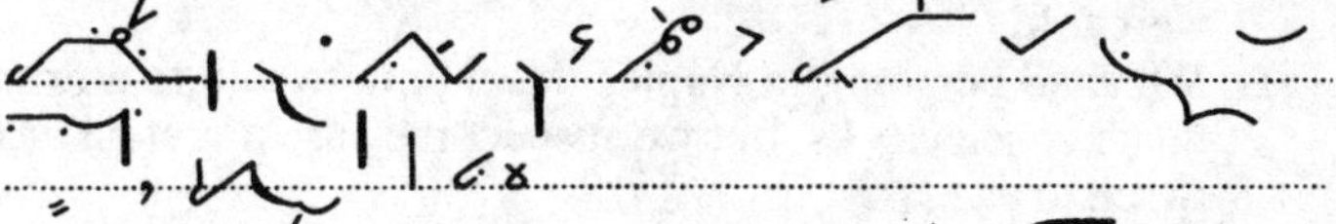

(*c*) 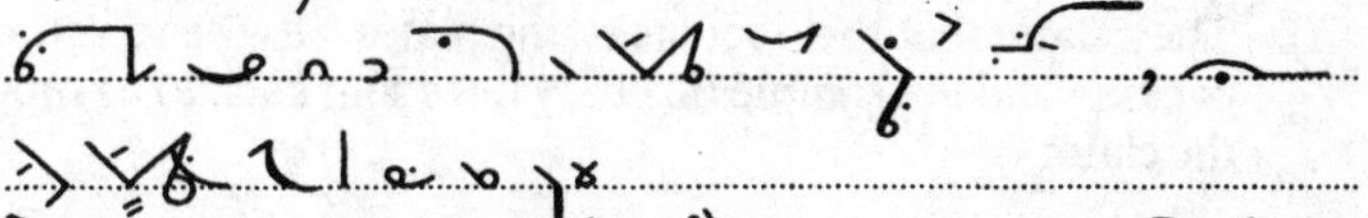

(*d*) 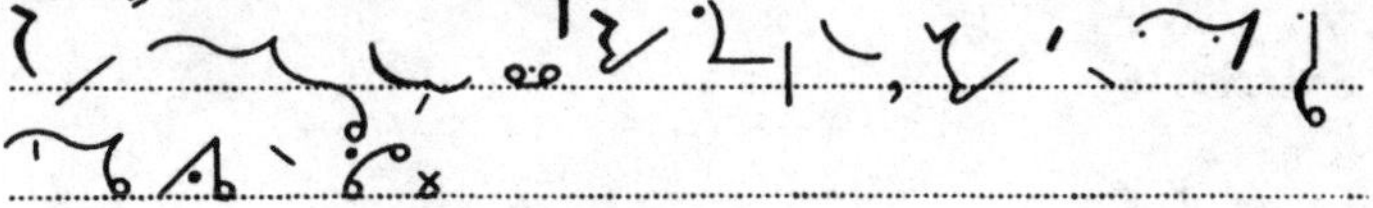

Section 4

Exercise 14

(*a*) We have some places left at the Globe for the play on Wednesday but I expect we shall sell them tomorrow at the Club.

(*b*) Will you get a red and black table cloth and a dozen glasses for us? They are in the same place as the plates were.

(*c*) I am asking Tom and Carol to label all the customs forms. They may be young but they are capable of doing this job for us.

(*d*) Cut the cable in two with this blade and attach a plug to a length of it.

(*e*) We are going to classes in making clothes at the local college and we think this will enable us to save a lot.

Exercise 15

(*a*) I would be glad to know that the ropes and cables we despatched to you on the local bus have got to your depot undamaged.

(*b*) We think we shall be able to repair the gold plate and glass vases for you, but it may take us a month to do the job.

(*c*) Are you able to let us know who they are yet? We know nothing of them, nor do any of the local firms.

(*d*) We have two models of pedal car for the young and both of them are safe enough for babes.

(*e*) We are told by all those who know them that they are manufacturers of top class clothing, and that they may let us have the coats and jackets we are asking for.

(*f*) Put the tablets in this glass of orange and swallow them as you were told.

(*g*) We shall be going to Naples this month to talk to a firm that make coach clocks, but we suspect they are not at all anxious to sell to us.

(*h*) They claim that the damage to the plates was the result of bad packing and the sample box they have sent back to us supports the claim.

Exercise 16

(*a*) 

(*b*) 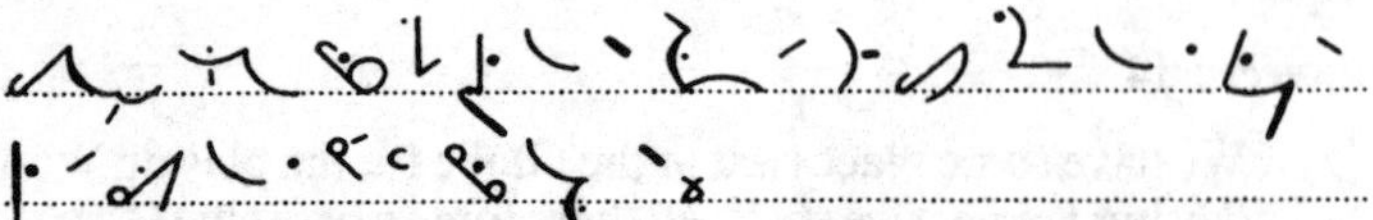

(*c*) 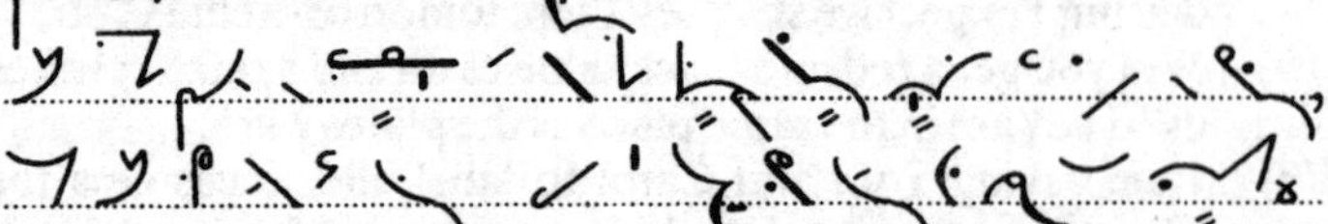

(*d*) 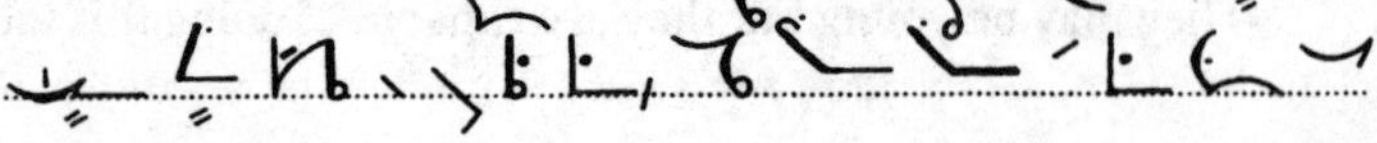

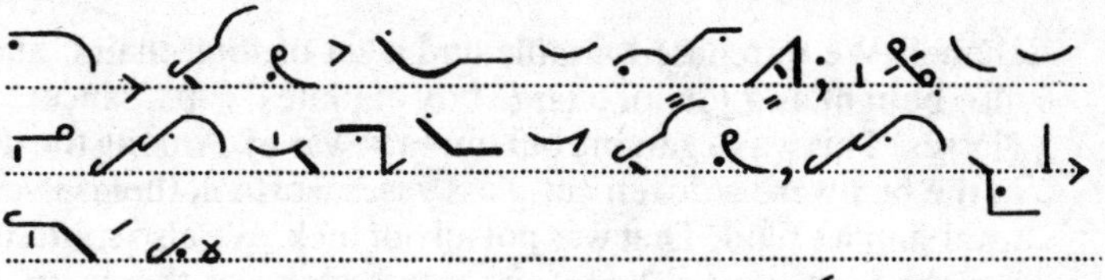

(*e*) 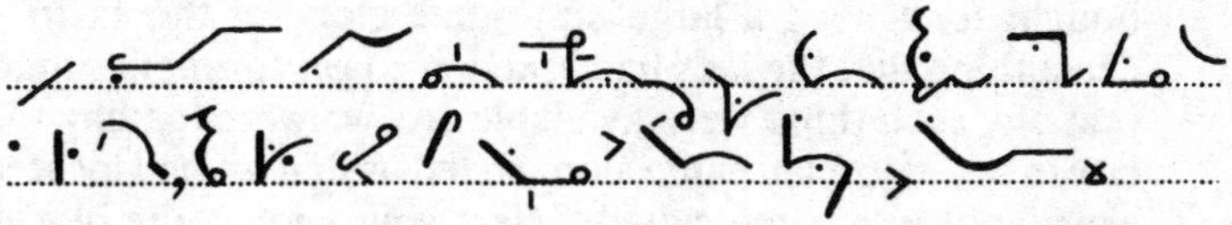

Section 5 – Review

1 We have an unexpected balance at the bank and we shall be able to pay our work force a bonus on wages in a month or two. We shall also set apart enough to enable us to erect a depot close to the railway and the road. The airport is not far away, and we shall arrange to despatch some things that are low in weight in this way. It is our purpose to add to our estate cars, too. We shall call on all our local customers with the estate cars. In this way they will get the things they ask us for at low charges. We shall have to pay to make repairs and changes to all doors as a result of the law that will take effect in March, but two-thirds of this sum will be paid for us. The law says that local resources will be called on to aid firms in making such changes as the law calls for.

2 Tom and Edna Edwards settled in this vale with Rhondda not far away. They had Welsh forebears and in young days they stayed with Welsh aunts and uncles. So they came to Wales and they have stayed. They go to chapel on Sundays and work for the chapel clubs on Mondays and Wednesdays. Tom takes the lads for wrestling and sports. Edna takes charge of the netball club. This month the club is top of the local netball table and will go to Wrexham to play for the Welsh Netball Cup. Tom is an expert angler and goes off to the lake on Saturdays. It is rare for Tom not to have caught some perch or roach.

3 We were at the market all day yesterday and we bought a lot of things. The shops in the market-place all have planks on trestles with canvas tops set up in the road exposed to the air and the dirt. But the old chapel that closed some months ago is also part of the market today and things like cakes and sausage rolls that would be affected with dirt and air are kept and sold in the chapel. We purchased a table and a set of four chairs, and we also bought as a job lot a large box of plates, cups, saucers, and glasses. This was a gamble but our luck was in. Among the things in the box were a dozen cut-glass vases worth in themselves the total sum we paid. That was not all our luck. We also spotted and bought for a song a large up-to-date globe of the earth – the exact thing that the lads had asked us to get for them supposing that any such thing were available. As we were loading the car late in the day, a lad came along to tell us that we had located the exact spot in a game called 'Select your spot in the plot' for a large bottle of Scotch, so we left thinking that this was our day.

4 We are unable, I am sorry to say, to let you have an answer. We have located the references you told us of but the fact is that all the boxes in which the notes were kept were so much damaged in a blaze some months ago that not a word of them could be read, so the Board sold them as junk to a local firm. Yet you may be able to get the facts, because we know that photos on a small scale of all the notes are available. We think that they are lodged in the bank vaults of the Bank of Naples in York. We are glad to enclose a form that the Bank of Naples has sent us which you may mail back to them asking them for a report on the notes that you have to have. They will charge for this, but we think you may well not object to that.

Section 6

Exercise 17

(*a*) The team will leave for a meal at six o'clock and we have booked places for them all.

(*b*) I think you ought to read this book as it tells of a part of the world that you know well and I feel you would be pleased with it.

(*c*) The finance necessary to erect this building is being raised in a month or two and the family will be purchasing shares in the firm that is doing the work.

(*d*) It is the policy of the family to use some of the money they make in the market on building and they are easily able to do this.

(*e*) We are asking each person who calls for money to purchase boots for the poor people in the Far East and we already have a good sum which we shall despatch to them soon.

Exercise 18

(*a*) Your business in Leeds will take you near the Selby Road and in that road Mrs Peel lives, I think it is at 428 Selby Road. We used to take care of Mrs Peel's business affairs so I would be pleased if you would call and see if she is well.

(*b*) She is a good cook and the curries and goulashes she makes are at the top of the class. But she has a limited range, and if she cooks for you for a week or two you soon come to those limits. Some dishes she will not attempt at all.

(*c*) The lads are saying that our team will lose on Saturday because Bill Blake will not be able to play owing to a chill and the paper in which it is published is the Daily Gazette.

(*d*) Food is our business and we are making a big attempt to raise our exports of meat puddings to Italy.

Exercise 19

(*a*) 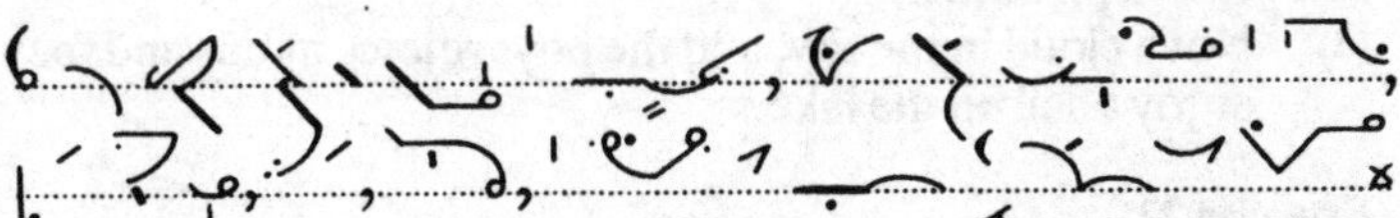

(*b*) 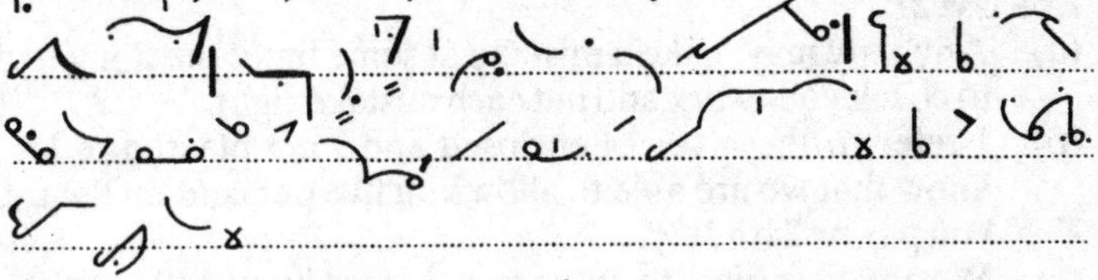

(*c*) 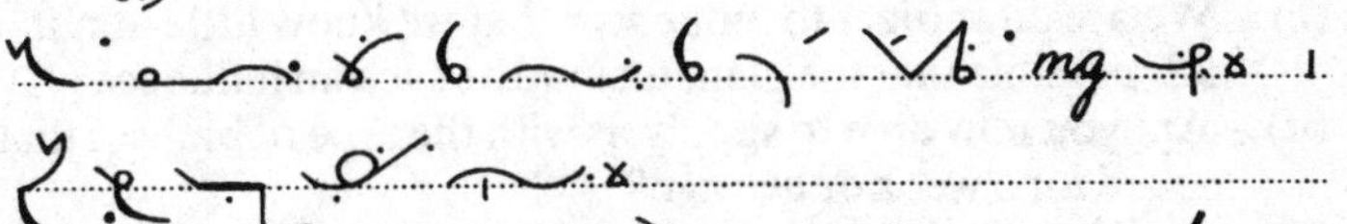

(*d*) 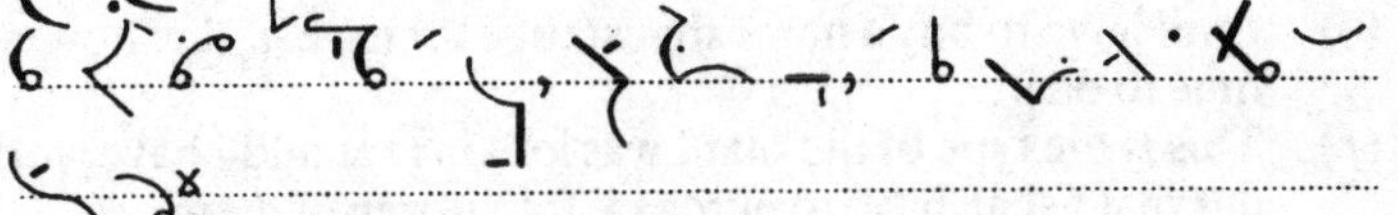

(*e*) 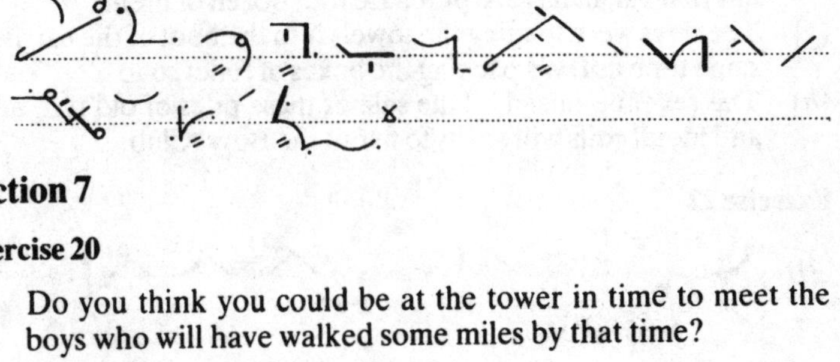

Section 7

Exercise 20

(*a*) Do you think you could be at the tower in time to meet the boys who will have walked some miles by that time?

(*b*) This type of couch is right for your lounge and you ought to buy it.
(*c*) It ought to be light by the time we get up for our voyage on the lake.
(*d*) This invoice shows that we ought to have received eight dozen of these toys but we are four short.
(*e*) The red blouse suits you and you ought to buy it now along with that tunic that is lying on the couch.
(*f*) A long queue of people was waiting to get into the Avenue Market.
(*g*) It seems that a part of your revenue is taxed twice, and you will have to argue your case with the tax authorities.
(*h*) Have you some tobacco in your pouch? I would like a pipe, if so.
(*i*) Make sure that you apply in good time for the job with the County Council.
(*j*) Not a cloud in the sky, and the boys rejoice at this and they will enjoy a sail on the lake.

Exercise 21

(*a*) Anybody may make a mistake at some time; the thing to do is to check your work and put each mistake right.
(*b*) I refer to the invoices enclosed and I am pleased to let you know that we are able to allow you five per cent on the total if you pay by 24th July.
(*c*) We are all subject to influences that we know little about, and it is possible that the planets could be such an influence.
(*d*) Are you now able to supply us with the type of blouses that we asked for a week or two ago?
(*e*) I will have to buy a new exhaust tube for my car, and now is the time to do it.
(*f*) This is the type of tile that I was looking for and I have worked out that I shall have to purchase four dozen of them.
(*g*) The boys were loading the towels into the boot of the car at the same time as I was packing the boxes of toilet soap.
(*h*) The revenue raised by the sale of these piles of old tyre tubes and metal coils will aid us to fit out the Boys' Club.

Exercise 22

(*a*) 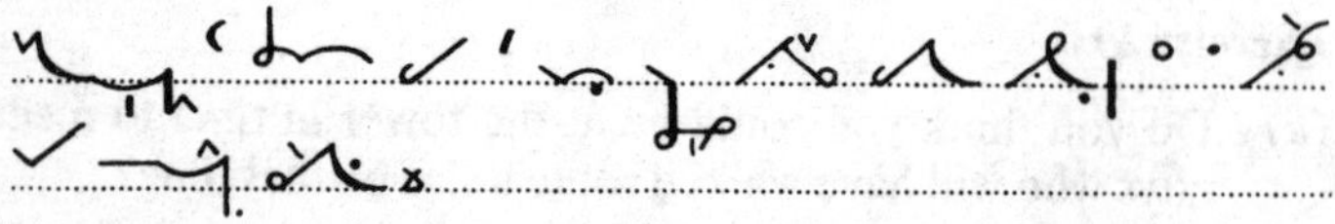

(*b*)
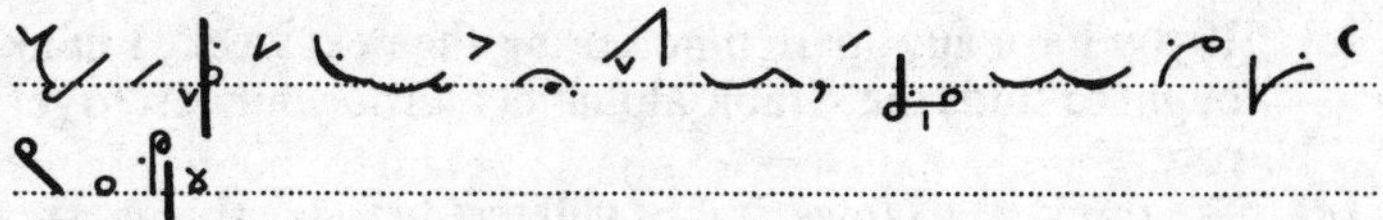

(*c*)
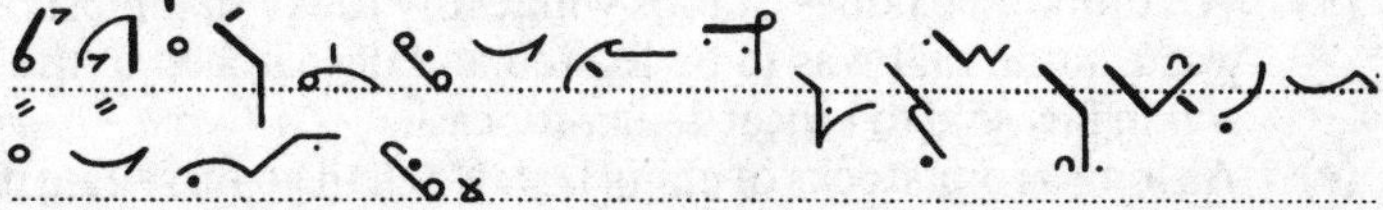

(*d*)
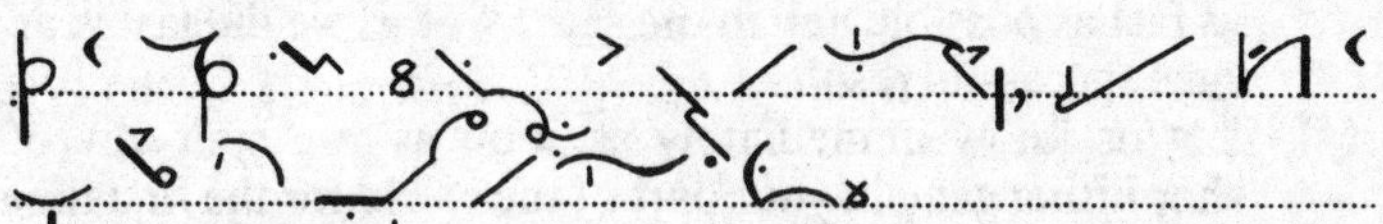

(*e*)
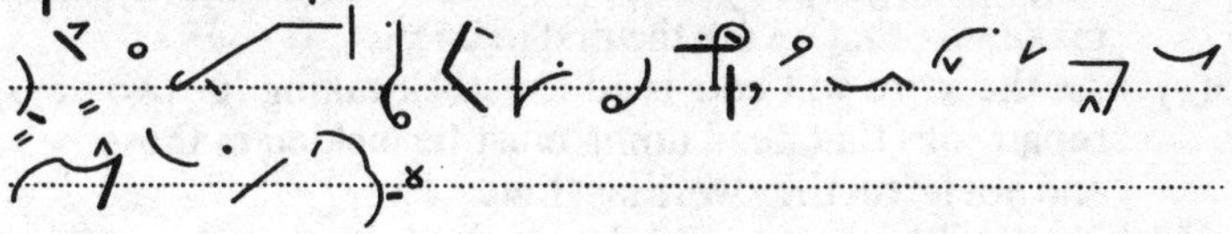

Section 8

Exercise 23

(*a*) Let me have a note of the cost of these toasters and also inform me how many of them we have in stock.

(*b*) Some of the statistics that we ought to have for the study of our factory costs for the past year are still not available, and we ought to write about this state of affairs.

(*c*) Will you please assist us to move these stores into the next room as the next stage of the work is to install some oak chests in this room.

(*d*) I have had receipts for the cassettes you bought in Manchester and I still have just enough time to finish the books by tomorrow.

(*e*) A person who cuts vast blocks of stone into fantastic shapes is not necessarily artistic.

Exercise 24

(*a*) First of all we ought to stack all the cups, plates, and saucers in these tea chests and we should have the job finished by lunch time.

(*b*) We need to set a first-class standard of work because our work force in Chester will take this standard as a model for them to copy, and they made a thousand last year.

(*c*) If you have any spare time during the next week, I think you ought to study the Arabic alphabet and do your best to get it by rote.

(*d*) We think that James Stubbs will testify today that most of the waste stone that was to be loaded and despatched to the port was in fact sold to a local dealer for cash.

(*e*) As long as our stocks of china last, we shall go on selling it just as fast as possible and in the same way as we did last year with such successful results.

(*f*) Let us know immediately as soon as you spot any of this shoplifting gang in your part of the world for the first time and make sure that we are the first to know.

(*g*) As the store will be closed for stock-taking for two days, the repair jobs that need doing must be tackled in those two days and not left as they were last time.

(*h*) You will be able to get the stock forms that you need at the post office, but you had best get them today as they were almost out of them late yesterday.

(*i*) The largest stocks of steel rods of all sizes are at the Railway Works, so I suggest that we send a reliable chap to the works to select the best in the standard sizes we need for the job.

(*j*) It must be the best result for a month's trading that we have had for the past few years and most of it is due to the work put in by our sales force.

Section 9

Exercise 25

(*a*) First of all, I would like to say that last year we assessed the value of the legacy at $8,000, but now it must be twice as valuable.

(*b*) In the local post office I saw a notice saying that the zoo might have to close because the area on which it is sited is to be sold to a large sawmill business.

(*c*) I should really like to have a report on this subject as soon as possible though I realise that the policy of the agency is to delay as long as possible in sending you all the facts. Ideally, I should like to have it sometime in the next week.

(*d*) It was easy for them to do the work set in the spare time they had at the end of each day's classes, but we had essays to write, so we had to work far into the night.

(*e*) We really think that they ought to co-operate with us in making a video called 'How to Type'. They have the right camera, and we have all the audio gear.

Exercise 26

(*a*) We hope you will be able to come to the New Homes Show. We usually have garage space available, and we shall be happy to keep a space for you in the car park and a room in the hotel if you let us know in time which day you will be coming.

(*b*) A new highway is to be built and some old houses and the rugby team's clubhouse will have to be bulldozed. They will all be unhappy about this, but new homes and a new clubhouse are to be erected nearby.

(*c*) It is hard to get rid of a bad habit. The thing to do is not to let such a habit develop. Yet it is possible by hard work and will power to shed the most deep-rooted habits.

(*d*) We now have eight vehicles and four warehouses and depots, two of which are leasehold and two of which we own.

(*e*) You ask me about Tom Hall. I met him first of all on a horse-riding course at Harrogate and I liked him immediately. As for Hannah Hall, I met her a year or two ago in the Black Horse Hotel and I was captivated by her charm and beauty.

(*f*) If he is still in New York, you should send him a telex immediately, and I hope that it will be possible for him to visit Harry Hawke in the hospital, which is a few miles outside New York.

(*g*) I hope he will adhere to the scheme as we wrote it at the time and not attempt to change it in any way at all.

(*h*) We have a lawyer for all our legal business and he is the best person with whom to discuss the purchase of the two houses and of Hill Farm which, I hear, is in need of extensive repairs.

Exercise 27

(*a*)

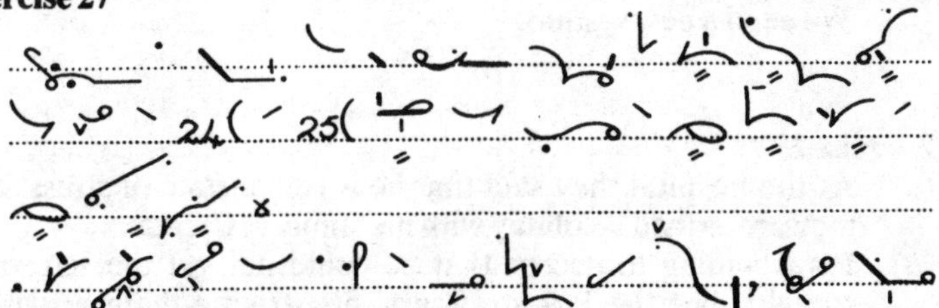

(*b*)

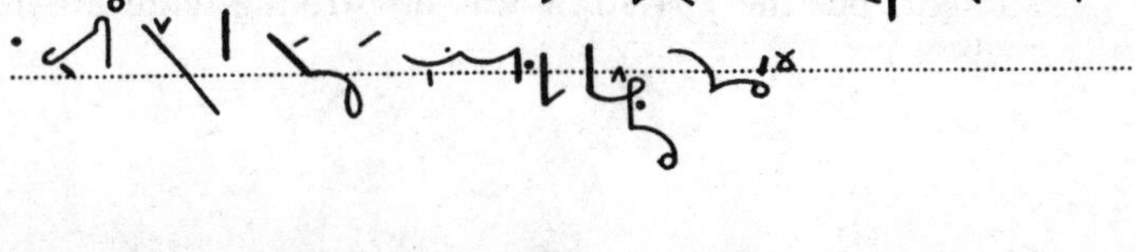

(c) 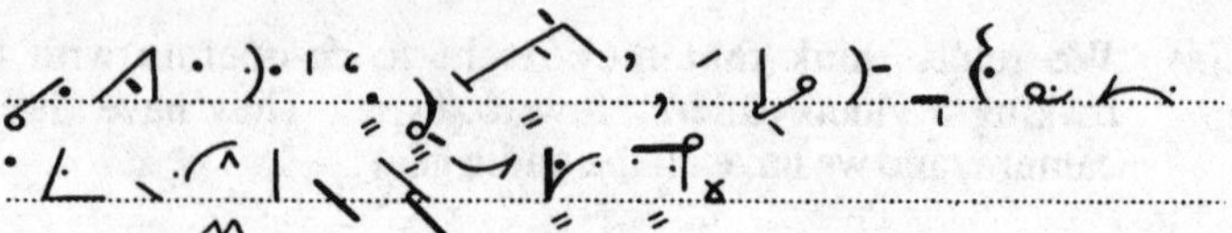

(d) 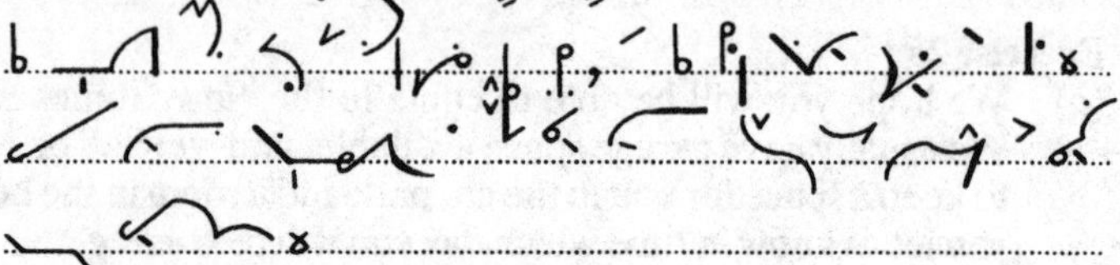

(e) 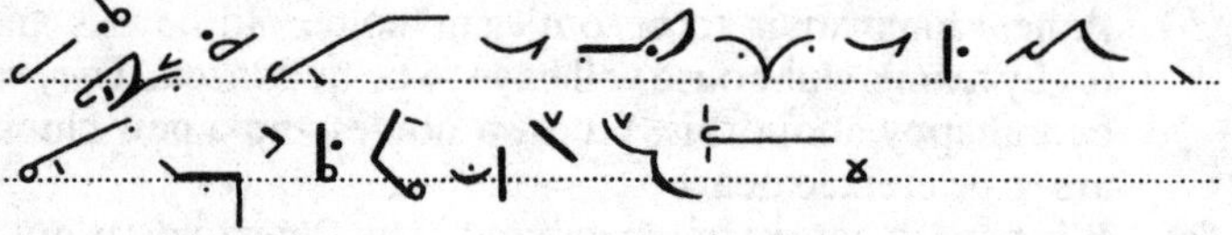

Section 10

Exercise 28

(*a*) Our problem is that the price of these crops is too high for us to buy them just now, yet we shall be in trouble without them.

(*b*) The group now embraces several firms and shows an impressive growth, now that we have works managers of vigour and a labour force interested in producing to get bonus wages.

(*c*) We have increased the number of word-processors in those offices that have a great deal of repeats and duplicated work to do.

(*d*) We manufacture soft drinks and in October and November we faced serious problems because our water supplies were cut off for several days. At the same time, as the result of a transport dispute, we could get no sugar.

(*e*) As our sales have increased, we have had to take on labour in the registry to cope with the filing and the extra ledger entries. We need a new system.

Exercise 29

(*a*) At the hospital they said that he was in a state of stress, and they prescribed a holiday with his family in Cyprus.

(*b*) I was willing to accept that he could not get the screws in straight, but the last straw was his striking them in with a mallet.

(*c*) He subscribes to the view that it is better to segregate boys and girls at this stage though he admits you sacrifice a lot by so doing.
(*d*) I regret that we are unable to duplicate this fabric or replace present stocks.

Exercise 30

(*a*) This shop window display is interesting and attracts the notice of most passers-by. It gets its message across in a bright and direct way and has increased the sales of the products that are displayed.
(*b*) Dear Madam, We thank you for the interest you show in the gold bracelets we have on show. A leaflet is enclosed telling you all about these low-priced products. Yours truly
(*c*) The number of persons of school age is falling and so it was agreed at a meeting of the council that the number of teachers in the employ of the local authority should be reduced.
(*d*) Dear Sir, I am sorry that you have had trouble in getting your hedge-cutter to work properly. We think that this booklet will instruct you in the correct method of adjusting the cutter. Yours faithfully,
(*e*) I think that this branch has really worked hard at the problem of reducing the total volume of paper used and a decrease of 27 per cent for the period February to April inclusive illustrates this well.
(*f*) Please leave your address with the girl at the desk and we will send the parcel of Christmas crackers on to you as soon as it arrives here.
(*g*) The Wholemeal Loaf Company Limited sells first-class bread and so, according to the trade papers, business is growing larger month by month, in particular here in the south.
(*h*) The purpose of asking all these people here today was to get them to subscribe money to express support for our candidate, Mr. Mark Strong, but the trouble was that we allowed too great a liberty to our speakers who spoke for too long and lost the interest of the crowds in the hall.

Exercise 31

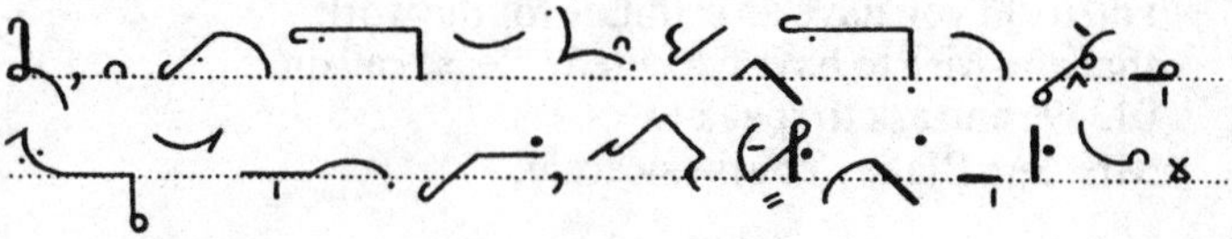

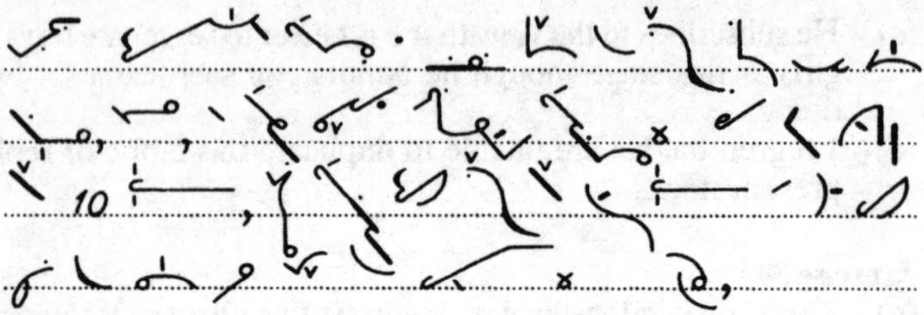

Section 11 – Review

1 Dear Sirs, Thank you for your prompt reply to our **10**
note about your paper supplies. We are sorry that the **20**
type of paper which we have supplied you with for **30**
so long is not available. The manufacturers tell us that **40**
the trade has ceased to ask for this particular paper **50**
because of its high cost. They do add though that **60**
they are still prepared to make this paper at the **70**
same price if you will take a gross of reams **80**
at a time. Will you please let us know if **90**
you agree to this. In the meantime we shall send **100**
you tomorrow a dozen reams of the type we suggested **110**
to replace the paper you always buy. We are sure **120**
that you will like it. Yours faithfully, **127**

2 Dear Mrs. Rogers, We are told by Mr. Peter Baker **10**
that you are looking for a reputable firm of long **20**
standing in the trade to modernise your home in King's **30**
Cross. According to Mr. Baker, the principal task is to **40**
unite the present lounge and breakfast room into a larger **50**
lounge, and also to build on to the rear of **60**
the premises a large glass and cedar wood sun lounge **70**
with a light-admitting hard plastic top. We have had **80**
21 years of this type of work and, although **90**
it may seem an exaggerated claim, we assure you that **100**
we have always managed to satisfy all our customers. They **110**
are happy with the excellence of the work and also **120**
with the prices charged. May we call on you at **130**
a time suitable to you, to discuss the subject? We **140**
shall be glad to show you our leaflets and files, **150**
and to let you have an estimate for the work **160**
that you wish to have executed. Please call on **169**
013496 and ask to speak to **180**
Mrs. Sue Blake. Yours sincerely, **185**

3 In the last two decades, the most popular way of **10**
taking a bath has become (if I may put it **20**
this way) to take a shower. Showers are now installed **30**
in 72 per cent of the country's bathrooms, and **40**
in some English-speaking countries, the percentage is still [higher. **50**
Showers have become popular for several reasons. A thorough [washing **60**
process is much easier in a shower. Less water is **70**
used. At the end of a bath you are lying **80**
in – not to mince words – dirty water. In the shower **90**
the water is always clear. A shower is invigorating, too. **100**
You step out feeling a new person. A last merit **110**
of the shower is that you may shampoo your hair **120**
and scalp at the same time. **126**

4 Dear Miss Crow, Thank you for applying for the post **10**
of medical secretary to the Senior Registrar of this hospital **20**
and for the detailed notes you sent us of your **30**
successes in your college course and the report signed by **40**
your Principal. We think it a most impressive record. We **50**
hope you will be able to come for a short **60**
two-minute test at a hundred words a minute at **70**
two o'clock on Thursday, 15th September. The test will be **80**
followed immediately by a talk with the Senior Registrar and **90**
the Hospital Secretary. We shall pay for your fares and **100**
your lunch. Will you please call me on the office **110**
number at the head of this sheet to let me **120**
know if you will be able to come. We look **130**
forward to seeing you. Yours sincerely, **136**

Section 12

Exercise 32

(*a*) It is known that this man will need a loan if he is to buy the two vans that he has to have for his work.

(*b*) He earns his money by dealing in old iron and he now has a fine business.

(*c*) The unions object to these new machines because, they say, the men who work them should get extra allowances.

(*d*) The judge was asked to assign marks up to a maximum of 10 based on the excellence of the taste of each sample of jam and to telephone the results of his marking to the paper.

(*e*) In Venice I had an illness and was rushed to hospital in an ambulance. They examined me and announced that I would be able to leave on the next day.

Exercise 33

(*a*) I hope to arrange a settlement of the debt owed by Mann and Sons and I shall use the trust fund for this purpose.

(*b*) I expect payment to be made for the plot of land soon, as I have reminded them that they still owe the money.

(*c*) The patient is now on the mend and we hope to arrange for her discharge if we get the Registrar's assent.

(*d*) His gallant act has added to the fame of the regiment and, I fancy, is sufficient to earn him an award.

(*e*) I lent my landlord a copy of the Land Act of 1980 in which a tenant's rights and duties are listed, but I fancy he found that document hard reading.

Exercise 34

(*a*) We are particularly pleased that you will be able to make the arrangements for the main event to be put on not too late in the evening.

(*b*) I am arranging for your party to have an excellent lunch at the Fine Foods Cafe and then to be brought to the venue for the game by coach.

(*c*) It must be said that in the past year we have earned larger sums than in the last year of trading, and we have also paid back all our loans.

(*d*) The last time we met was in the post office because I recall that you had your van waiting outside and asked me if I would care for a lift to Union Lane to watch the big match.

(*e*) As a business man, you ought to take steps right away to raise the finance you will need for the purchase of heavy wire fences for which the local authority will make you an allowance.

(*f*) We are arranging for the new machines to be picked up by a heavy van some time tomorrow, and I will let you know by telephone immediately the van leaves.

(*g*) I had to pay a fine of two hundred dollars, one hundred on the spot and the balance within four days, and I also had to promise to keep silent about the money I had found.

(*h*) Dear Sir, Now is the best time to invest in the Alliance Investment Trust as the share market is rising and will rise, we think, for the next two months. We will arrange the sum you invest in any one of six ways, the details of which are shown in the enclosed booklet. Your money will be in safe keeping and we guarantee an interest rate of at least eight per cent for the year. In fact, we expect it to be much higher than that. Yours truly,

Section 13

Exercise 35

(*a*) I think you can win this race if you run as fast as you did yesterday in training.

(*b*) To maintain all the machines that we use in this factory, it is necessary for our men to follow a regular routine, and they begin work as soon as the day shift have done work for the day.

(*c*) This region is largely urban and so we have a good bus and train service running into the main cities.

(*d*) All our residences are fitted with the most modern appliances and the response to our sales campaign has been most encouraging.

Exercise 36

(*a*) Spend the next few seconds counting up how many one pound coins you find in your till.

(*b*) It is important for us not to depend too much on any assistance we can get in painting the club house, but make plans for doing the whole job alone, possibly with nobody to lend a hand.

(*c*) I asked my assistant to look back at the correspondence we had with Tony Kent about the proposed training programme that we intended to run at that time.

(*d*) I want you to find out for us the extra distance we have to go if we decide to go round by the lake instead of using the main road.

(*e*) I think this is Dan's handwriting without any doubt, and so we have to accept that he took his chances and by some means made his way to the Lebanon and was in that country on 14th June.

Exercise 37

(*a*) The responsibility for the sales department is your own for the whole of next week, and the campaign that begins on selling cans of soup will be in your hands.

(*b*) Poach some eggs and open a tin of beans. I do not think that we have time for anything better than that if we are to reach the training camp by noon.

(*c*) We have been asked to return the screen of the VDU to the makers as soon as they can get one to us to replace the faulty one, so that we shall be able to carry on without a pause.

(*d*) I think this appliance is much better than the one we tested in June, and so it has been decided to return that one and buy four of these, even though the expense is greater than we expected.

(*e*) Please let us have at once full particulars of all residences you have for sale in this region, particularly those with large kitchens and well maintained.

(*f*) The ice dance programme is due to begin at seven o'clock and so we must arrange to adjourn our meeting at least an hour earlier than that to enable us to watch it.

(*g*) Go round the shops of the whole region and record the prices in each shop of all the paints in this list. They will not all stock the lot, but it is important for us to get our own list of prices and not to be dependent upon the lists handed on to us by the sales department.

(*h*) Our expenses this week are higher than they were last week, but that is because we have been going longer distances to get the kind of assistants that we need.

Exercise 38

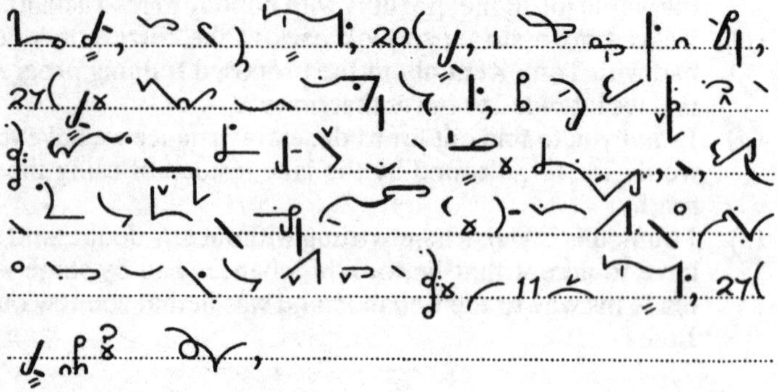

Section 14

Exercise 39

(*a*) I shall not make any payment of my rates until I have a new assessment on my property.

(*b*) The only argument he has is based on a document which may well be a fake if an analysis is made of its paper and ink.
(*c*) The department has just issued an announcement that only four appointments to the top grade of clerk will be made this year.
(*d*) The assignment that we were told to work on was to carry out experiments on the sample to test how strongly it was made and if the results of the tests shown in the document were wrongly based.
(*e*) Unless you change your plugs annually or at least make adjustments to the gaps, your car will go no better.

Exercise 40
(*a*) This experimental stretch of road on the A1 has been instrumental in helping us to devise methods of surfacing roads cheaply.
(*b*) We need these supplies urgently and we are wholly and totally dependent on them for the maintenance of our departmental work.
(*c*) My son diligently studied the arts and skills of a monumental stone mason, and he has certainly made a great success of it locally, having trebled his business in two years.
(*d*) We became aware recently that we were working increasingly hard in the shop for smaller returns, so, not surprisingly, we began to suspect one of our assistants of dishonesty.
(*e*) Mentally and physically my uncle is much better than he was ten years ago and his change of job has been principally instrumental in bringing this about.

Exercise 41
(*a*) I was particularly pleased to meet Sir Peter at the party and he talked to me for a long time stressing again and again that if we would take on the job he would make the money available.
(*b*) Ladies and Gentlemen, I am glad to tell you that our annual analysis of costs and expenses shows that we have once again been able to reduce these, although by only two per cent. The value of spending time on this assessment lies in increasing the efficiency of the firm. The argument is strongly against those who think that it is just a waste of time and money. In the four years that the experiment has been running, the analysis has been instrumental in saving us four times as much as the work has cost. It is a wholly viable project and rightly, in my view, it

is to be extended to our offices too, with the full agreement of our staff who stand to benefit by better and better ways of working.

(*c*) Dear Sir, Thank you for writing to us. We have persistently pressed the argument that the only way for the firm to rescue itself now is for drastic cuts to be made in many departments and the immediate appointment of a new manager. It is no use mincing words. Bad management at the top has been the root cause of our problems, and as a result our market has been diminishing for a long time. Yours truly,

Section 15

Exercise 42

(*a*) We have adequate supplies of all kinds of garden equipment to meet any requests you may make.

(*b*) Answer all these questions quickly as the time allowed for them is quite short.

(*c*) By the time he was only 20, he had acquired several languages and was well qualified as a teacher.

(*d*) The prices we quote do depend, as you will realise, not only on the quality of the goods that we stock, but also on the quantity that you require.

(*e*) What you will need when you get here is a square meal and somewhere to sleep while you are staying in the village.

(*f*) We are holding a day of aquatic sports to raise money for the victims of the earthquake, and we are requesting your support.

Exercise 43

(*a*) Year by year the pace of change quickens and our resources are inadequate to enable us to keep our equipment up to date. We shall require money quickly if we are to keep going.

(*b*) It would have been a better year altogether if we had not lost a large quantity of liquid oxygen and some machines only recently acquired.

(*c*) Thank you for your enquiry and for the acknowledgment of the safe receipt of the language books. We shall be enquiring in the United States for your requirements, but meanwhile we are despatching the books you urgently requested today.

(*d*) The question is: Where can we find cloth of the quality that we shall be requiring soon in the quantities that we will need? Squires Textiles said that they would be able to meet the firm's requirements but subsequently they were forced to acknowledge that the job was too large for them.

(*e*) We have to bear in mind that what we see as a sale is, in the customer's point of view, a purchase, and that we have to work together with our customers. If not, they will go elsewhere.

(*f*) She is a quiet child but a bright one, too. She is always wanting to know about things and asking such questions as: Where does the sun go at night? Why does a cat purr? Where does the Queen work? When did we learn how to speak? and What was I when I was not here?

Exercise 44

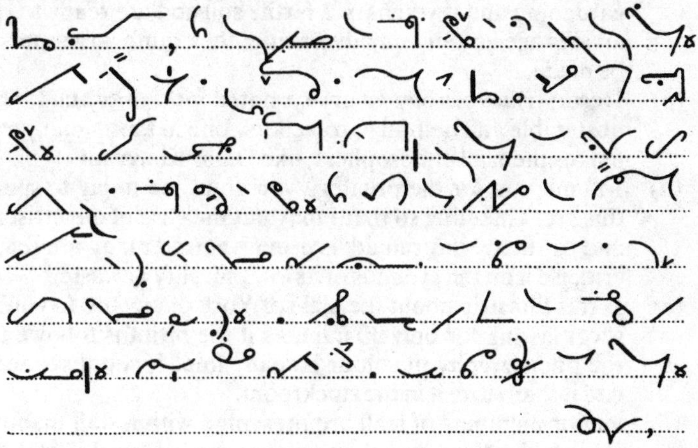

Section 16

Exercise 45

(*a*) I shall be free on Friday next and I hope to see you at the special general meeting of the athletic club when the new site for the hammer throw will be the subject to be discussed.

(*b*) I offered him two large crates of grapefruit at a favourable price, but he was afraid to accept them.

(*c*) During the war he rose to the rank of major in Royal Signals and he was flown to Vladivostok to attend the funeral of Marshal Donnell.

(*d*) The energy for mining the minerals in this region was supplied by a powerful hydro-electric scheme which operates pile-drivers and steam-hammers.

(*e*) A new measure is being discussed in the House to increase the penalties on car owners who fail to license cars, either by heavy fines or by other penalties not yet decided upon.

Exercise 46

(*a*) I think it would be better for us to pass the summer in the civilised environment of this farm than to stay in a noisy holiday camp.

(*b*) We have a short filmstrip about the art and skill of nursery gardening and if you have a fertile soil and are ready to spend an average amount on advertising, then quite large sums may be made.

(*c*) Desert tribes are almost always noted for civility and for being hospitable and helpful to travellers. Life in those lonely wastes makes them all philosophers, like Omar Khayyam.

(*d*) I thank you for the privilege you grant me today to speak at this great meeting so that I may put the case of advertisement and of those who run advertising when so many are ready to criticise it on the grounds of its low morality or waste.

(*e*) Is this filmstrip about the Vale of York of any use to you? It is short lasting for only 30 minutes if the script is followed, but the photography in colour is really fine. I would sooner you had it than store it in the stockroom.

(*f*) Junior members of staff are presented with a staff manual on joining the firm, and they are required to read it and know what it says. The firm promises to care for the welfare of its staff especially its juniors and it fulfils this promise as the manual reveals.

(*g*) Numbers in the Civil Service have been steadily reduced over the past five years, but no dismissals have taken place; the numbers have fallen through change of job, retirement, marriage and death.

(*h*) Flights to all parts of Africa are quite frequent and they leave both Heathrow and Gatwick. Once a week they run a non-stop flight either to Cape Town or to Johannesburg during the summer months.

(*i*) An official of the Foreign Office was sent especially to meet these delegates and to be helpful in any way that he could. The visit has the approval of all of us, and we hope that it will be beneficial to our economy.

(*j*) Free verse usually has no rhyme and no fixed rhythmic arrangement. This has led some persons to regard free verse as not verse at all, but in fact I hope today to show you some fine poetry, all of it written in free verse.

Section 17

Exercise 47

(*a*) A large cache of ancient silver coins from Saxon times has been discovered in an Essex field near Saffron Walden.

(*b*) The government has decided to celebrate the anniversary of the opening of the river barrier with a festival to be attended by a gathering of all those who took part in its planning and building.

(*c*) The photographer, Stella Grover, is famous for her shots of clouds and weather and for buildings reflected in water. However, she may not win the Society's Gold Medal, which is likely to be awarded to her rival, Jennifer Gulliver.

(*d*) It is shameful that such a clever novelist should have been so little esteemed in her own day, and the discovery of an unpublished novel by her is a notable event.

(*e*) The government cavalry were manoeuvring to cut off the rebels who were engaged in the removal of art treasures from the old royal palace.

Exercise 48

(*a*) Miss Grover has done very satisfactory work for us in the enlargement of shots for commercial photography from normal size prints using the most modern types of enlarger, and she is certainly more skilled in this type of work than she was before she joined us.

(*b*) I am very glad that we now have someone influential on the Board to argue the case for better treatment for them and their customers.

(*c*) They arrived at the camp sooner than we had expected and more than a third of our party were not present to welcome them on their arrival.

(*d*) In our view, this new crop can be raised in all parts of the world and there is no doubt of its commercial possibilities.

(*e*) It appears that we may have gone too far in extending credit to these customers and so far we have only been able to collect about a third of the sums owed to us.

(*f*) In the course of his talk, the speaker said that it is only possible to make an estimate of the manufacturing output of the new factories, and at the same time he warned those who owned shares in the group that it would be several months before we would have any more exact idea.

(*g*) Our customers have been very influential, dissuading us from taking any steps to cut down output for a month at least.

(*h*) In our own part of the country it is not possible to plant tomatoes outside until well into June and then there is less than four months to bring the fruit to ripeness.

(*i*) It appears that when they were about four miles along the road they decided that it was too far to walk all the way to their uncle's and so, of course, they called Tom, long-suffering as usual, who agreed to get the estate car out and pick them up.

(*j*) There is no doubt that there will be an acute shortage of green vegetables next month and it is only too likely that more will have to be imported from Europe and from Kenya.

Exercise 49

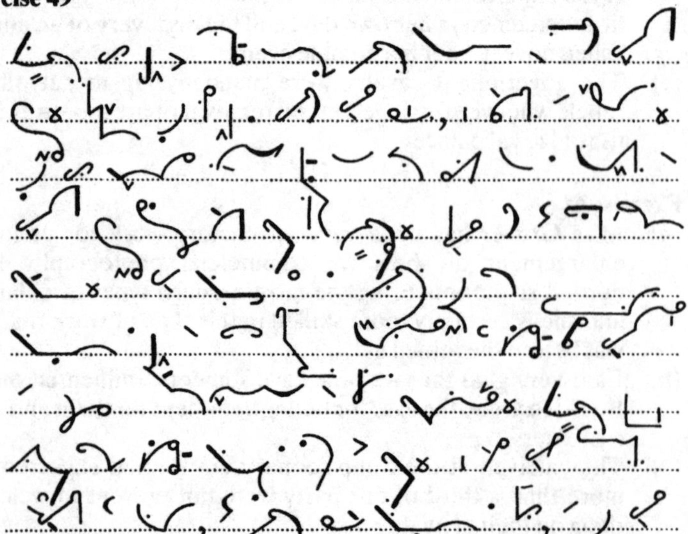

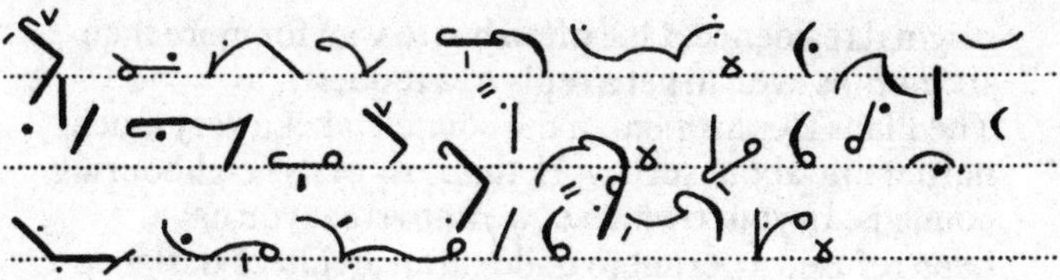

Section 18 – Review

1 While every care is taken to ensure the security of 10
these premises and of the car park, the management cannot 20
be responsible for any loss of or damage to customers' 30
property either in the hotel or in the car park. 40
Particularly valuable items should accordingly be handed in
[to the 50
clerk at the desk and receipts obtained. Our general security 60
measures work very well and we have an altogether
[satisfactory 70
record in this respect. The police carry out their annual 80
scrutiny of our security arrangements and the following is
[quoted 90
from the latest report: 'The Star Hotel has always
[implemented 100
measures that we have proposed to them and this has 110
been influential without a doubt in making them the safest 120
premises in our police region.' 125

2 Dear Mrs. Nelson, It is possible that there may be 10
a delay of about a fortnight in meeting your requirements 20
of special inks and pens as some of these have 30
to be obtained in the United States of America. However, 40
we do not think that they will be any longer 50
than that in reaching you and you may rely upon 60
us to get them to you as soon as possible. 70
We have already posted the art paper you specified and 80
we are pleased to tell you that there is a 90
5 per cent drop in the price of this paper, 100
so we shall make an adjustment when we send you 110
the monthly statement. Yours sincerely, 115

3 Dear Sir, You will not need to be told how 10
hard it is to get approval from this local authority 20
for any building work that modifies or adds to an 30

original residence. One often has to wait for more than 40
six months even to get a reply to a request. 50
The Plans Department of the council takes a very much 60
harder line about such work than any of its neighbouring 70
councils. In your own case, we know that you have 80
been refused a permit to build on an architect-designed 90
sun lounge to your premises. We have formed a local 100
residents group with the support of several local councillors
[to110
change the policies and attitudes of the Plans Department.
[Full120
details of our scheme are enclosed and we hope that 130
along with many others in your area, you will join 140
us in efforts to amend the present state of affairs. 150
Yours truly, 152

4 A country is no different from a family in the 10
sense that it has an income from various sources, and 20
then has to budget how that money will be spent. 30
Like a family, a country can raise loans, but then 40
it has to take into account the interest that has 50
to be paid on those loans and also the repayment 60
arrangements that have to be made over a period of 70
months or years to return the capital borrowed. Where things 80
differ lies in what happens when a family gets too far into 90
debt. Then the family will find itself faced by the 100
law and will be obliged to pay back all it 110
owes. A country may pay its debts by increasing the 120
supply of money. But if it does, disaster is likely 130
to follow. All prices of goods and services rise with 140
the most serious effects on employment and on all
[commercial150
interests. At the end of the day, the government of 160
any country has to be as financially accountable as a 170
family, if the people are to prosper. 177

Section 19

Exercise 50

(*a*) Vaccination against smallpox and inoculation against yellow fever are available on one day's notice at this health clinic.

(*b*) An extension of the time allowed for entry to this examination has been requested and the authorities will decide whether to grant this at a secret session on Friday.

(*c*) There is to be a national census of the population next year, and the public will be informed about it by means of a series of television programmes. They should attract a lot of attention.

(*d*) British people seem crazy about abbreviations and create a profusion of them, some of which endure like VAT and others of which quickly fade away.

(*e*) Inflation creates an illusion of prosperity, but it is false, and relations between various groups of the population are only made worse by inflation.

(*f*) It is not surprising that so beautiful and talented a woman should exert a great fascination on men and attract the admiration of both men and women. She is a highly successful professional lawyer and dresses fashionably at all times.

Exercise 51

(*a*) The oppression of some sections of the population is the cause of our present hesitation to go to the help of this government of so-called national socialists.

(*b*) I am glad that your persuasion was successful and that he agreed, though grudgingly, to the exclusion of these four illustrations because they would without doubt have been regarded as exceptionable by many.

(*c*) This new edition of the book with many emendations and additions will enable you to offer additional tuition to your classes.

(*d*) The job specification makes it clear that applications will be accepted only from those with 'A' level qualifications, even though it is only a vacation job.

(*e*) Your occasional co-operation in our operations to clear the cellars and basements of junk will be much appreciated, and will enable us to get on to the restoration of these vaults to their proper use once again.

Exercise 52

(*a*) Prompt attention to these provisional propositions for the acquisition of the Texas Oil Corporation ought to ensure our leading position when the final decisions are made.

(*b*) We are in a time of transition in our business when more people each week are realising the revolutionary sort of changes that are taking place in all office organisations.

(*c*) The notes you sent are unsatisfactory, and I want you to seek out much fuller information about all our living pensioners.

(*d*) We shall introduce some relaxation of our requisition procedures next month to cut down on the time wasted on waiting for decisions to be made before goods can be supplied.

(*e*) For your own protection, we strongly urge you to make reductions in your purchases and in your stock, and to take on the modification of all job specifications.

(*f*) I hope the sensational success of this new edition of your book will have given you satisfaction and that you will now go on vacation and accept the invitation to visit our tea plantations in Kenya.

(*g*) The word 'navvy' means a man trained in hard work, and it comes from 'navigators' – those men, often Irish, who came here two hundred years ago to build the inland navigation of the rivers and canals.

(*h*) Write an application to the Council for the erection of an additional hut on the site, and mark its exact location on the plans, attaching a specification of the hut.

(*i*) Ask the reception clerk whether it is far to the corporation offices as we have to put in an additional quotation by 4 o'clock for more supplies they need.

(*j*) Dear Sir, Thank you for sending us particulars of your educational qualifications and experience with the Bowman Paper Corporation. We are enclosing a copy of the job specification. The position is still open and we should like you to come to see us for a final selection meeting on Monday 15th April at 10 o'clock. All expenses will be paid. The selection meeting will end at 12.15 and we extend you a cordial invitation to join us for lunch. Only one other candidate has been selected. Yours truly,

Section 20

Exercise 53

(*a*) I approve of the chief points in this report, but I wish the survey had been made in more detail.

(*b*) The Salvation Army is very active in many fields of service and deserves our full support in its work of tracing missing relatives.
(*c*) The young musicians gave an attractive performance and deserved the applause of the audience especially for their sensitive playing of Brahms.
(*d*) At the cafe, they refused to serve us, and gave us no reason why we were thought to deserve such treatment.
(*e*) Like the previous party held here, it was a festive occasion and guests were active in seeking autographs from the stars who were present.

Exercise 54

(*a*) I had no difficulty in getting their active approval to our proposal to buy her some attractive gift to celebrate her anniversary.
(*b*) We are out of stock of a number of the items that you have asked us to reserve for you and in particular silk handkerchiefs.
(*c*) Will you please reserve for me a copy of the new juvenile magazine which will appear for the first time next week in spite of difficulties over the printing. It will be called 'Young Achievement'.
(*d*) One thing that we have learned in our survey of the traffic passing through our chief city in the West is that we need to provide more one-way facilities in the city.
(*e*) My wife has a number of male relatives who have served in the armed forces and she knows very well how restrictive such a life may be from a social point of view.
(*f*) I want you to observe this instrument closely. It is very sensitive and it will register every change in the graphs you see on the visual display unit once every five minutes. You will record the changes in pressure, heat level and flow of water as they flash up on the screen.
(*g*) This aircraft will take off at 6.30 pm and the flight will last for ten hours giving each pilot five hours of duty, but they will share the time as agreed between them.
(*h*) He is a tough but attractive-looking man, talkative but always ready to listen and much more sensitive to any situation than he seems to be on the surface.
(*i*) We have a new range of fine kid gloves now available at all our branches and it would be to your advantage, if you have a little

time to spare, to inspect them. These gloves, which have been bought as part of the stock of a warehouse damaged by fire, are of very high quality and are being sold at a low profit margin.

Exercise 55

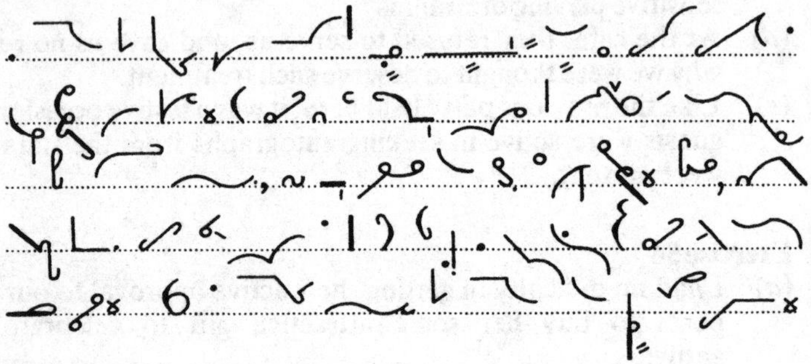

Section 21

Exercise 56

(*a*) Thank you for your letter and for your order for two new electric motors for the stand-by lighting in your theatre.

(*b*) In the manufacture of clothes, natural materials have largely given way to alternatives like polyester and terylene which are man-made.

(*c*) I shall attend for another interview for this post at the International Trust Fund and I suppose I have a moderately good chance of success.

(*d*) Julius Caesar was really the inventor of our modern calendar and largely the builder of the Roman Empire, too, carving out the frontiers in the north and west of Europe.

(*e*) The arterial road is sure to be very crowded at Easter and neither of us wishes to stand for hours in long traffic tailbacks so I suggest we take another day's holiday and go by the alternative route on Thursday.

Exercise 57

(*a*) If you are a good operator on a typewriter, it is easy to become a good operator on the keyboard of a word processor.

(*b*) The printer tells us that he cannot get more than a quarter of the copies we need off to the distributor today.

(*c*) If you use the duplicator, then I expect to see your signature in the book which is inspected by the directors quarterly.

(*d*) At the end of this quarter our agriculture will be producing 62 per cent of all the food we eat, and further expenditure on tractors would increase this still more.

(*e*) Our local MP will give a lecture tonight in the Crucible Theatre on the structure of agriculture in this country and the outlook for the future.

Exercise 58

(*a*) I think there is good reason for his sister and his father to refuse to surrender to him their rights to his mother's effects.

(*b*) One of the most outstanding features of life in some country villages is the way in which the people are always ready to help one another in the event of a need arising.

(*c*) My dear Madam, In reply to your enquiry we can use an alternative material for tiling the floor of your kitchen, but it is much more expensive. We enclose another revised estimate. Yours truly,

(*d*) What a wonderful January we have had with the temperature not falling below freezing point on a single day, and no wintry weather at all, and a moderate amount of sunshine.

(*e*) If there is some other way of getting to this hill farm that avoids a long journey along the arterial road, especially when towing a tractor, I hope somebody will tell me.

(*f*) The quarterly returns on all furniture, fixtures and fittings in this public house with the addition of any further items added since the last returns were made, are now due.

(*g*) A porter was at work changing the indicator board at Waterloo Station. It was a quarter past eight and the station was thronged with people – typists, WP operators, directors of firms, clerks – all scurrying to be first on the underground trains.

(*h*) The doctor told her to take 5 ml of the mixture twice a day, and on the subject of food he said she must alter the whole nature of her diet.

(*i*) We have been there before and as a matter of fact the last time we were there, you may recall that neither of us could think of the name of the farm.

(*j*) It is only natural that, if we owe him this money and the debt is a long-standing one, he should send us a reminder. According to the calendar, he has been waiting for his money for eight weeks.

Section 22

Exercise 59

(*a*) I hope this conference will be conducted in a way that will be congenial to all those attending.

(*b*) The company is facing some very complex conditions in the next few months and it is important that the new computer should be installed as quickly as possible.

(*c*) I am confident that the committee will give you constant support during the weeks of difficult work ahead, and that you will complete the task and come to a satisfactory conclusion of your mission.

(*d*) We must concentrate our whole attention on a satisfactory drafting of the terms of the contract because the Board is concerned that it may not be ready in time.

(*e*) In spite of all the TV advertising, you have to recognise that most aircraft seating is uncomfortable and cramped, and that better arrangements should be made, particularly on long hauls, to reduce this discomfort.

(*f*) It is incumbent on you to take the lead, and I recommend that you prepare a short speech in which it is recognised that our annual grant has been an encumbrance on the estate for too long.

Exercise 60

(*a*) We hope to bring the harvesting of the wheat to a successful conclusion notwithstanding the damp conditions.

(*b*) You have paid too much income tax this year and I shall continue to press for the inland revenue officers to consent to an immediate rebate.

(*c*) Although modern technology enables a computer to communicate with another computer without the need for human intervention, nevertheless it remains true, contrary to what some people believe, that the computer requires human skill and brains to actuate it.

(*d*) I recommend that this line which has suffered a considerable fall in sales over the past year should be discontinued.

(*e*) In connection with the report by the Communications Committee published a week ago, we have received a number of comments which call attention to errors of language and also of contents, and these are a matter of serious concern.

(*f*) The radio commentator was constrained to make an unconditional withdrawal of off-the-cuff remarks that he made at the conclusion of yesterday's programme called 'Conquest of the Unconscious'.

(*g*) The book consists of a complete history of human communications not confined to language only, but giving considerable space to non-verbal communication, too.

(*h*) In order to complete the contract, the company sent out a convoy of heavy trucks loaded with all the rest of the supplies that the contractor had ordered and we were congratulated on a successful conclusion to a very difficult enterprise.

Section 23

Exercise 61

(*a*) The meeting arranged for 4th February is now to take place on 3rd March and it will commence at 10 am. Lunch will be served at 1.30 pm.

(*b*) Special care is needed when dealing with figures. It is easy to see a mistake in a word, but much more difficult to see a figure error.

(*c*) Two million, four hundred thousand tons of coal have been imported this month and that is a rise of one hundred and fifty-two thousand tons since last month.

(*d*) Nine hundred thousand persons are unemployed in this region.

(*e*) The aircraft will take off at 0400 hours and is due to arrive in Palma at 0600 hours.

Exercise 62

(*a*) It is illogical to suppose that an illiterate and immature person could open this door since the method depends on the ability to read.

(*b*) It is unnecessary to remind you that the cause of the burst water–pipe is still unknown, nor have we yet found out who immobilised the repair truck and how the person who did it got through the gates unnoticed.

(*c*) Your replies to the questions asked by counsel were indefinite, incorrect, and sometimes quite unbelievable.

(*d*) He admitted his authorship when the penmanship of the manifesto was compared with his own writing.
(*e*) We hope that the friendship and fellowship shown here today will long continue.

Exercise 63

(*a*) She has an old-fashioned attitude to fashion, and the outfits she wears remind one of the sixties.
(*b*) They are proposing to substitute art for metalwork at the evening institute.
(*c*) The crash of a Trident aircraft at Slough undermined BA's confidence in this type and they are all phased out today.
(*d*) If the attempt had been made to give prompt attention to the symptoms, this death could have been averted.
(*e*) Treat all his empty boasts with contempt. He is no more exempt from the duty on imported goods than we are.
(*f*) Please hang my coat up in the hall cloakroom and lay out my dress suit and my only good white shirt.

Section 24 – Review

1 Dear Miss Constable, As a result of the recent spell **10**
of dry, clear weather, we have been able to make **20**
good progress on the construction of the twelve lock-up **30**
garages. Indeed, we have advanced the programme so well [that **40**
I am now sure we shall complete the project well **50**
ahead of our penalty clause date. Would you, therefore, [according **60**
to the terms of our contract, please let me have **70**
your cheque for a further £7,000, which is **80**
the sum agreed as the last instalment of our total **90**
costs of construction. I am pleased to hear that you **100**
already have a waiting list of tenants for all of **110**
the garages. Yours truly, **114**

2 Dr. Johnson, the famous eighteenth-century writer and [compiler of **10**
the first full dictionary of the English language, used to **20**
say that the weather had no effect on people's minds **30**
and attitudes. Experience suggests, however, that in this [instance he **40**

was not right. Most of us are cheered up by **50**
a bright, sunny day and depressed by a gloomy wet **60**
one. When the barometer is rising we feel better and **70**
work better. When it is falling we are not so **80**
capable of good work. In a country like Great Britain **90**
which is subject to constant change of weather, it is **100**
not surprising that the weather is a regular subject of **110**
conversation and comment. This is a point often noted by **120**
visitors from other countries which have a much more stable **130**
climate than ours. **133**

3 I am glad to inform all members of staff that **10**
the new cafeteria is almost completed. It will be open **20**
from Monday, 5th April, and a range of midday meals **30**
will be available at two sittings, the first at **40**
12.30 pm and the second at 1.30 pm. **50**
The whole operation of the cafeteria will be run **60**
at cost by a Staff Catering Committee consisting of three **70**
elected members of staff and three management members.
[Details of **80**
this arrangement will be published shortly. The company will
[subsidise **90**
the finances of the cafeteria by thirty per cent of **100**
the total. The cafeteria will be open from 10 am **110**
until 5.30 pm daily, and light refreshments **120**
will be available at any time. I hope that every **130**
member of staff will make use of this new amenity. **140**
All suggestions should be submitted in writing to the Staff **150**
Catering Committee. Miss Christine Baker has agreed to act
[as **160**
honorary secretary to the Committee. **165**

SHORTHAND
PITMAN NEW ERA

PITMAN

This easy-to-follow, shorthand course has been specially compiled by experts at Pitman to make self-tuition both simple and stimulating.

The rules of shorthand, along with exercises, facility drills and dictation tests, are comprehensively covered over the twenty-five lessons. This book will be indispensable to anyone – young or old, in private or professional life – seeking a first or refresher course in New Era shorthand.

TEACH YOURSELF BOOKS

SHORTHAND

[illegible]

[illegible]

TEACH YOURSELF BOOKS

TYPING

PITMAN

A complete self-instructional course in touch-typing, compiled by experts at Pitman.

This book takes the beginner, at his or her own pace, from the first principles of typing to mastery of the QWERTY keyboard – the keyboard utilised by modern computer and word-processing systems, as well as the manual and electric typewriter. At each stage, exercises provide extensive practice in keyboard operation and technique and, for the secretary, practice also in the layout of business correspondence and tabular and display work. The book also includes advice on punctuation, spelling and abbreviations.

The emphasis on accuracy and technique makes this an invaluable first or refresher course for everyone who uses a keyboard at home or at work.

TEACH YOURSELF BOOKS

SECRETARIAL PRACTICE

MARY BOSTICCO

A comprehensive guide to the role and responsibilities of the secretary, with special emphasis on the day-to-day activities which are central to the efficient operation of a modern office.

This introductory text and reference handbook describes the whole range of secretarial duties, explaining the basic principles and procedures before going on to consider the applications of modern office technology, particularly in telecommunications, reprography and information processing.

The book stresses the importance of personal organisation, self-discipline and clear, concise communication, oral and written. It includes examples of business correspondence, memoranda, minutes and reports, with practical guidance on style, layout and punctuation. The book covers all the topics common to first-level secretarial courses, and the emphasis throughout is on the qualities and skills expected of a competent secretary in today's office.

TEACH YOURSELF BOOKS